Caress Of
The Bête Noire

Samuel P. Frearson

Copyright © 2023 Samuel P. Frearson

All Rights Reserved.
No Part of this book may be produced, stored in a retrieval system, or transmitted by any means without the author's written permission.

ISBN: 978-1-916954-49-6

DEDICATION

I want to dedicate my book to the following people:
To my Children who went through hell and back with me.
And the forgiveness they gave me for not knowing when
they needed protection.

Mum: For her unwavering support.

To all our therapists who helped my family and me unpack
and navigate the fear, stress, and emotional trauma we suffered
and continue to endure.

To our lawyers who defended and protected us.

To the men & women of law enforcement who serve, protect,
and enforce the law. Especially to those who responded in cases
of domestic violence calls, as they never know what they could
be walking into—stay safe out there.

Table of Contents

ACKNOWLEDGMENTS — 1
FOREWARD — 2
PROLOGUE — 4
PREFACE — 7
Chapter One: When Life Crashes to a Halt — 9

PART 1: Memoirs of a Marriage

Chapter Two: Once Upon a Time — 15
Chapter Three: As the Door Opens — 18
Chapter Four: Blue Blood and Castles — 24
Chapter Five: To Catch a Thief — 26
Chapter Six: A Summer of Incubators — 29
Chapter Seven: A Dog's Bite — 32
Chapter Eight: My Little Social Butterfly — 34
Chapter Nine: Moving to the USA — 36
Chapter Ten: Dream Catchers — 38
Chapter Eleven: Cruise — 40
Chapter Twelve: The Real Estate Agent — 42
Chapter Thirteen: Dumpster Diving — 44
Chapter Fourteen: Her Brother's Story — 45
Chapter Fifteen: It's Margarine? — 49
Chapter Sixteen: Assaulted — 52
Chapter Seventeen: A Friend's Divorce — 56
Chapter Eighteen: Child Protective Services — 58
Chapter Nineteen: Credit Problems — 60
Chapter Twenty: Sports and Activities — 62
Chapter Twenty-One: Arguments — 64
Chapter Twenty-Two: Move to Florida — 66
Chapter Twenty-Three: Cell Phones — 67

Chapter Twenty-Four: Broken Finger	68
Chapter Twenty-Five: Gout	70
Chapter Twenty-Six: Descent into Madness	74
Chapter Twenty-Seven: The Reconciliation	77
Chapter Twenty-Eight: The Business Partners	79
Chapter Twenty-Nine: Piano Lessons	84
Chapter Thirty: Separate Bedrooms	86
Chapter Thirty-One: How About Now?	88
Chapter Thirty-Two: Hanky-Panky	91
Chapter Thirty-Three: Organic Farming	94
Chapter Thirty-Four: A Wedding and a Funeral	96
Chapter Thirty-Five: Christmas Before the Final Move	100
Chapter Thirty-Six: An Interlude Regarding Sam	102

PART 2: Memoirs of a Divorce

Chapter Thirty-Seven: The Shit Show	106
Chapter Thirty-Eight: One Hell of a Trip	127
Chapter Thirty-Nine: Fannie is Now Sophie	137
Chapter Forty: Fear and Security	139
Chapter Forty-One: Filing for Divorce	144
Chapter Forty-Two: TRO Violations	148
Chapter Forty-Three: High Conflict Preparation	154
Chapter Forty-Four: Family Court Services Mediation	158
Chapter Forty-Five: The Deposition	160
Chapter Forty-Six: Ascension from Madness	174
Chapter Forty-Seven: Revelations	179
Chapter Forty-Eight: Tattoos	190
Chapter Forty-Nine: Therapy	192
Chapter Fifty: Sophie's Story	196
Chapter Fifty-One: Breathe	200
Chapter Fifty-Two: Narcissists	202
Chapter Fifty-Three: Custody	212
Chapter Fifty-Four: Barging In for Rubbish	220

Chapter Fifty-Five: Becoming my Mother	222
Chapter Fifty-Six: The Kavanaugh Hearings	223
Chapter Fifty-Seven: Divorce Settlement	225
Chapter Fifty-Eight: Online Dating	229
Chapter Fifty-Nine: Abusive Relationships	232
Chapter Sixty: Fraud	235
Chapter Sixty-One: Foreclosure	241
Chapter Sixty-Two: Coronavirus	245
Chapter Sixty-Three: Sold the Farm	247
Chapter Sixty-Four: Red Flags	251
Chapter Sixty-Five: More Lies Come to Light	259
Chapter Sixty-Six: Creepy Porn Lawyer?	260
Chapter Sixty-Seven: The Greenhouse Rubbish	262
Chapter Sixty-Eight: The Crazy Cat Lady	267
Chapter Sixty-Nine: Life's Doldrums	270
Chapter Seventy: Delay Tactics	275
Chapter Seventy-One: Finalizing our Divorce	278
Chapter Seventy-Two: Retrospectus	287
EPILOGUE	292
COROLLARY	295

ACKNOWLEDGMENTS

It is problematic to thank those who helped my family and me through the events described in this book without jeopardizing the notion of our anonymity.

To all my aunts, uncles, cousins, siblings, nieces, nephews, and friends not mentioned herein, I love each and every one of you. Yet, association with or inclusion in this type of story is not an aspiration any person should desire.

I joined a writer's guild with many established and published authors. They accepted me with open arms as I began my authoring journey. I had a compelling story when I first joined their guild. Yet, to say my grammar and literary acumen were lacking would be the understatement of a century. I thank each of you for your help and counsel regarding proper writing etiquette.

The guild suggested two resources to help improve my writing technique: *The Elements of Style* by William Stunk Jr. with revisions by E.B. White and *Self-Editing for Fiction Writers* by Renni Brown and Dave King. These two books have proved to be invaluable references.

Samuel P. Frearson

FOREWARD

"CARESS OF THE BÊTE NOIRE" is a remarkable fractured saga of resilience and redemption. The honest style of expression tells the reader about the depth of a determined human spirit. This emotional truth (Adult memoir) will take the reader on a roller coaster ride through the author's unbridled life, offering a glimpse into the darkest corners of the human soul and the eventual emergence into the light of hope and healing.

The narrative opens with raw honesty, and the author courageously confronts his painful memories and suppressed emotions that have haunted him for years. This book appears to be a cathartic release for the author and serves as a precedent of courage for those battling their own struggles. In other words, someone's tragedy can hopefully be another person's inspiration.

One of the most striking aspects of this memoir is the author's memory. This is a story of suffering, clearly expressed as a means of therapy. As readers, you may witness the author's transformation from a place of despair to one of empowerment and self-discovery.

The author's use of anonymous pseudonyms for people and places ensures respect for other people's privacy, no matter how appalling their conduct may have been. This also maintains the honor of the story. This level of selflessness and self-reflection adds depth and genuineness to the narrative, making it even more relatable to anyone who has faced adversity in their own life.

The author's writing style is quite engaging, while simultaneously, it's indicative, allowing people to visualize and feel the emotions as if they were right there.

Beyond personal cleansing, the author's primary motivations for sharing the story appear clear: to help others who may be trapped in a similar or their own unique toxic misery of relationships. It's more like a sincere apology as well as a warning. It's not easy for anyone to liberate themselves from the net of a narcissist. At times, it takes a lifetime to understand that one has, in fact, been living with a narcissist! Hence, this narrative is no less than a potential lifeline for such souls going through similar ordeals.

In "CARESS OF THE BÊTE NOIRE," the author's journey from darkness to light is heart-wrenching and, at the same time, uplifting. It serves as a testament to the strength of the human spirit. The powerful storytelling within this book, on the other hand, has the capacity to help others heal wounds with the deepest scars. Stories of this nature regularly inspire change. This extended memoir is not just a tragic tale but a beacon of hope for those seeking their own path to healing and transformation.

If you're looking for a deeply emotional and thought-provoking read concerning the complexities of relationships, personal growth, and redemption, then "CARESS OF THE BÊTE NOIRE" is a must-read for you. It might leave you with a renewed sense of existence and emotions, with the hope that healing and redemption are possible and that life has endless opportunities to offer.

Sabrina Miller
Senior Editor—Lincoln Publishers

Samuel P. Frearson

PROLOGUE

This book tells a painfully personal story. Some in my family would prefer I did not share it with the world. Over the past four years, I have faced and dealt with my feelings. If you ask my children, they will say I spoke too much about these trials and tribulations, either with them or with strangers. Talking about my feelings and these events was my way of releasing my suppressed or bottled-up emotions. I have been through Hell, and although scarred, I survived.

I also found rehashing these past events, stories, and feelings psychologically exacting and painful. And yet, at the same time, I was formulating how to pen them down in words on paper coherently, making it easy for one to visualize and feel the same emotions.

Every conflict has two opposing sides. The truth between these adversarial parties always lies somewhere between the two. The prevalence of the facts usually tends closer to a midpoint between the two factions. Trust me when I say my story emerges as a very one-sided one. Nobody is perfect, and heaven knows I am not without foibles. Even though, at times, I may paint myself in a brighter light than I deserve, this book is not some hagiographic account of my life. Instead, it is a criticism of all the actors in this dark narrative. No bright lights were shining upon any individual. I attempted to portray everything honestly from my viewpoint as I understood it at the time, without adding any embellishments.

But here's the rub: all the events documented in this book did happen and are true. They are recounted from my perspective and recollections as I remember them now. I have not fabricated any incidents, and with this story covering a thirty-year lamentable relationship, I chose to leave out many circumstances. I changed all the names of people and places to obscure our identities and remain anonymous. Only three people were made up or fictitious characters in my story to help further enhance the narrative and protect our privacy. Adding these fictional individuals did not change the story or the events.

I was always a water baby. During my entire life, when I went swimming, if I stopped moving and tried to float, I would sink—because I was a little on the dense side. The history of my relationship with Lucija teemed with red flags. However, because I am a little dense, I failed to notice these warning signs, and I sank into a cold, dark place under her subjugation without even realizing it.

By no means was writing down these events meant to punish or demean anyone. Consequently, I ask you to abide by my wish to remain anonymous. If someone figures out who we are, I ask them not to post the information to the general public.

First and foremost, the main reason for authoring this manuscript was an additional means of therapy for me. An outlet to help me cope with some of the lingering pain and suffering that Lucija put me through. I will add this book to my collection of genealogical materials for my descendants to read in the years to come, should they ever choose.

The second reason for writing my story was that it gave me hope that it could help others experiencing similar situations. Suppose my narrative only assisted one person from a life caught up in a narcissist's grip, and it helps them get the aid they require and ultimately break contact entirely with their tormentor. For me, it would vindicate all the time and effort involved in writing my book.

Throughout my relationship and marriage with Lucija, several people brought to my attention the existence of her affairs and thievery. At the time of each incident, I thought those people were crazy. I did not believe them and eventually forgot each event within the tenebrous recesses of my mind. Also, because enough time separated these incidents, I never connected the dots between them. I know they were right in black-and-white terms by virtue of the hindsight and knowledge gained these past four years. Unfortunately, I played the fool–totally in the wrong. As much as I wanted to reach out and apologize to those who tried to warn me, I decided not to, as I did not wish to open any of their old wounds. If we ever cross paths in life, I will talk to them at that time and let them know my regrets for not seeing the truth in their words. This state of affairs leads to the third reason for writing these memoirs–my feeble attempt at using this roundabout and indirect method of apologizing to those people for my incompetence.

The final reason for writing the book was, of course, economic. My current financial situation is in shambles and ruin. It would be nice to sell a few books, pay off my debts, buy my dream farm, and live happily ever after.

I know this is a bit of a fairy tale or pipe dream, yet I like to dream big. Heck, you will never reach your true potential unless you set your goals high.

Instead of using exact dates, to a certain extent, I organized the timeline relative to the moment of my decision to divorce Lucija. The era of my life I called "The Shit Show." It was my ground zero, the point at which my life and marriage fell apart. As a result, this story includes roughly thirty years from when I met Lucy leading up to when I filed for divorce–followed by another three-plus years of incidents from filing for divorce to finalizing the divorce. Oh my gosh, it took almost four years to divorce myself from this nightmare of a woman. I cannot say if my chronological format renders a more coherent story for the reader to understand and follow. I hope it does. I believe the story flows smoother when told how I perceived and witnessed it.

I have gone to great lengths to preserve everyone's identities. Therefore, again, I ask you to allow us to remain in the shadows of anonymity.

PREFACE

A little bit of levity before I get into the painful details of my story. Why does the abuser get a cool term labeled to them? As the word 'Narcissist' rolls off your tongue, consider how it sounds rather elegant in juxtaposition to the relatively vile person/condition it defines. This book is less about that wicked person and deals more with the people damaged, broken, or hurt in the wake of a narcissist passing through their lives.

I have not seen any stylish labels for us in everything I read, merely referred to as the narcissist's target, the person preyed upon by a narcissist, or the narcissist's victim. Typically, the focus is placed on the nasty person labeled a narcissist.

Suppose you have a narcissistic person in your life; you know of their condition and always make an effort to keep them at arm's length. It is kind of like a narcissist afflicts you. Therefore, 'Narsafflicted' would be an apt term for you.

If you are like I was, unknowingly enthralled under the spell of a narcissist's allure, under their control and, in essence, doing their bidding, I call this condition the 'Narsenthralled.'

When you have achieved a complete break in contact and exorcised the narcissistic demon from your life, I call it 'Narsorssized.' This term is my favorite of these three neologisms.

These fabricated suggestions are my way of saying, "Hey world. A little more attention and focus here on us silent, broken victims, please."

In my opinion, we are more noteworthy than those victimizers. We are much more meaningful and offer more to society than those narcissists who lurk within our communities and only know how to take and destroy.

Chapter One

When Life Crashes to a Halt

So, how do I set the scene for you?

How do I tell you my story and all the bizarre events I have witnessed without explaining too much about her?

I married Lucija, whom everyone calls Lucy, twenty-five years ago. I always had a firm belief in our loving and loyal relationship together. I felt that we were one of a kind, meant for each other, in a category of love that was nothing less than magical. My Lucy was everything I ever wanted in a woman, everything a man could ever dream of having.

We raised our five children to be polite and respectable. We endured some bumps along the road of our times together, some bumps larger than others. But, through thick and thin, I always thought of myself as the luckiest man in the world to have Lucy by my side and in my life as my wife.

Four years ago, in January, I left my job as a computer engineer at a large aerospace company and bought an Apple Farm in Walden, New York. I moved away to the farm while my wife and our three youngest children planned to follow me in June, at the end of the school year. We agreed to list our home in Titusville, Florida, for sale in the spring.

My oldest daughter, Cassandra, married a few years earlier and resided in White Plains, New York. That summer, my second oldest child, Maggie, moved to my mother's home in London, England, to attend university. My sons, the twins, Gilbert and Clifford, moved to the farm in July.

My wife, on the other hand, stayed behind. It seems she kept finding excuses not to move for four years. It was astonishing how strange it felt. Some of her reasons made sense, but others were questionable.

Our four-thousand-square-foot home in Florida remained unlisted and never placed for sale with a realtor. As a consequence, my wife and our youngest child, Fannie, never moved, and our house in Florida never sold. At no time did our financial plan ever include the ability to maintain two residences. This was a situation I found myself trapped in, and my frustration was extreme. So, we lived apart these past four years, yet another one of those bumps in the road we were required to surpass.

Two years ago, the twins followed their sister to London to attend the same university. So, I had three children enrolled in a foreign university simultaneously. Thank God my mother has a big home and a huge heart. I could not afford this without Mum providing the kids with a place to stay.

This year, my entire family gathered to celebrate Christmas and New Year's at my eldest daughter's home in White Plains, New York. My three university students visited us here from England during their winter break. My wife, Lucy, and our youngest daughter, Fannie, also visited from Florida. It was exciting to have the entire family together. All the more delightful, finalizing our plans to move Lucy and Fannie from our old Florida home to the farm in New York.

As a family, we all agreed that I would fly back to Florida in late January to pack the remaining items from the house into a moving rental truck, and we would then drive back to the farm in early February. We relocated most of the contents from the home to the farm the previous summer with a moving company on a fully loaded tractor-trailer.

I flew to Florida on a Wednesday night about ten days before our drive to New York. Lucy picked me up from the airport. I placed my suitcase in the back seat of our SUV, next to a baby's car seat with a sizeable lifelike doll strapped into it.

"Oh, is Fannie now doing the school parenting exercise her sisters previously did?" I commented.

Lucy quickly agreed with an "Uh-huh."

I scheduled the moving truck for a Friday pick-up. Yet, when we got to the house, I discovered nothing ready or packed for the move. Lucy demanded more time to pack and asked me to delay renting the moving truck for a few days. There had only been four years to prepare for the move, and she had nothing done. While discouraged, with some reluctance, I agreed to change the rental date to Monday, placing us on the road by Wednesday morning.

I drove Fannie to her high school the following morning, then returned to pack. When I returned home, Lucy said, "I have some errands to run."

As a result, she disappeared for the entire day in a car she borrowed from a friend and left me to pack everything myself.

That night, after I picked Fannie up from school, my daughter began to tell me a whirlwind of unfathomable stories about her mother, Lucy, and what happened in the past. Things like her mother having affairs, hitting and hurting her and her siblings, shoplifting, stealing from friends, lies, and a copious amount of secrets. Then Fannie told me she attempted suicide two years prior when she was thirteen.

Suicide? How could I not have known?

Fannie divulged an abundance of details to me. Yet, each incident she related to me conflicted with what I thought I knew of this woman I loved, trusted, and found myself attracted to both physically and emotionally.

A day later, I found a stash of guns and ammunition hidden behind the door on the floor of the walk-in closet in the master bedroom. I say hidden, but the bag that concealed them lay in plain sight. In brief, I felt marooned to contemplate the meaning of these weapons, this person, and my marriage.

After all of Lucy's delays, she turned a five-day move into ten days. And to top it off, she did not help with any packing. We were finally all packed and ready to go on the tenth day. However, on this glorious morning, Lucy pretended to be sick with fake coughs. She forced Fannie to play along with her hoax in another attempt to delay the move further. Fannie told me about the planned ruse moments before it started. Because her ploy did not work, Lucy began to pinch and hit Fannie's leg out of my view. She attempted to make Fannie cry to garner feelings of guilt within me for continuing with the move.

While I gathered the last load from upstairs, Fannie appeared in the doorway and softly told me, "Mom said she's thinking of committing suicide."

At this point, I had had enough. I kept Fannie close to me, under my wing, with my hand on her shoulder. I grabbed the bag of guns and ammo I had found a few days prior and locked the bag in the back of the moving truck. Fannie and I drove off in the moving truck while I called 911 to inform them of the hidden weapons and Lucy's threat to hurt herself.

I arrived back at the house shortly after the police did. The officer told me he finished his interview with Lucy, and she denied any suicidal thoughts or claims. I gave the officer the two handguns, which he took for disposal.

As the officer and I finished, Lucy came out yelling, crying, and full of accusations. Considering the circumstances, I found her performance out of place and a complete overreaction—was she being theatrical on purpose? During Lucy's hysteria, the officer told her that Fannie and I were leaving with the moving truck, and Lucy had to decide whether to stay or go with us. With considerable reluctance, Lucy agreed to go with us. Fannie and I waited in the truck for roughly two hours before Lucy finished packing and joined us for the drive to the farm in New York.

The first two and a half hours were quiet and uneventful, with Lucy red-faced and brooding. The uneasy stillness broke when I saw Lucy say something to Fannie, which evoked an immediate stream of tears down my daughter's cheeks.

I pulled over at the next gas stop, somewhere in Georgia, to fill up the truck. While Lucy busied herself buying drinks and snacks inside the station, Fannie came over to the gas pump and told me, "I cried earlier because Mom said, 'I have a gun, and if I have to die, I am taking the two of you with me.'"

My heart skipped a beat as my mind yelled, "What the fah?"

Suddenly, you, the reader, experience the screeching sound of squealing tires as I stomp on my story's brakes, and then, in my awkward style, I cut away to another part of my tale.

Who in their right mind starts a story at the climax when the proverbial car crashes into some life-altering event? I guess, perhaps, a burgeoning author like myself. Nevertheless, my children, extended family, and I suffered through and survived this charmer's cruel and destructive embrace.

My story does not begin or end here. Instead, this moment was the precise point in time when all my clarity and fears began to coalesce, taking shape in a palpable form.

Whoa, to ye of wee conviction,[1] let us now fade back to where this mess all began. I invite you to read on and dare to learn the depths of my despair and the peaks of her depravity.

---

1. I took, modified, and combined two bible verses, then added a touch of Scottish flair. "Woe to ye" and "O, you of little faith." I wanted my readers, especially those who may doubt my story so far, to take a pause, make them reflect, and then have them read on. I am uncertain how well this sentence fits in my book. However, in my mind, it was a clever method to convince those who may not quite believe this could happen to read on. Woe to me for typing such a distracting sentence.

Samuel P. Frearson

PART 1
Memoirs of a Marriage

Chapter Two

Once Upon a Time

I imagine I should start my story with an introduction. The following will sound like the beginning of an Alcoholics Anonymous (AA) meeting, not that I ever attended one. I have only watched AA meetings depicted in movies.

So, here we go:

"Hello, my name is Samuel Frearson, and it has been over four years since I was a narcissist's thrall. My friends call me Sam. So, Sam I am."

My story begins in London, England, where I first met Lucija roughly thirty years ago. As I mentioned earlier, everyone calls her Lucy, and we married around five years after we first met, or about twenty-five years ago. We did not move to the United States until four years after our marriage.

We have five children. Cassandra, my daughter, from a previous relationship. Maggie, our firstborn daughter. She was born about one year before we married. The twins, Gilbert and Clifford, my two boyos, were born three months premature. And our youngest daughter, Fannie. She is a US citizen and our only child born in the United States.

I suppose you could say I come from a multicultural family. My father's side of the family has roots from all over the British Isles, and my mother's side comes from France and Western Europe.

When I was twenty-one years old, my nineteen-year-old girlfriend became pregnant. These were quite embarrassing times for her and her family, so much so that she did not want to keep the baby. On the other hand, as scared of becoming a parent as I found myself, I could not shirk my mantel of responsibility. I felt I had an inexplicable obligation towards my unborn child. Before the baby's birth, I envisioned walking down a country road in autumn. The trees were a myriad of colors. Leaves rustled on the ground in the breeze. I could hear the sound of water in a gentle stream nearby while my child's tiny hand grasped my pointer finger. This mental image had a two-year-old version of my yet unborn child walking down this country road with me. Not bad for a dumb and immature twenty-one-year-old.

After Cassandra's birth, her mother left her at the hospital for adoption. However, I successfully blocked the adoption process, and Cassandra came home with me directly from the hospital at the ripe age of seven days old. She became my world. My life consisted of completing college, working, and raising my daughter. I could not imagine my life without her.

I did not start dating anyone until two years after Cassandra's birth. Unfortunately, the two most serious relationships I entered did not go well. The first was with a girl I dated who was far too immature for my circumstances. Before long, she grew jealous of Cassandra and of the time I spent with my daughter. So, without any regrets, I ended our relationship.

The second was a woman I dated, who was a lousy drunk, even violent at times. It was a rocky relationship that was on-again-off-again in nature towards the end. Ultimately, I learned directly from her lips when she said, "I don't even like your daughter."

I remember my immediate thought process as I mused, "So what is the point of us staying together?"

There was no possibility of solving the problems in our social engagement after a chasmal statement like that. So, I ended our companionship, even with her repeated attempts to rekindle it.

I never looked back at either of those two relationships. I was not searching to replace my daughter. I wanted a partner to join my family—my daughter and me.

After those two unfortunate relationships, I reckoned, "Who wants to be with a single father?"

I figured, accepted, and made peace with the inevitability that I would be a bachelor for life. So, I decided to stop the courting process and went back to solely being the best father I could be for my daughter, Cassandra.

I met Lucy shortly after I stopped looking for a kindred spirit to share my life with. It felt as though she fell from Heaven and right into my lap.

Chapter Three

As the Door Opens

"There's a new girl working at your grandfather's," my father told me enthusiastically. Then, with his signature coy smile, he suggested, "Maybe you should go over and check out the young lady."

I knew my parents cared for me and worried about my happiness. My father was looking out for me. But it was the last thing on my mind.

"I'm not interested, Dad." I brushed off his playful recommendation. I had already made peace with and resigned myself to bachelorhood.

My father's sister had schizophrenia and often visited my grandfather. Usually, her visits did not cause any problems. However, sometimes, she dropped in for a visit during a schizophrenic episode. During these incidents, my father would drive to my grandfather's home to evacuate my aunt.

Like my grandfather, my father was a barrister and solicitor. In American parlance, they were lawyers. Several months after Dad's suggested social match, which I had dismissed and forgotten, I received a phone call from my father. He was busy closing a large and significant real estate transaction for a client. So, he requested my help to remove my aunt from my grandfather's place.

It took me about forty-five minutes before I arrived at Grampa's home. As the solid oak arched front door of his Tudor mansion opened, Lucy greeted me. I only saw her head pop through the doorway. She wore a ponytail on the very top of her head. It stood tied straight up, maybe three inches high, before it fell back down, reminiscent of an *I Dream of Jeannie* hairdo.

The voice inside my head said in its best David Lee Roth impression, *"Wow, she's beautiful."*

I remember the following with vivid detail. I said, "Hi, I'm Samuel Frearson," then thought to myself, I am such an idiot because that was the name of her employer. It was my grandfather's name.

I assumed she must have thought, "No, you're not."

I then stammered out, "I am not the Samuel Frearson. I am his grandson Samuel Frearson, and I came to help remove my aunt from the premises."

I learned from this young lady named Lucy about my aunt's departure some minutes before my arrival. As a result, I went upstairs to enjoy a half-hour visit with my grandfather. We watched some sports on the telly. When I came downstairs, Lucy invited me to join her for some tea. So, I stayed, and we talked for hours until late at night. Needless to say, visiting my grandfather once every few months soon escalated to an almost daily event.

Lucy was like a godsend. She was beautiful, charming, and intelligent. She spoke six languages and was studying English as her seventh. Her voice carried the cutest accent, and best of all, her fondness for my daughter, Cassandra, and me appeared genuine.

Several months after we started dating, I learned Lucy was already married. She came to England three years prior at the age of nineteen, chasing a boyfriend who had previously immigrated to England from Croatia. They entered into a civil marriage, allowing her to stay in the country. Eventually, he grew tired of her and asked her to leave one day. This guy was not an awful person. Still, I never had a particular cordiality for him, mainly because he was the competition. Their marriage was short-lived. I met Lucy when she was twenty-two and lived separated from her husband for some time. I believe they separated one or two years earlier. I always believed his stupidity in throwing her out was "His loss and my gain." I repeated this slogan many times throughout our marriage to many people. Each time I repeated it, I reaffirmed that I could not have been happier. It meant this beautiful, gentle, and caring woman was all mine.

Lucy frequently talked about how she played piano back in Croatia, and I often requested to hear her play. Later, she added more details to her story. She used to play music with her high school boyfriend. Unfortunately, her boyfriend committed suicide at some point, and Lucy vowed to give up playing the piano in his memory. Over the years, I tried to sit her down in front of the ivories a few times. She would stretch her fingers and touch a couple of keys, yet never made a single note. Even though I wanted to hear her play, I was impressed with how devoted she was to her pledge. Her unwavering commitment made me love her even more.

After a while, her estranged husband started to make overtures of his love for Lucy, insisting he had made a mistake and wanted to get back together. You can imagine how much stress this placed on our relationship. However, one of our friends told me it was all hogwash. She explained to me that her estranged husband spent all his time with a new girlfriend. I did not particularly appreciate how he played mental and emotional games with Lucy.

One day, he would not answer Lucy's phone calls. She was worried about his health and well-being. I knew and told her he must be busy with his new girlfriend. So, I decided to drive Lucy to his apartment complex. Lucy had me wait in the car while she went up. The first time I ever saw Lucy so angry and boiling over with rage occurred as she returned from his flat thirty to forty-five minutes later. She returned bloodied with some nasty scratches. Her hair was all messed up, and she had two broken fingernails—I mean, her fingers bled from the tears into her fingers' nail beds.

As she calmed down, she commented on her sore scalp as she pulled wads of loose hair from her head. Lucy told me how she tailgated someone through the locked doors of the apartment complex's lobby and gained access to the building. She found his flat door unlocked when she got to his apartment unit. Lucy opened the door and walked in. She discovered her husband and his girlfriend both naked in his bed. Lucy explained why she had lost her temper. It agitated her that her thirty-year-old husband fooled around with an underage girl. She complained of a sore head because he pulled her by the hair to separate the two girls from battle.

I thought the problems with this guy were over, except two weeks later, he began another round of cooing. He declared his love for Lucy. He portrayed the other girl as a meaningless one-time fling, a mistake. Then he blamed Lucy for their breakup and placed the guilt on her for being with me.

I only waited briefly until the next time he would not answer her phone calls. Then I drove Lucy back to his place. She went up alone again, and this time, nobody answered the locked door to his apartment. Fearing a medical emergency, Lucy found and convinced the building superintendent to let her into her husband's apartment. The superintendent unlocked and opened the door. She caught her estranged husband and his underage girlfriend with their pants down for a second time. I believe the fighting this time comprised, for the most part, verbal stabs, although Lucy came out of the building in a rage once again.

After those two battles, I never heard anything about him trying to get Lucy back. Yet, for some reason, Lucy wanted to remain good friends with him. This was something I struggled to understand as I felt he had hurt her. So why would she feel the need to stay friends with him?

Several months later, Lucy and I went to my family's summer country lodge for the weekend. We scheduled it all for ourselves. But Lucy wanted to bring her ex-husband along to show him they could still be friends. For the life of me, I do not know why I agreed to it or what I rationalized. I should not have acquiesced, and the weirdest weekend of my life ensued. They went for long pedal boat rides and left me alone at the lodge. One time, I walked into the kitchen through the exterior side door. I saw them kiss. I know I saw his hand down the back of her bikini bottom. I saw it, only for a split second. I slammed the door and ran off.

She followed and found me, maybe half a mile away. Ultimately, she convinced me I saw things wrong, and it was not what happened.

I allowed myself to believe her story. I let myself accept my eyes deceived me. To my knowledge, it was the last time we saw him. He disappeared from our lives. It seemed like he consistently lived in other parts of the country from that time. As a matter of fact, I had consigned the events of this weekend vacation to oblivion until now, while writing the book. It is curious. Or is it alarming? What the mind will allow you to forget and continue in your perceived normal state.

Lucy found a flatmate to move in with, which lasted maybe half a year. I guess these two women could not get along adequately. While we packed to move her out, these two ladies started to fight over who owned four plastic cups. These glasses they fought over were free gifts from the petrol station. I am attempting to convey that these two grown women faced each other, ready to go fisticuffs over some worthless items. I separated them and, at the same time, berated them both over this junk fetish they seemed consumed by. And by separate, I mean I grabbed Lucy by the waist and carried her to her bedroom. I closed the door behind us in her flatmate's face and held it closed until they both gave up.

From this point on, Lucy and I lived together. I bent my knee and proposed to her shortly thereafter. Our wedding plans and wedding dates kept getting pushed down the calendar for various reasons.

Lucy became pregnant and gave birth to our daughter, Maggie, around one year before we married. So, our two children walked up the aisle with us as part of our wedding procession. Doubtless, it was a strange situation for many people. Although, for me, it was an exceptional experience to have our kids participate in the ceremony.

We were married in a cozy country Catholic Church, followed by a reception held in a rustic old-style restaurant. Our guests consisted of over one hundred family members and friends. We reserved the restaurant exclusively for us for the entire evening and night. My father paid for an open bar after dinner, and everyone had a great time.

The evening ended on a strange note. I had to drive the disc jockey (DJ), a Croatian friend of Lucy's, home after the party. It was odd and upsetting. Yet, that was Lucy. She always thought of other people and did what she could to help them. And maybe that was another quality that drew me to her.

When we arrived at our hotel room, Lucy wanted a bath alone. And that was how our wedding night concluded.

Chapter Four

Blue Blood and Castles

Since the first week I met Lucy, she talked about her family's castle in Croatia. As the story goes, Lucija's grandmother was the last family member to live within its walls. Lucy was a descendant of nobility and royalty dating back a few hundred years. The castle's original purpose was more of a fortress or garrison than a castle, and the keep lay in ruin. Since the Second World War, it has remained vacant.

The Communists took away all land and ownership in the country after WWII. Her family never successfully reinstated their rights to the castle since the country's freedom from communism. She seemed deeply melancholic about it.

Her story went on further regarding the time her grandmother passed away. Her father inherited the paperwork for the castle and the thousands of acres of land surrounding it. In contrast, his siblings inherited money, jewelry, works of art, and other immediately tangible things. She explained that her father's siblings often laughed and made fun of him for inheriting nothing. The communists did not recognize an individual's right to land ownership.

According to Lucy, her father held the paperwork to prove his rights to the castle and land. She claimed that after the fall of communism, the local government quasi-recognized her father's claim. Except, the country's government would not approve his property rights nor reinstate the family's ownership. Lucy recounted how her father spent much time in court attempting to reacquire his inheritance.

She described a story of two suits of armor. Her father possessed one set of knight's armor, which he kept buried somewhere, and his brother owned another ensemble of plate armor. The brother traded his suit of armor with some Russian person in the Communist Party to gain favor and join the party himself. She even described these two suits' headgear, adorned with long feathers, along the helmets' crests.

Lucy had another story regarding a large oil painting from her family's castle. The artwork in question depicted a victorious ancestor of hers, his sword drawn as he rode on horseback in the middle of a panoramic battlefield. She described the composition as life-sized. My mind envisioned the canvas as eight to ten feet tall and at least twenty feet wide. Lucy claimed the Germans had stolen her family's work of art during WWII. Her account went on to impart how her father had traced the painting to some museum in Germany. It was not on display. The museum kept it as part of its collection in storage, away from public view.

Lucy told all sorts of childhood stories regarding the castle. She spun tales that involved dangerous catacombs and tunnels below. Some of her more contemporary accounts concerned greedy land developers and architects. These people tried to steal the castle and land from her family for some development projects by going through the country's legal system. She accused them of wanting to line the pockets of some government officials and their own with money.

After Lucy's father passed away, new details emerged regarding the castle. Lucy announced that her father transferred the titles of both her parent's home and the fortress to her on some legal documents before she originally left Croatia for England. She repeated these new details often enough.

Chapter Five

To Catch a Thief

It seems like money regularly went missing. It disappeared from my dresser and my pants pockets. I was losing my mind over this. I thought cash fell out of my pants when I purchased things or removed my hands from my pockets. I tried to be extra vigilant about keeping the bills at the bottom of my pockets to avoid their loss. Nevertheless, it kept happening, and over time, I slowly became accustomed to losing money.

Cash often disappeared from family members, particularly from my mother's purse. Once, my mother thought the instant teller, now called an Automated Teller Machine (ATM), shortchanged her. She took money from the ATM, went straight home, and never spent any of it. She complained to the bank about the missing money, and they reimbursed her for the £120 missing out of the £300 she withdrew.

It is disorienting to suffer a burglar in your midst. At first, you do not realize the thefts. Then, when you suspect a crook lingers in your life, you suspect everyone other than the culprit. Not until some bigger heists take place can you narrow it down to the accuracy of an individual.

Over two thousand pounds sterling disappeared from our bedroom during Maggie's baby shower. I nailed it down to two suspects. After a priceless painting my family had conserved for generations vanished from its frame at my parent's home, I finally realized our thief was Lucy's best friend from Croatia. Naturally, Lucy did not want to believe it. It was not until her friend offered to hold Lucy's purse while Lucy tried on her wedding dress that she began to recognize the crook. Lucy peeked through the slats in the door from inside the changing room stall and observed her friend rummaging through her purse.

Soon afterwards, I set up a hidden video camera in our living room and caught her best friend as she stole two £20 bills from the hundred pounds sterling of marked £20 banknotes I placed in Lucy's purse. I watched her do it in real time from the video feed. I recorded it on the camera and another VHS player upstairs. I switched the videotape in the machine to continue recording, and then I went downstairs to confront her.

I accused her of stealing the money.

Then, in a screechy voice, she exclaimed, "What, Sam—NO!"

It was a curious thing that happened when she stopped talking to me, as if I had ceased to exist. Instead, she switched to the Croat language and only spoke all her denials to Lucy. While she spoke with Lucy, I played the video of her pilfering from Lucy's purse. Then, the second strange event transpired.

Speaking in English, all in a flash, her story changed from denial to, "Yes, I stole from you, but only this one time."

Laughing, I mocked her and said, "Oh no, you've stolen from us many, many times," and named some of those instances.

She continued to deny stealing from us before this day.

So, I bluffed her with, "Would you like to watch another video?"

She left our home running, crying, almost screaming. Maybe an hour later, she returned to our front door as the third bizarre incident occurred. Her story again evolved to claim that she only stole £600 from us. She insisted that she kept a written record of each time she stole from us and knew the exact amounts. She dropped £300 at Lucy's feet, probably from an ATM.

It was amazing to observe how other people reacted to the news. Some of our friends refused to watch the videos and sided with Lucy's friend, the thief. These so-called friends grew upset, and some were even angry with me for recording the crime.

She and her husband lived in an on-again, off-again relationship of separation. After viewing the two videos, his voice, hands, and body visibly trembled. The first video of her stealing. The second recording of the confrontation and her admission.

Shaking, he exclaimed, "This is the last nail in the coffin [for their marriage]," and immediately began to divorce her.

And to me, that seemed to be the end of all this "tomthievery[2]" business.

Since I am talking about Lucy's friend, the thief, I wanted to mention how I still remember Lucy and her best friend consistently ridiculed how I danced.

---

2. Tomthievery is my little play on words with tomfoolery.

Chapter Six

A Summer of Incubators

Roughly a year and a half after our marriage, Lucy went into premature labor while pregnant with the twins. When we arrived at the hospital, Lucy's water had already broken. She was dilated and in full contractions. She was only in her twenty-seventh week of pregnancy. The hospital could not take care of babies delivered at this early stage of development. It lacked the proper specialized equipment.

The hospital placed Lucy on a magnesium Intravenous (IV) drip to stop the contractions. They also arranged to relocate her to another hospital suitably equipped to handle the extreme nature of our expected premature babies.

At this stage of pregnancy, babies do not possess fully developed lungs, which presents a host of potential and significant problems. To help develop my babies' lungs, the hospital wanted to immediately give Lucy two injections of steroids while the babies remained within the womb. These drugs' names, as I remember, were Stilbesterol and Chlobesterol. While writing this book, I researched these drugs and found that Stilbestrol is a hormone, not a steroid. I could not find anything about Chlobesterol. Are these drugs discontinued? Or does my memory loosely recall homophones of the drugs' names? It does not matter. My point is that both babies required time for these drugs to help develop their lungs.

The doctors explained to us how lucky we were. Lucy had only lost a bit of water. The break occurred at the top of the amniotic sac, allowing the membrane to reseal itself. Eventually, the magnesium drip reduced the contractions and, several hours later, finally stopped them altogether. Every hour and every day, the babies stayed within Lucy's womb; the more their lungs developed due to the steroids, the better their chances of survival with fewer complications.

With the contractions ending, the urgency to transport Lucy to a different hospital had passed. So, she remained at this hospital for observation for three days before returning home.

A week and a half later, Lucy complained about painful contractions again. Her contractions came about an hour apart. We raced to the other better-equipped hospital to deliver our preemies, and it was an hour's drive away. Within minutes of driving, Lucy's contractions became three minutes apart and over a minute long each.

Then, she yelled out, "My water broke," and bit me on the shoulder.

My fears concerned the babies' survival. If Lucy bore them in the car, their chances of survival became slim. I raced the entire journey and safely ran through some red lights.

When we arrived at the emergency entrance, hospital personnel helped me get Lucy out of the car and onto a stretcher. Before entering the emergency front doors, I heard someone say, "The head has already crested." Gilbert was already almost here.

Both twins were born in the hospital's emergency room, three months premature, roughly a week-and-a-half after Lucy's first labor episode. Gilbert was delivered moments before Clifford. The pair came out kicking and screaming—they breathed on their own! The hospital staff took our two boyos from the emergency department to the Intensive Care Unit (ICU). We spent the summer with our identical twins, who remained in incubators.

Both were perfect in every sense, yet on a much smaller scale than normal. The pair of them fit in one of my hands.

No real big scares happened after this. The hospital placed my twins on respirators, even though they both breathed independently, on their own. Gilbert skipped a breath or two one night, and the ventilator kicked in. Each of my boys experienced a bit of jaundice, and the ICU used bilirubin lights to treat them. My miracle babies were healthy.

Chapter Seven

A Dog's Bite

We visited with some friends when the twins were a week away from turning two years old. The adults barbecued in the backyard while the kids played inside. Gilbert and Clifford ran around in diapers at our friends' home. Suddenly, we were startled by a child's loud screeching emanating from inside our friends' house.

I ran into their home to find out what had happened. Maggie stood in frozen terror, screaming at the top of her lungs. Then I saw Clifford on the floor, crying and bleeding. There was so much blood.

Our friends had a large dog named Smokey, and for no reason that I can fathom, their dog savagely mauled Clifford.

Clifford's right ear hung practically torn off from the side of his head. He suffered puncture marks on the top of his head, below his jaw, and on the back of his shoulder. One puncture wound lay straight under his right eye. Because of the swelling, I thought a tooth had pierced his eyeball.

Lucy had not seen his injuries. She only knew the dog had bitten him. Lucy completely lost it, which, by the way, did not help the situation. She yelled and argued with people. She never inspected Clifford's injuries and did nothing to help or comfort him.

I wanted to get medical attention for Clifford as quickly as possible. So, I held him against my chest, hiding the extent of his worst injuries from Lucy. I did not want her to see the dangling ear and his deforming eye.

As heart-wrenching as it was to view his horrifying wounds, he needed care. Knowing Clifford required a hospital emergency room, my sole purpose was getting him there as quickly as possible. Our friend's mother suggested we go to the doctor's office and offered to drive. I agreed since I did not want to aggravate Lucy's panic further. The mother drove Clifford and me while Lucy followed in our car with the rest of our children. Once on the road, I asked if she could take us to the emergency doors of the closest hospital, and she took us there.

Clifford was remarkably fortunate to be alive. The bite's punctures were close in proximity to his neck. The doctors sewed up his ear with five stitches. There remains only a tiny scar along his hairline. His eye was not pierced despite the dog's tooth passing between his eyeball and the bone in his eye socket. Instead, the force of the dog's bite chipped the bone of his eye socket. Over time, the various other puncture marks on his face disappeared or became barely detectable.

Maggie was so traumatized by what she witnessed that day that she immediately developed a severe phobia of all animals, which lasted until her early teen years. She could not be around dogs. She would shake and cry if a cat or even a squirrel got within ten feet of her.

This chapter highlights Lucy's extreme reactions to such critical situations. I do not remember why I knew about her intense and non-beneficial outbursts to crises at this early stage of our marriage. Yet, by way of this example, the evidence clearly exhibits my awareness, and it shows I adapted my response to help mitigate the inappropriate scenes she created during these crises. Each time Lucy plunged into a tirade, handling the unfolding circumstances was troublesome and obstructive.

Chapter Eight

My Little Social Butterfly

Lucy was very personable, and she had a warm, approachable charm. She had a knack for picking up on strangers' conversations, and then she would interject herself into these other people's discussions and then into their lives.

Always quick to pull other people into our world. She continually surrounded herself with "good friends." Yet most of her good friends were people she had recently and randomly met. She would call herself "Aunt Lucy" to the children of these people she had just encountered, sometimes even the same day she stumbled upon them. She always seemed considerate of others and bought little gifts for their kids each time we visited.

Lucy often proclaimed, "I am a Social Butterfly."

And I must agree she had the gift of gab. Lucy had a very outgoing personality, and I liked this quality of hers. She was comfortable meeting and conversing with new people under almost any circumstance.

Lucy loved the local flea markets, and there were several nearby. We visited a bazaar at least once a week, and each time, we spent a half-day browsing the rows of stalls at any market. She loved to haggle with the vendors and usually bested them at their own games. Most of her purchases occurred around closing time because, as Lucy once explained, the merchants did not want to repack and transport things back to where they came. So, this twilight hour presented the prime time for her best deal-making.

Outside of flea markets, I felt embarrassed when she would enter negotiations. She pushed too hard and could never make the deal, or once an agreement was made, as a lost liter for the other party, she would add that she did not want to pay the tax. For example, I could not buy a car if she was in attendance. I have had car dealers walk away from us because Lucy wore them down for hours and pushed the deal deep into the red.

Chapter Nine

Moving to the USA

I started to work for an aerospace giant as a contractor in the late nineties. For an entire year, I flew back and forth across the pond. I worked three weeks in Houston, TX, and then one week online from home in England. Finally, after a year, this company decided to hire me as an employee. I negotiated with them a full relocation package. They applied for work permits that allowed for a path to residency and then petitioned for our Green Cards–Permanent Resident Status.

How can I adequately describe my desire to be in the United States? I do not think most Americans appreciate how lucky they are. Your country is beautiful and comprises open space in abundance. From the first time I came here, my impression was that the people were warm and welcoming. Back in England, people were much more socially conservative. Meaning when I walk down the street, strangers do not generally make eye contact or greet each other.

Here in the United States, a stranger walking down the road will look you directly in the eye and say something similar to, "How are you doing?"

Exquisitely straightforward, yet I love it. You also revel in a great deal of opportunity here, and I am not only talking about work and money. You enjoy a much wider variety of things to experience, from leisure activities to sports. While partaking in the American melting pot, you can savor various cultures, traditions, and cuisines.

I negotiated a much higher pay rate while remaining a contractor to give this aerospace company some extra incentive and hurry them along with my work permit application. I yearned to become an employee of theirs, then a permanent resident, and eventually a citizen of the United States.

My employer paid to relocate my family and me while I continued to work as a contractor. The visa application process took over a year. I became a full-time employee at this company the day after receiving my work visa. The acquisition of my Permanent Resident Status took almost five years. Nonetheless, it was all very much worth the wait. Only one goal remained in my quest–to become a US citizen. Yet, to this day, I have not applied and must get around to it.

When I become a citizen of the United States, I will do my rendition of a little Irish Jig. My happy dance, if you will. Reminding me, I do not believe Lucy ever danced once with me since we moved to the United States.

Americans have curious terms and sayings. I had never heard of this catchphrase before, yet it stuck with me. I thought it had to do with melons. My neighbor and I were going to go to a paintball park. However, he asked me to help him finish his wife's honeydew list before we could leave. I did not understand what he was talking about, so I helped him. I must apologize to my readers. I will never write it as a honey-do list. For me, it will forever be known as a honeydew list. So please bear with this minor quirk of mine.

Chapter Ten

Dream Catchers

I always had a vivid imagination and dreamt of many wondrous and fantastical things. I often claimed that "I dreamed in technicolor."

I even believe that, at times, my conscious and subconscious could interact with each other while dreaming. A form or sense of self-awareness within the dream, able to interact and manipulate the dream.

Several times during my life, the answer to some complex problems would come to me in my dreams, and I was lucky enough to remember the solutions when I awoke.

Lucy brought several dream catchers into our bedroom. A large one that was roughly twelve inches in diameter and three or four that were smaller, each around four inches in diameter.

Dream catchers are over-commercialized versions of the Native American Asibikaashinh talisman meant to catch nightmares and negative thoughts while you sleep. Some Native American tribes believed that harmful thoughts and dreams traveled through the night air and that the dream snare talisman would catch them, much like a spider's web catches flies. The dream catcher would only allow peaceful and positive thoughts to pass through its center hole so you could enjoy a soothing and restful sleep.

Soon after Lucy brought the dream catchers into our bedroom, something changed. Something sinister began to occur. I began to lose my ability to dream, and eventually, I did not dream whatsoever. I did not believe in the supernatural, but I could not deny the possibility of the unexplained. As my sleep became unsatisfying and non-renewing, I felt like I was transforming into some form of zombie. These concerns were possibly a little dramatic, but the trinkets had an impact that affected me. I thought these dream catchers took all my dreams and stole the capacity of my subconscious to help solve problems.

I spoke with Lucy about my inadequate sleep and loss of dreams. I blamed her dream catchers for my malaise. Then, I removed these sleep charms from our bedroom and placed them in a storage box.

Eventually, my dreams returned, and my sleep felt better. But it was a long and slow recovery.

Ever since this episode with dream catchers occurred, I have considered them bad medicine and will not allow them to remain in my vicinity.

Chapter Eleven

Cruise

Lucy and I went for a ten-day cruise through the Caribbean on a new ship, whose maiden voyage was less than a year earlier. We enjoyed several great destinations aboard this beautiful ship.

One day, the ocean liner cruised through gale-force winds and waves that rocked the vessel. That morning, I ate a large muffin with coffee for a quick breakfast. The acidic mess churned in my stomach as this massive ship rocked and rolled in the waves. It did not take long to make my stomach ill. After throwing up once, I became seasick for almost twenty-four hours. I returned to our cabin to lay in bed before 10 a.m. I felt like a wretched, green-faced landlubber. I had never experienced seasickness before. I was no stranger to open water, frequenting small lakes, large lakes, rivers, and a couple of oceans on a regular basis.

Lucy only stayed with me for a half-hour before she went for lunch. She brought me crackers after her lunch, and then, to all intents and purposes, she vanished. I got up around 9 p.m. and wondered where Lucy had disappeared. Even though I felt ill, I walked back and forth along the ship's length on several decks, searching for her. I checked all the restaurants and lounges. I scoured the out-of-service pool area, which closed due to the foul weather, and then explored the dance and theater areas. She was nowhere to be found. She did not return to the cabin until after 4 a.m. She left me sick and alone for over twelve hours.

I felt as though I was "left for dead."

The next day, Lucy explained she loitered at the piano bar most of the time. She got to know the piano bar singer. His work shift finished at midnight, and they walked the upper deck talking afterwards. She minimized and made light of my feelings of abandonment. All I knew was that she was not in the piano bar when I passed through it, searching for her.

Some months later, Lucy told me the piano bar singer reached out to her. He wanted to meet her in a nearby port. She agreed to visit him with our daughter Maggie. However, he wanted, even insisted, that only Lucy go to see him. She told me she decided not to meet him because of his questionable demands.

Chapter Twelve

The Real Estate Agent

From the first time I met this fellow, he seemed much too touchy-feely around my wife. However, when it came to real estate, he was on the ball and persistent.

Lucy told me that sometimes she saw him having lunch with other married women. Lucy also shared her belief he and these other women cheated on his soon-to-be wife with whom he lived.

During our Caribbean cruise, my parents came from England to stay at our place to watch our children. The real estate agent knocked on my door in the middle of the workday, looking for Lucy.

My mother recently told me, "How odd it was." Then her explanation continued, "Having this gentleman arrive at your home, looking for your wife, during your usual work hours."

My oldest daughter, Cassandra, started to work for him at some point, delivering fliers door to door.

Our family went to his parent's place for a party. Days later, Lucy told me he tried to shag her in the bathroom of his parents' home. But she focused her anger on me. Lucy raised her voice and began yelling at me. Her catalog of complaints included that I didn't even care. What was she talking about? He tried to fornicate with my wife in the bathroom, and somehow, she thought I did not care. Wait, hold on, these were preposterous accusations. How could I have even known? She had not told me about this before. Why was I the bad guy and had to explain I did not know? I did not understand the anger she directed towards me. Needless to say, our friendship with this fellow came to an abrupt end.

Despite our terminated friendship, this individual kept showing up. For example, Lucy told me that while taking one of the children out of the car seat in public, he walked up behind her and grabbed her underwear, the thong sticking out the back of her jeans.

She told another story that he asked her, "What will it take for us to have sex? Do I have to get you a ring?"

His brazen offer of an engagement ring to my wife with the expectation to engage in sex. Outrageous!

From the time I realized he was Mr. Creepy, I often warned Cassandra how I wanted her to stop working for him. It felt to me like he groomed her with the clear ambition to become her sugar daddy when she turned eighteen. Cassandra kept working for him for a while because she wanted the money. Lucy did not help to stop it. She would only report to me when Cassandra worked for him. I required this guy to be permanently out of our lives. But, like a bad case of herpes, he just kept showing up.

Not until sometime after his marriage did he seem to disappear from our lives.

Chapter Thirteen

Dumpster Diving

Invariably, we collected too much junk in the house. It routinely overflowed into my two-car garage. Lucy often held yard sales, except she would never sell much. She either set her price too high for things or decided something was placed outside in error as someone was about to buy it. I think the only things she ever sold were my personal items.

Be that as it may, the rubbish we amassed had to go. On occasion, maybe twice per year, I ordered a dumpster and filled it up with refuse, such as broken furniture, unused toys, ripped or worn-out clothing, rotting food from the garage, and the regular trash.

It was typical for Lucy to become upset and even mad about the disposal of debris. She usually recovered things out of the dumpster. More than once, she climbed into a dumpster looking for all her precious garbage. It was crazy, and I would laugh it off in unease with our children. However, I found this particular aspect of her behavior weird, eerie, and disconcerting when it occurred.

Chapter Fourteen

Her Brother's Story

Lucy had one sibling, a younger brother named Franko, and we called him Frank. I never met him as he lived in Croatia. Once or twice, I conversed on the phone with him. However, we only spoke a few words each time since he could not speak English.

Sometime after Lucy and I married, Frank found a job and began to work at the local jail. The police force operated the jail system in the country. As a jailer, he did not carry a firearm. I was not aware of a formal training period. It seemed to me that his job paid a reasonable salary because he bought a BMW.

Now that Frank had a job and owned a BMW, a much more prestigious car than the old Mazda MPV I drove. Why did a requirement remain for me to continue to send money to her family in Croatia? I never received a satisfactory answer to this question. However, a need remained for more money to float over to her family in Croatia routinely.

Her brother married sometime after we did. His marriage, ever so brief, lasted about one meager year. They had one son together. The story, as I understood it, Frank's crazy wife threw him out. I never discovered why she threw him out. Lucy alluded he did not help enough with raising their son, and his wife's pregnancy affected her mind. His mother-in-law moved in with his wife and child, and the evil mother-in-law would not let him see them.

In the immediate aftermath of their separation, I heard stories about his new girlfriend. He and his new partner moved in together, and she became pregnant soon after. Frank had a second son out of wedlock with his live-in companion. His two sons were born less than two years apart.

Sometime later, his employer fired him from his job. They terminated her brother for cause. I never knew the actual reason for his firing. Lucy never explained.

Instead, she blamed "The crooked system in Croatia."

According to Lucy, almost everything in Croatia seems to involve corruption.

Soon after Frank lost his job, Lucy's stories focused on the police. They searched for and wanted to arrest her brother. According to Lucy, his BMW was the marriage of two stolen cars welded into one, and she now disclosed he bought the BMW from some shady chop shop. The authorities wanted to repossess the vehicle for bearing invalid identification numbers.

I heard her proclaim things like, "Oh, my poor brother," "He paid good money for his car," or "How could he know he bought a stolen car?" and "The system over there is crooked."

When not in use, her brother hid the car. He parked his car in the garage at various friends' homes to conceal it. He chose a different location after each outing.

Then we heard her brother died in an accident. He lost control of his BMW while the police chased him. He went off the road and hit a tree. The car split in two, exactly where the chop shop welded the two vehicles together.

The ambulance took over two hours to arrive and pick him up from the accident scene. They took him to the hospital, where he underwent surgery for a broken leg. Sadly, he died while under anesthesia during the operation on his leg.

You can imagine my wife's hysteria. Her baby brother died around the age of thirty. So, right away, I bought Lucy an airplane ticket with an open-ended return date so she could attend her brother's funeral. And then she could spend as much time with her family as needed.

Lucy's brother and his wife separated five years earlier. They never divorced. But his wife immediately withdrew all his work and insurance benefits for herself. She left me in the lurch to pay for his funeral expenses. Then, to add salt to the wounds, his wife, whom he never divorced, still, to this day, would not allow anyone from Lucy's family to visit with Frank's son.

Lucy stayed in Croatia for no more than two weeks, a much shorter visit than I expected. While there, she visited many friends and relatives from nearby villages and towns. A few days before her return, Lucy told me over the phone that someone had attempted to mug her while taking an evening stroll through her hometown. The thug hit her in the head, although Lucy assured me she was all right. Lucy told me how she fought the attacker off, threw rocks, and yelled at him. I was concerned for her and proud of her effective resistance against the assailant. I even told some of my friends at work.

Her brother's funeral occurred years ago during the pre-digital age of photography. We took the rolls of film to the local parking lot booth, a Jiffy-Photo-Mart type of place, for development. We waited a few days to retrieve and view the pictures, and they weirded me out. Different cultures practice different customs. However, photos of everyone gathered around an open casket struck me as a little morbid. I only saw a display of grief on Lucy's face in one or two of the photos while she stood beside her brother's open casket. The remaining pictures showed Lucy smiling from ear to ear, grinning with her teeth showing, and making two-fingered peace symbols. In other images, she stood with her mother in a group of relatives. They all grieved. Nobody else smiled. Yet Lucy beamed for these funeral parlor glamour shots while everyone else mourned. I know everyone deals with grief in their own way, yet I always deemed those pictures as no less than peculiar.

Lucy had conspiracy theories galore regarding the circumstances surrounding her brother's death. According to her, several hospitals in Croatia harvested organs from dead bodies without permission. As part of the conspiracy, ambulances took their time before reaching an accident scene. This delay allowed younger and healthier people to pass away from their injuries before arriving at a hospital.

To further explain her viewpoint, Lucy said, "Young and healthy organs are worth more money."

Another part of the conspiracy was that these hospitals used a specific drug to stop the heart of victims while under anesthesia in surgery. She claimed they harvested all her brother's organs, including his brain. Lucy described the thick black thread used to sew up the incisions around the top of Frank's head. She said the stitches were garishly visible while he lay in repose at the funeral home within his coffin.

These conspiracy stories went on for years. Lucy added new ghoulish details on a random basis, such as hundreds of bodies being exhumed and tested for the heart-stopping drug and later stories of court cases to halt the exhumations. While her descriptions appeared outlandish, I believed Lucy and what she claimed happened to her brother.

Chapter Fifteen

It's Margarine?

This story of hers followed a kind of progression. While in Croatia for her brother's funeral, I shared Lucy's attempted mugging account with some of my friends from work. Lucy became quite angry with me when she learned I spoke with co-workers about the news.

By the time she returned home to Houston, her story soon changed. She confided to me, "I was raped."

During the mugging attempt, the assailant raped her. A few weeks later, she told me, "I just found out from the doctor that I am pregnant."

"She tested positive for pregnancy—with a rapist's child!" my mind screamed in agony.

I wanted the rapist brought to justice. Lucy explained that her aunt had taken her to the hospital, and she filed a report. Hospital or police report? I do not know. Lucy's explanations were nebulous at best, and I never heard any specific details. But she had been through a lot, which explained the cagey depictions.

No one besides Lucy, her aunt, and I knew about the rape. She was embarrassed and traumatized by her rape. In her usual way, Lucy avoided talking about the subject. The rapist got away, and she could not identify him. We lived on a different continent from the perpetrator. Lucy wanted me to let it go.

I wanted an abortion performed. We knew nothing about the rapist, and there could be anything from genetic problems to drug problems. Who knew? Lucy was dead set against terminating the pregnancy and would not kill the baby.

I struggled with the next issue and did not share my concern with Lucy. Could I raise and treat this child as one of my own? It took me a couple of weeks to come to terms with it, and throughout the years, not only have I treated Fannie like my own daughter—she is my daughter.

At some point during this ordeal, Lucy told me one of her mother's old sayings, "It's not butter, and it won't melt away."

The "it" referred to a woman's private parts–her vagina. I assumed Lucy communicated this phrase to me, worried I would no longer want her because of the rape.

I loved my wife, and this rape would not lessen that feeling.

Still, I perceived her statement as baffling and thought, "What an unusual and strange expression."

Lucy made me swear never to reveal the circumstances of her rape to anyone, to cushion herself and the baby from all future harassment. I agreed, and I kept my word. I never told a soul until around ten years later, when my world started to fall apart. And I will tell you that story later.

There are five stages of grief: denial, anger, bargaining, depression, and acceptance.[3] I think I went through four of those stages. I do not remember being depressed, although I was undoubtedly worried and concerned.

Lucy had a bruise on her forehead and said she was hit on the head and knocked half-senseless. Thinking back, it wasn't a legitimate bruise. It exhibited no swelling, no breaks in the skin, no blood, and no scabbing. Instead, it appeared as a discoloration

---

[3] Elisabeth Kübler-Ross authored On Death and Dying in 1969 based on her near-death studies. In this book, she postulated her theory of the five stages of grief, now known as the Kübler-Ross Model.

of the skin. The bruise resembled a triangular mark precisely in the middle of her forehead and a little above her eyes. It took close to a year for it to fade away and disappear.

Lucy talked about her need to go to the doctor to get tested for AIDS and Venereal Disease (VD). I guess there was a stigma with the term VD, which was deprecated. What is it called now, STDs (Sexually Transmitted Diseases)? Wait, this expression also fell into disfavor, and they changed it again to STI (Sexually Transmitted Infection). Sorry, I went off on a tangent, making fun of all the label changes over the years. I grew up attending a private Catholic High School under the fear of VD, so it will always be VD to me. Anyhow, I do not remember anything about Lucy being tested for VD or any results.

We named our daughter Frances in memory of Lucy's brother Franko, who died nine months earlier. From as early as I can remember, we called her Fannie.

Chapter Sixteen

Assaulted

Lucy kicked our daughter Cassandra out of her bedroom and doubled her up in her sister Maggie's bedroom. Then, she rented Cassandra's bedroom to a single mother and her daughter. One evening, I came home from work to find these people had already moved into my home.

Eventually, I learned this single mother worked as a waitress at a local bikini bar. I do not know where Lucy found these people, although she said they were like-minded and met in the organic section at a grocery store.

One day, while this occupant wore a tank top, I observed scars all over her arms and shoulders. Several dozens, maybe even over a hundred, of these inch-long scars, large white welts all over. I could not help myself and asked her about the marks.

I considered her explanation mind-boggling. She used to cut herself as a troubled teen. I had never heard of anything like this except in the movie Doom. When Goat cut himself for uttering a profanity against God, he sported around six scars on his forearm. Yet this girl in my house sat in a league of her own, way beyond Goat's condition. I found it concerning and disturbing that someone with these types of issues lived in our home close to our children.

One of her boyfriends started coming to our home nightly. He stayed upstairs in her bedroom until the wee hours of the morning. This individual radiated the demeanor of an unsavory character. He appeared disheveled, dirty, and smelly. He dragged his feet as he walked and always seemed nervous and agitated.

I called him "the Meth Head."

I found it extremely uncomfortable with this individual in my home. To deal with these distressing circumstances, I set rules. She could not bring men or anyone upstairs. If she wanted visitors, she could meet with them downstairs or outside.

I guess my rules did not sit well with her. She decided to move out about a month later. On the day of her move, the Meth Head and another obese and out-of-shape friend came to take her things. Even if their lives depended on it, these two clowns could not safely move large items. I helped them carry the weightier pieces down the stairs, out the door, and to their truck to save my house from damage. I helped them with mattresses, bookcases, dressers, and whatever else required my assistance.

As I walked up the slope of my front lawn towards my home, after I helped them with the last load, the Meth Head stepped between myself and my home. He stood higher on the slope than I. He was rising and lowering on the balls of his feet as he got right in my face. I could smell his skanky breath as he leaned towards me, inches from my face. Then, with his chest pressed against mine, he told me, "Lucy goes to the [bikini] bar a lot, trying to pick guys up."

I did not realize it at the time. It appears this person espoused the sole purpose of wanting to fight with me.

I remember the surprised look on his face as I responded with a dismissive tone, "Just leave."

I walked around him, and then, out of the blue from behind me, he sucker-punched me to the side of my head. It happened so fast that I could not fully comprehend what was occurring. The next thing I knew, we faced each other, although he was on top and tried to knee me in the head. I used to wrestle in high school and university. I positioned myself so his entire leg hit me across the chest with his foreleg–the femur part of his leg. I did not get hurt, the point of his knee did not hit me, and I took no strikes to my head. While his ineffectual bashing on me wasted most of his energy, he finally picked me up, held me upside down, and threw me to the side.

By tossing me to the side, he separated us. Now, my adrenaline kicked in. My fight mode engaged less than thirty seconds after his first sucker punch. He was younger and smaller than me. I figured I could give him a trouncing with ease. Then, I contemplated my situation. I lived in the United States on a work permit with my Permanent Residency application in progress. I did not want to risk my work or our legal status over the likes of this shady individual. I assessed all of these thoughts in the blink of an eye.

He no longer stood between the house and me, so I decided to withdraw. I turned around, entered my home, and dialed 911. The police caught him a few blocks away. He ran off on foot, carried no ID, and would not give his name. They took him in for fingerprinting and identification—I love our first responders.

I began to feel a nagging and painful ache in my hip while the police interviewed me in my home. I pulled up my shirt to discover one of the ugliest bruises I had ever witnessed. When he threw me, my hip struck the edge of the concrete walkway. This prominent circular bruise grew and spread across my buttocks all the way up past my ribs. It consisted of yellow, red, and purple concentric circles resembling an archery target. I showed the officers my hands and knuckles to prove I never threw one punch.

As I recounted the attack's details to the two police officers, I relayed he threatened my family and me.

I remember bursting out crying in front of the officers as I told them, "He knows where my kids go to school."

I did not want to press charges out of fear for my children, and I asked the police to tell him, "Leave us alone. We are not pressing charges."

I told Lucy I never wanted someone else living in our home again. Would you believe it? A few weeks later, she rented Cassandra's bedroom all over again. Coming home from work that night felt incredibly awkward, and renters were already half-moved in as Lucy excitedly explained things to me. Both times, Lucy brought strangers into our home without my consent or foreknowledge.

Chapter Seventeen

A Friend's Divorce

Lucy met Sadia and her husband Rifah years ago before Lucy's brother passed away. She got to know them at Sadia's family-owned beauty salon. She found their business located in a strip mall close to our home. Both Sadia and Rifah worked at the parlor.

Our families soon became friends. Lucy often watched their two sons during work hours. In addition, Lucy and our children visited them on a regular basis, and she often brought home a plate of Bangladeshi cuisine for me to eat when I returned from work.

Less than two years after Fannie was born, without warning, Lucy unexpectedly became quite upset with me one day. She accused me of not buying Fannie enough toys. That same day, Rifah gave Fannie an outdoor playhouse as a present.

To start, Lucy rubbed the details of his gift in my face, "Rifah bought her a playhouse as a gift," and then she said, "Isn't he nice."

When I mentioned how strange it was for him to buy our daughter such an extravagant gift for no particular occasion, asking "Why, out of the blue, would he spend so much money on our daughter?"

"He bought it for his boys, but they were too old for it. So, he gave it to us." Lucy explained.

Years later, Lucy informed me that Rifah and Sadia were facing marital problems. Sadia called me sometime soon after, crying on the phone. She said, "People have seen Rifah and Lucy together, spending time at the malls, shopping, and having lunch together at restaurants."

As she continued to weep on the phone, she told me, "Lucy is having an affair with my husband."

Now, I do not want to sound racist or anything, although it may appear as such. All I could think was, "Why the hell would my beautiful wife, who has and loves me, want anything to do with that little man?"

Sadia's story sounded ludicrous to me. I found her insinuations ridiculous, sad, and amusing in a strange way all at the same time. I figured Sadia felt distraught as her marriage fell apart from under her feet. Not knowing how to react or what I could say to console her. I took my leave from this uncomfortable phone conversation in the politest approach I could muster.

After they divorced, I never heard much about Sadia. But every once in a while, I learned the latest news of Rifah or their sons.

Samuel P. Frearson

Chapter Eighteen

Child Protective Services

Child Protective Services (CPS) conducted separate interviews with Maggie and the twins at their school.

The twins were young at the time, and they only remember CPS asking questions about their mother. Gilbert remembers telling the CPS worker a story about him and his siblings being left alone at home, afraid, and wondering where Mom went. The twins were in grade one or two when questioned.

Maggie's only memory of the incident was going to the principal's office for an interview. She does not remember the context or the questions. She studied in grade three or four.

Cassandra said CPS never interviewed her. She only found out about it many years later. Cassandra believes she may have already resided at college, living in the dorm away from home. But as I calculate it, she must have been in High School around the eleventh grade.

CPS never contacted or spoke to me, and I knew nothing about the interviews, the case's topic, or the case's existence until after it had closed. They interviewed Lucy, and after the case closed, she explained that a neighbor had filed the complaint. Lucy described how she dealt with CPS when they appeared at our door. Without any problem, she invited them in, spoke with them, and gave them a tour of our home. She explained to CPS everything was all right.

I do not know if the following ties into the CPS story. Maybe it fits better under the heading of affairs or abuse. However, when we lived in Houston, Lucy often gave Cassandra some money and compelled her to walk her siblings to the local fast-food burger joint. This place included an indoor play area of its own. With each visit, Lucy gave Cassandra explicit instructions to remain there all day. When the kids returned home, it was common for Lucy to become angry, complaining they did not stay long enough.

I knew that Lucy often sent the kids to the burger joint under Casandra's supervision. But, until a short time ago, during the second part of my story, I did not realize the duration or frequency of these trips or Lucy's anger concerning our children's return.

Chapter Nineteen

Credit Problems

The first time I refinanced our home, we had over $80,000 in additional debt beyond the mortgage. More than sixty-thousand dollars that Lucy amassed in revolving credit card debt. The remaining twenty-thousand dollars was our two auto loans. After that, I refinanced the home another two times due to the crushing debt she kept incurring.

Lucy applied for credit cards in my name without my knowledge. Some I found out about, but most she kept under the radar. At one point, she held two Victoria's Secret cards, both in my name. I can unequivocally state that I do not wear Victoria's Secret clothes. I do not shop at that store. Except once or twice, in the company of Lucy or my daughters, when I paid for their purchases. I never applied for a Victoria's Secret credit card. Lucy once explained she required the card to purchase bras online, as the stores never stocked her size, 32 Double D.

I never noticed when my wife went from no maintenance to high maintenance. Thinking back, she always required more money than I made. Yet, she seemed to make do with our available resources. At least until she felt comfortable using my credit and bank cards and then applying for credit cards in my name. Finally, she seemed to make due all of the debt, forcing me to refinance several times.

I worked eighty to ninety hours per week, and we never had extra cash. Lucy's excuse for the excessive debt and not curbing her shopping practices?

"Everyone else is doing it," as she pointed out friends or neighbors who she claimed suffered similar credit and debt problems.

I guess you can figure out my response to her was, "I don't care how our neighbors get themselves into credit card problems." Then I continued with an example, "If they jump off a bridge, I am not going to follow them down that same failed trail."

Needless to say, my explanations never helped, and she remained hell-bent on spending everything–and more–on herself.

One time, I became furious. Lucy co-signed for a friend's credit card with a $5,000 credit limit. Lucy was involved in several Multi-Level Marketing (MLM) businesses. And her meritless explanation to me afterwards was her friend was supposed to buy five-thousand dollars' worth of Lucy's products. However, this lady immediately maxed out the credit card on other things and then disappeared. This debt and her disappearance left me stuck carrying the load. I canceled the card and paid off its balance. Lucy and credit cards were an issue I always had no control over, and I often got burned by her credit schemes. I was so angry that I threatened to divorce Lucy if she ever co-signed for anyone again. I must point out Lucy had only known this friend for a few weeks.

Chapter Twenty

Sports and Activities

Long ago, my father taught me to keep the kids occupied so they do not become loiterers and fall into other bad habits. Following my father's advice, we enrolled our children in many activities. They participated in sports like soccer, hockey, t-ball, volleyball, and swimming. They joined their high school orchestra, played the violin and piano, and took dance lessons, including ballet, jazz, and hip-hop.

Lucy registered each of the kids for multiple activities at the same time. She would share some of the duties. However, I was the principal contributor and did most of the driving. At this point in my life, I worked over sixty hours per week and drove our children all over the place each weekend. I could not even watch most of their games because I transported our kids to and from them. I am not complaining. I loved watching my children play and enjoy sports the same way I now love watching my grandchildren play. However, due to the amount of driving, I never got to stop and enjoy smelling the roses, as it were.

I coached soccer as the assistant coach for one year and head coach for the next two years. I also refereed soccer for two years—well, truth be told, only as a flagman on the sidelines.

When it came to the twins playing hockey, I was the only parent who performed the driving. I am not sure if Lucy ever attended a single game. They participated in a weekend tournament out of town, and Lucy refused to go. As a consequence, I drove my boyos to their competition, and we had a great time. Clifford even scored the first goal of his life during the tournament. It was the game-winning goal, and I still have the puck.

Chapter Twenty-One

Arguments

The first several years I knew Lucy, it seemed that we were almost always in sync on virtually every topic, and I do not believe we ever argued.

While we lived in the United States, Lucy slowly became quarrelsome with me. Eventually, she graduated to a belligerent level and later to combative. I don't know when she started using these tactics, and I only started to notice it after it reached an atrocious pitch.

In an argument over one thing, Lucy would go on the attack over fifty other things. She would talk too fast for me to keep track of all the various complaints, faults, and blame she hurled at me. She would wear me down to a nub. Verbal clashes with her were always a losing proposition for me. I would typically give up based on the sheer volume of persistent complaints and accusations.

As the years progressed, she began to yell over me. I am not talking about being loud. She would scream her vitriolic babble for minutes on end until I acquiesced. It was difficult for me to get two words in during these episodes. She was always on a mission with a purpose.

More than once, I successfully interjected into a tirade of hers, "Would you please stop yelling."

Lucy would immediately deny any yelling, then demonstrate the difference between her talking loudly and screaming by yelling at me, "This is loud," and then screaming, "And this is screaming."

The only difference I could detect between her examples of talking loud and screaming was the shrill-pitched voice she added to the screaming.

I always felt burned, tired, and devalued after one of her scathing outbursts. Like many things regarding Lucy's behavior, she continuously ratcheted it up a notch after each time I became accustomed to the previous level.

It regularly felt to me as though she was organized chaos. I liken it to the Tasmanian Devil's whirlwind from Bugs Bunny's Looney Tunes cartoon. Of course, the whirlwind itself was a chaotic mess. However, it had a method and purpose, and Taz invariably beat Bugs to the destination.

Chapter Twenty-Two

Move to Florida

Years ago, around sixteen years ago, my employer moved us from Houston, Texas, to Titusville, Florida. It was an executive-level type move, all expenses paid, and they would even buy my home in Houston for an agreed-upon price if I could not sell it.

I moved ahead of the rest of my family when our Houston house sold around February of that year. I drove our SUV and towed a U-Haul trailer full of valuable items.

Cassandra was away in her second year of college in New York, so she was never a part of the move.

Lucy planned to stay behind for thirty days with the kids. They would fly out once escrow for the new home in Titusville closed in March. She and our children remained with a neighbor. However, after escrow closed and the Titusville house belonged to us, Lucy decided to stay in Houston until the kids' school year finished.

Even though her sudden change of plans was upsetting for me, it made sense from our children's schooling perspective. So, I did not make an issue out of it.

Chapter Twenty-Three

Cell Phones

Lucy adopted cell phones before anyone else in our family. She wanted it for her Multi-Level Marketing (MLM) businesses. As a result, she created a service account in her name. I did not acquire a cell phone under her account until we moved to Florida.

Every year, Lucy traded in her cell phone with the latest model for herself while I continued using her old original hand-me-down flip phone until the screen stopped functioning. Even with a broken screen, Lucy would not allow me to get another phone. For years, I paid for her cell phones and the service, the typical monthly payment in the range of $600, although many times well over $1500. Finally, I went to the cell phone store to buy myself a new phone. They would not allow it.

I could not purchase a new phone to replace the broken one for my existing phone line on Lucy's account. She clutched the account and held it in lockdown. Lucy secured her account with an iron fist. Eventually, I was able to purchase a new phone and add it to her account. But only because the provider called Lucy, and she permitted it for this one time.

Whenever I needed something done with the cell phone service, a nightmare ensued.

Years later, it would dawn on me that Lucy probably had my name barred from accessing her account.

Chapter Twenty-Four

Broken Finger

While lost in reverie as I mowed the lawn in the backyard with hearing protection, Maggie startled me as she suddenly grabbed my arm.

Crying, she tugged at my side and said, "Come inside, Fannie is hurt, and Mom is going to kill Clifford."

I rushed to Fannie in the house. She stood alone in the kitchen and held her hand close to her chest. As I attended Fannie, I became aware of an unfolding scene forty feet away in the living room. I could see Clifford crouched in the corner. He cried and cowered with his arms covering his head. Lucy stood over him, howling the most vicious insults and swinging her arms in wild attacks focused on him. I think I saw her pause for a moment, looking for an opening before making a direct punch at him.

I yelled at Lucy in a commanding voice, "Stop it. You're making things worse."

Meanwhile, I saw the tip of Fannie's middle finger hanging from a bit of skin from the fingerprint side. It appeared to me that the finger was cut almost entirely off—directly below her fingernail.

I needed to get Fannie to the hospital fast. Clifford was traumatized by his mother, and he felt guilty about the accident of slamming his bedroom door on Fannie's finger. I wanted to keep

Clifford close by and safe as well. So, we all got into the car and headed out, despite not knowing the hospital's location, as we were new to the area. We called 911, and they asked us to pull over at a specific gas station and wait for paramedics. A full-size fire truck pulled into the gas station less than one minute after us. Talk about excellent response time. They checked Fannie's finger and explained how to get to the hospital. I guess they could see the confused look on my face, and they offered to escort us there—I love our first responders.

We learned from the emergency room doctor that Fannie suffered a crush injury, and he also showed us the x-ray displaying the broken bone at the tip of her finger. They stitched up the end of her finger and placed a metal splint around it. This brace was more to protect her finger from bumps than to hold things together.

They assured us, "Her finger should heal up fine." Then, he referred us to a specialist.

That night, after we returned home, Lucy apologized for her tirade against Clifford, explaining, "I just don't know what came over me after Fannie got hurt."

Lucy never apologized to Clifford for her horrific behavior.

Some days later, we visited the specialist. He inspected her injuries.

"Your daughter should regain full feeling in her finger," he said, "Her finger is already healing very nicely."

Chapter Twenty-Five

Gout

One morning, I woke up in excruciating pain. It felt like my foot was on fire and broken. The simple act of the bed sheets sliding over my foot hurt like hell. When I removed the linens to look at my foot, I found it red, swollen, and burning hot to the touch. But touching it, even ever so slightly, sent shock waves of pain through my entire body. The pain was debilitating, and I felt crippled by it. I could not walk. I could not put on a shoe or even a sock.

I did not go to the doctor's office for several days. I thought the pain and swelling could go away as quickly as they appeared. Shortly after I arrived at the clinic, the doctor told me, "You have a nasty case of gout there."

"Gout?" I argued with the doctor, "It can't be gout."

I did not live a life of extravagant eating. Nobody else in my family, cousins, uncles, or great-uncles, ever lived with gout.

"This is a classic case of gout," the doctor restated as he gently applied a slight pressure on the knuckle of my big toe, making me flinch quickly from the sharp pain his touch produced. Then, he prescribed some anti-inflammatory pills.

A friend of mine from work, who suffered from gout for years, told me he endured regular flare-ups in his feet and elbows.

He also told me he used some drugs that were on the market for decades and were safe to use with no side effects.

After a week, I returned to the clinic. The anti-inflammatory drugs did not work, and my foot grew worse. I saw a different doctor who assured me the anti-inflammatory medications would not help. Instead, he prescribed a potent steroid dose. I took a different number of pills every four hours for seven days. He gave me detailed instructions, warnings, and cautions regarding their use. Steroids. Oh my gosh, they worked! The next day, my foot's swelling vanished. Some pain remained, but I could walk. Not only that, I felt like Superman, with strength, endurance, and an incredible feeling of well-being and invulnerability. With these newfound superpowers, I could get the entire honeydew list done. Despite feeling indestructible, I followed my doctor's orders of no additional activities and restricted myself to mowing the front lawn.

After my second encounter with gout four months later, I decided to change my diet to control it. Outbreaks occurred in the big toe of my right foot about twice a year, and I managed these flare-ups with steroids. Cheese is my kryptonite. I love cheese, and avoiding it is a challenging task. You will find it in most prepared meals, a staple of the American diet. So, I gave up cheese, and I only risk eating one slice of pizza per year. I also gave up drinking beer. Oh, how I miss my Guinness. I do not think I drank more than four beers in the past ten-plus years since my first bout with gout. Sometimes, I required a second round of steroids for the more severe flare-ups.

Believe me when I say, "All flare-ups are bad, but some flare-ups are more bad than others"—my gout rendition of George Orwell's 1945 novel Animal Farm: A Fairy Story.

Over the years, these flare-ups became progressively worse and more frequent. Gout developed in my ankle, little toe, and the long toe beside the big toe. I often required three or four courses of steroids to clear it. At four rounds, my doctor would not prescribe more steroids. Since I was in the middle of a painful cycle of gout, there was absolutely no way I would remain in a perpetual state of agony.

I found a new doctor, got a steroid injection, and another seven-day pack of steroids to clear it up. He also put me on two drugs, Allopurinol and Colchicine. Unfortunately, I reacted to both drugs. One drug reduced my liver function to dangerously low levels, and the other gave me memory and attention problems. I thought I was in the beginning stages of Alzheimer's disease. These memory problems went away two weeks after I stopped taking those drugs.

You may be asking yourself, "What does an account about gout have to do with narcissists?"

Gout plays a prominent role in dealing with a horrible situation later in the story. From a chronological standpoint, describing my condition with gout fits in well, telling it in the book here.

Spoiler alert! After I filed for divorce (yes, I eventually woke up and filed for divorce). I saw a video ad on the internet for some product claiming to help with gout. I did an internet search because the knuckles of my big and little toes were persistently sore and considerably deformed. I am not one to jump on miracle cures or believe everything I find online. However, the explanation in the video made sense to me. At the very least, it seemed to be a plausible solution worth trying.

I bought a thirty-day supply of Carbamide and Arginex. The video claimed these two supplements would scrub and clean out my kidneys, allowing my kidneys to perform their normal functions and hence reducing my gout. The next day after taking those pills, I detected a difference in the frequency and amount of pee I spouted. My God, man, the floodgates had opened by the third day. I do not remember urinating this often or with this volume at any point in my life. The uptick in frequency was not from a lack of bladder control. My bladder filled up six to ten times a day and in the middle of the night. I filled the toilet each time I peed. After three weeks, I felt a faint yet sharp pain around my kidney area, and I stopped taking the products.

I must tell you, these supplements worked for me. I did not once suffer a single full-on flare-up for over four years. Since then, when I encountered soreness in my foot, I took one pill a day for two or three days, and the pain went away. The other thing I found overly pleasing was that the deformity of my foot slowly retreated. Those two knuckles were not back to normal. However, the bumps were no longer discernible. I could wear shoes all day again with minimal pain, although I continued to wear flip-flops most of the time.

These two products were a game-changer in my twelve-year struggle with gout. I do not know if they are suitable for everyone with gout. Try it and see if it helps. What do you have to lose? My only wish here is to help others who suffer from this terrible condition. Perhaps I should add a disclaimer here—I am not a doctor, this is not medical advice, and I am not affiliated with any company selling these products. Consider it a dietary supplement suggestion. You should seek out your doctor's opinion and proceed from there.

After four years, I began to experiment with my diet. Unfortunately, many of these diet trials did cause several flare-ups, and I now refrain from all the foods that cause issues.

Chapter Twenty-Six

Descent into Madness

Once, when Lucy wanted me to fix the email program on her laptop, I found a long email letter, approximately three pages' worth of printed text from Lucy to Rifah. In it, she proclaimed her love for him, asking, "Why do you mistreat me?" She also wrote, "You hurt Fannie's feelings."

When I confronted Lucy with the email, she explained that she wrote the letter because Rifah talked about killing one of his sons for being gay, and he also felt suicidal. She further articulated that she tried to save him by sharing her love with him. I almost swallowed her nonsensical story. However, something either in the email or elsewhere tipped me off. Rifah was Fannie's biological father, and no rape occurred in Croatia.

Lucy got on her knees in a praying position right in front of me, begging for forgiveness. She almost prostrated herself. She did not lay flat on the ground; she remained on her knees with her face and elbows on the floor. Her hands moved up and down in a praying gesture. She swore they slept together only once, during her confusion while traumatized by her brother's death. She promised to do anything, and as hurt and confused as I was, I could not accept her offers as recompense.

I hid my crying and tears at work, burying my nose in my computer screen. I kept my back towards anyone who passed by my cubicle. Ultimately, I spoke with my manager, an accommodating gentleman. I explained my situation, my inability to perform my work, and the embarrassment I felt as I wept at my desk. Finally, I told my boss about Lucy's sexual assault story, which I recently discovered covered up an affair. He consoled me, wrote down the company helpline, and gave me the rest of the day off. Informing him of this story was the first time I ever told anyone about Lucy's fabricated tale of rape from twelve years earlier.

While I drove home bawling, I started experiencing chest pains and possibly some form of a panic attack. I pulled onto the highway's shoulder and then called the helpline. They wanted to get me an ambulance in case of a heart attack. After a few minutes of talking with the person on the helpline, I started feeling well enough to continue on my way home once again. I do not remember how many days I took off from work, probably an entire week.

Lucy would become pretty upset if I called her betrayal and lies an affair. She seemed disassociated from me and my feelings. The gravity of the situation did not seem to register with her. She gave me the impression that she treated it like water under the bridge or as though it never happened. I contemplated divorce, but I honestly did not want to lose the love of my life.

I cried a lot, uncontrollably at times. It was more feeling sorry for myself than anything else. She turned my world upside down and did not seem to care.

She told me more than once I needed to "grow up," "man up," or "get over it."

She also wanted and demanded we never talk about it again.

One morning, during this time off work period, I remember while showering, I wailed like a madman, and snot ran down my face. I don't know how to give an accurate description of the moment. It felt like I wept for myself while a second me, or a voice inside my head, thought about how much of a wretch I looked. My internal monologue also spoke of ways to commit suicide. It refrained from talking about actually committing suicide, solely of ways to do it. Then the other me considered breaking the shower door glass and using a shard. Suddenly, I felt the real me wake up a little, frightened from the train of thought I had contemplated a moment before. I got out of the shower, still sobbing in a snot-filled pathetic trance. Dripping wet and naked, I called my employer's corporate helpline. They told me help was on the way. At some point, I remembered I stood there naked. Still dripping wet, I put my track pants on. I sat down on a step stool and continued my solitary spectacle of sorrow.

I remember the police knocking on the bathroom door. I do not remember opening it. I remember the paramedics taking me away on a stretcher. I do not remember getting onto the gurney. I cried the entire trip to the hospital. They placed me in an isolation chamber while I remained in a dismal state of disillusionment. They performed drug tests. I do not remember them drawing blood.

Until this point, I had been lost, marooned within the isolated island confines of my tormented, sorrowful thoughts.

Then, a doctor came in after a while and started talking to me. The first voice of reason I heard came from him.

In a straightforward manner, he said, "Stop crying. It isn't helping anything."

Thus marking the turning point at which I started the gradual end of my miserable display of tears and the re-acquisition of my composure. The doctor's single statement was the beacon or the lighthouse I clutched for safe return.

I did not realize it at the time. Never in my life have I experienced this magnitude of despair. I will expand on these feelings later in the book. Due to the pernicious aspect of Lucy's demeanor, a part of me momentarily lost the will to live.

Before releasing me, a hospital therapist interviewed me. I told her about Lucy's rape story and disclosed everything I had recently discovered regarding the affair. The hospital discharged me the same day they admitted me. I called my wife and asked if she could come to collect me, and she did. I felt a glimmer of hope. She still loved me enough to pick me up.

Chapter Twenty-Seven

The Reconciliation

Lucy was stubborn and kept the cell phone account locked to herself. However, she gave me the cell phone bills to pay. On intuition, I went through these bills and checked the list of calls and texts for any suspicious numbers. I found a bunch of numbers looking like Rifah's or his family's. I confronted Lucy with the information I discovered in the listings. I told her for our marriage to continue, she must break all contact with Rifah and his family. Maintaining any form of communication or relationship with any of them would be an outright betrayal of my trust.

She argued some of his relatives were regular customers of her MLM businesses, and they bought some of her health products. I did not care; we did not need their business, and all contact must end. Shortly thereafter, Lucy stopped asking me to pay for the cell phones, and in due course, the bills disappeared from the house.

Lucy told me Fannie had no idea about the affair with Rifah, and she made me swear never to reveal her biological father's identity. I did not wish to harm our daughter, so I agreed not to divulge this information to Fannie.

During this phase of my life, I went to see a marriage counselor alone. Lucy refused to attend, and I soloed most of the sessions. I told the counselor about Lucy's rape story, which I found out a short time ago, covered up an affair. However, with some pressure, I convinced Lucy to attend. Another one of those absurd events from my life ensued. It was the only time Lucy made an appearance with the marriage counselor.

While there, she dropped several one-liners I had not heard before, commensurate with, "I'm a child of the light" and "I found my spiritual awareness."

She talked at length about being a woke spirit. She expressed nothing about our relationship, the affair, or causing my despair. During the same session, I blamed myself and my job for the distance between us. I also talked about how I did not want to lose her.

There are five stages of grief: denial, anger, bargaining, depression, and acceptance. I think I went deep into all five steps, although I went through depression before bargaining with Lucy.

Life with Lucy deviated from normal at this juncture. She seemed nice again for a short period, and then conditions in due time became worse. Lucy seemed more distant than before I found out and confronted her about Rifah. I felt like a frog sitting in a pot of comfortable water, and the container sat upon a hot burner. And—I never noticed how I succumbed to the pain, agony, and anguish.

Chapter Twenty-Eight

The Business Partners

Lucy met Loqueesha when we first moved to Florida, and they became good friends and business partners. For years, Loqueesha would spend a few hours at our house almost daily. Chronologically speaking, I added her story here because, on this occasion, I observed Loqueesha's open contempt for me. Years earlier, Lucy became a director in Loqueesha's company, and Lucy led me to believe she received signing authority. One of the Multi-Level Marketing (MLM) businesses that Lucy operated funneled all its money through Loqueesha's company, giving it cash flow. Lucy possessed a bank debit card to the business and took her money out with the card.

Loqueesha registered her company in the District of Columbia.

You may be asking yourself, "Why would Sam add this little tidbit of information to the book?"

It will become quite clear later during the Deposition of Lucy.

One day, I went through the mail, ripped up, and threw out all the unsolicited credit card applications. Many of them were also in Lucy's name.

Loqueesha observed my undertaking and made a nasty "hrumpf" sound.

Maybe she even made some comments (I don't remember). She then proceeded to go through my garbage and collect any torn mail addressed to Lucy.

While sneering at me and red-faced, Loqueesha handed the recovered garbage to Lucy, gruffly spewing aloud, "Here is your mail," with the voice of one of Marge Simpson's sisters from the cartoon The Simpsons.

"Gadzooks, this is preposterous," I thought.

Her behavior was unbelievable. She disrespected me in my own house. Yet, I remained polite and did not say anything, even though I wanted her out of my house to never return.

When I brought up my misgivings about Loqueesha's behavior with Lucy later that night, she completely dismissed my feelings and arguments as she stated, "Loqueesha is simply a very protective friend of mine."

Lucy had a second business partner, Tim, who I did not plan to add to my book until after a development occurred during the second part of my story. It was as simple as a friend of mine sending me pictures of Tim and Lucy together at some hotel party. These pictures jogged my memory of some past troubling events regarding him.

To call this individual "a piece of work" is an understatement.

I always regarded him in low esteem, and my daughters all disliked him with a passion since the first time they met him. My two oldest daughters believed he persistently tried to hook up with their mother.

Anyone associated with an MLM business knows cross-line sponsorship is verboten. Around six months after Lucy joined a particular MLM, she met Tim at a conference. He convinced her to also enlist under him as her sponsor in the same business. He made all sorts of promises to help her line grow. I trust you fathom how their relationship blossomed from an unethical union.

Within the first year of meeting Tim, he got in trouble with the corporate office. They censured him and placed his enrollment with their company in limbo while deciding if they would expel him. While at a conference, a local news station video recorded him in an interview promoting the business' products. His interview sparked complaints against him to the company. He had dressed up in a white smock-like shirt and hung a stethoscope around his neck. He pandered himself as a doctor to bolster his sales of their health products. Lucy rallied many friends to help save his job, and they each wrote letters to the MLM's head office in support of him.

Tim lacked moral character, integrity, honesty, and ethics. He often demanded money from his down-line members to cover his travel expenses. He stole potential clients from his down-line for himself, similar to how he stole Lucy from a cross-line sponsor. Why did Lucy gravitate to these types of people?

Her Business Conduct

The next bit does not concern her business partners. Instead, it relates to Lucy's business behavior.

Her businesses, partners, clients, and customers eventually came first. As a concurrent side-effect, our family became a distant afterthought.

She would be on the phone until midnight, seven days a week. None of our children nor I could talk to her. She would get upset with us if we tried to interrupt her discussions. However, she would instantly drop a conversation or phone call with us for any of those people. Eventually, it became virtually impossible to reach my wife over the phone. She would immediately decline my calls. My children experienced the same difficulties, and Lucy would often be several hours late picking the kids up from school.

Her business calls were more social events than anything else. She would talk for hours with I do not know who and get angry if we tried to speak to her. And later, she would berate us for interfering with her businesses.

Many of her MLM products were expensive. The corporation offered an option to apply for a credit card to help with the initial purchase. Lucy assisted people in completing the information on these applications. She also retained the credit application forms, and Lucy would fax the application along with her clients' purchases to the corporation.

Lucy often told her clients, "My partners and previous clients all call me Mother Teresa."

I winced every time I heard her say these words, and I would tell Lucy not to say this. I once sat Lucy down to explain the impropriety of it.

"If other people want to call you Mother Teresa, let them. But you don't do it yourself," I told her.

Then I described how it was unbecoming of her to brag about such things herself. I even compared what she said to wearing a stethoscope in my attempt to make her understand.

Less than a week later, I overheard Lucy on the phone boasting to a prospective client, "I help so many people. They call me Mother Teresa."

I gave up trying to help with her businesses and avoided all her business dealings and gatherings. Whenever she had customers or clients in our home for demos or seminars, I would disappear and retire upstairs to my computer room. I witnessed entirely too many untenable circumstances, which I perceived as unethical. Stepping away was my approach to evading blame. I felt like a politician attempting to achieve plausible deniability.

I began to witness some bizarre performances. Lucy used different voices for distinct audiences. On a side note, I am certain Lucy acted in this manner all along, but I only became aware of her conduct and never recognized this behavior until soon before I moved from Florida to the farm. I heard Lucy use an unreal-sounding voice I had never heard before, and nobody talks like that.

Jeepers creepers, hearing that voice sent shivers down my spine, similar to nails on a chalkboard. When Lucy was on the phone with a creditor, she used an annoying, monotonous-sounding speech. It was a fake nasal sound she created in her throat.

Not until much later in the future did I realize she had several different intonations. Most of the vocalizations she employed had subtle differences. I do not think this was multiple personalities. I believe it was part and parcel of her well-practiced false pretenses. Without a doubt, this charmer also used these voice techniques to manipulate her creditors, clients, business partners, friends, our children, and me.

Chapter Twenty-Nine

Piano Lessons

Lucy had an exceptional and long-term friend from Croatia named Iva. Iva raised her daughter by herself and cared for her dying mother, who lived with her. Lucy helped Iva's mother until she passed away.

For years, Fannie took piano lessons with Iva. After Iva's mother passed away, she restricted her business to in-home instruction, and Fannie received her tutelage in our home for around the next two years. According to Lucy, our son Gilbert once went through Iva's handbag, looking for candies. Gilbert thought it was Lucy's shoulder bag he foraged through. Furthermore, Lucy told me how much it upset Iva. Lucy's story soon morphed into how she did not want Iva ever to accuse me of going through her purse. Then, to protect me, Lucy demanded I remain upstairs in my computer room each time Iva came to our home to teach Fannie piano. I never understood how Lucy's ludicrous concerns leapfrogged to me, yet I was more than happy to avoid their "girl talk" and play computer games with my two boys or help the kids with their homework.

Fannie's lessons were always Iva's last teaching class of the day. After each session, Iva stayed to visit Lucy. They would chat over a pot of tea for around an hour.

One day, towards the end of these two years of in-home lessons, a loud commotion developed downstairs. I could not hear what had gone on. However, I learned from Lucy that Iva stormed off upset.

Lucy came upstairs and told me, "Iva hid a camera in her purse," set to record. "When Iva went to the bathroom, I saw her purse open and unzipped."

Lucy told me, "Iva accused me of stealing from her. But I only zipped it closed."

The entire situation sounded so ridiculous to me. My tech giant employer paid me a handsome salary as a computer engineer. We were well off, and I considered us making an upper-middle-class standard of living. So why the hell would Lucy steal from her friend? A single mother, nonetheless. It made no sense whatsoever to me. I brushed it off as Iva being a little crazy and needless to say, Lucy and Iva's relationship fell apart, and Iva immediately disappeared from our lives.

Chapter Thirty

Separate Bedrooms

Lucy set up the downstairs guest bedroom for herself years ago, and she would occasionally sleep there instead of with me when she had cramps or other ailments. However, over time, she added additional reasons. So that she would not wake me up in the middle of the night, she slept downstairs on the nights before leaving on a business trip or returning from a business trip. This process of no longer sleeping with me spanned a period of roughly four years. She eventually stopped sleeping with me altogether. Remaining in the downstairs bedroom became her nightly norm.

Her rationale to occupy the downstairs bedroom initially began with her ailments and, after a couple of iterations, finally evolved to claiming I snored too much. In the end, she claimed she could not sleep. Her excuse sounded outrageous to me. Snoring, sure, maybe a little, but as a justification to no longer sleep with me? In disbelief, I asked each of our children about it, and they all confirmed that I did indeed saw logs at an awful pitch and volume. They claimed they could hear me through closed doors on another floor of the house.

I had a sleep study performed, only to find out I sustained hundreds of events per night with potential danger to my health. Incidents in which I skipped a breath, spiking my blood pressure.

I was not obese or overweight, so the results surprised the doctor. He prescribed a Continuous Positive Airway Pressure (CPAP) machine. When I started using the CPAP, Lucy slept with me for only one night. Her ensuing complaint was that the device made too much noise. She also made plenty of unkind remarks regarding how I looked wearing the mask.

As it turned out, I sustained a significantly deviated septum. It was S-shaped and located deep inside my nasal cavity. It blocked one nostril and restricted the other by over eighty percent. The doctor performed surgery for the deviated septum. I guess they extracted most of the cartilage from the septum.

A week after the operation, the doctor removed all the tubes and gauze from inside my nostrils. Instantly, I could breathe unrestrictedly through my nose. What a strange sensation. I don't think I could breathe freely since a sporting accident in college. Not only could I breathe with ease through my nose, but I could also smell things.

"So, what is that aroma I sense in this hospital hallway?" I thought as I left.

"Why, it is old lady perfume," I surmised.

As I stepped outside, I caught the intense scent of cut grass. "Uh, oh, I need to buy allergy pills in case of a severe, unfettered sneezing fit," I told myself.

Lucy started sleeping with me again, but only on the far side of our king-size bed. Her latest excuse was that she became too hot when I slept close to her.

Chapter Thirty-One

How About Now?

I genuinely believe that intimacy and sex are personal subjects between two people, not spoken of outside of the relationship. Yet here I am, blurting out to the world the very topic I feel is taboo to discuss.

In the beginning, Lucy and I had sex almost daily, oftentimes more than once a day. However, from around the time right before we married, it seemed the frequency with which we enjoyed lovemaking diminished at a gradual pace over the years.

After Lucy's brother died, she told me her Croatian rape story. I did not remember the following until I wrote this section. Due to the physical and mental trauma that she feigned to have suffered, we did not have sex for almost two years. Of course, you already know that no rape occurred. Instead, she had engaged in a so-called one-time affair. Afterwards, for about ten years until I bought the farm in 2014, intimacy between us only materialized maybe once or twice per month.

At some point during my late thirties, Lucy started using tampons every day of the month. I often joked, "You're on your period five weeks a month."

Usually, when I asked for sex, in an aggressive tone, she would reply, "No."

Sometimes, she would pull out her tampon and rub it in my face, saying, "See."

That was so disgusting and gross. Lucy smeared her pigstick across my lips.[4] And she did this to me dozens of times over the years.

"We are too old to have sex," was a new excuse Lucy started saying during my forties.

I honestly don't remember when I started using my own little signal for Lucy.

I would ask her, "How 'bout now?"

Most of the time, her responses were negative for the various reasons explained above. However, she would be agreeable every so often, and we would go upstairs to our bedroom–well, to the master bathroom.

Over time, another deprivation developed. I cannot recall when it started. Lucy stopped having sex with me in bed. During those rare occasions when she was agreeable, it could only be in the master bathroom, most times in the shower or in front of the sink. Looking back now, it no longer felt to me like love—it began to feel as though it were only an impassive sexual act.

For the last four years of our marriage, while I lived on the farm and Lucy in Florida, we had sex no more than twice per year. Although I must confess, Lucy only visited the area at the most twice per year, and she still threw out her excuses for no sex. Therefore, I guess a more honest estimate would be we had intercourse at most once per year.

A joke from my teens or early twenties comes back to mind. It was a parody I found quite funny, and I swore up and down would never happen to me. The skit goes as follows. A TV show host asked his audience how frequently they had sex.

"How many people enjoy sex once a day?" more than half of the audience raised their hands.

---

[4] A sinister play on words from the Charles Schwab firm's 2002 commercial phrase "Lipstick on a Pig."

"Okay, next is, how many people do it once a week?" A large portion of the audience extended their hands.

Then the host asks, "How many people engage in sex once a month?" Only a few hands are displayed here and there in the audience.

The host then exclaims, "One last question remains." He doesn't know why he should ask it but does anyway. "How many people have sex once a year?"

One old guy jumped up from his seat, hopping around, as he said, "Me, me."

Astounded at the elderly gentleman's enthusiasm, the host asked him, "Why are you so excited about having sex only once a year?"

The old man, still standing, his hand even now in the air, answered aloud, "Because tonight is the night!"

Life can be extremely brutal. She turned me into the pitiful old guy I swore I would never become. As a result, I no longer find this joke as funny as I once thought, now that it has become a painful reminder.

The last time I participated in intimate or sexual activities with Lucy. No, let me back up a bit. I have not had sex or amorous relations on any level with anyone other than Lucy since I saw her open the door at my grandfather's home the first day we met. Having said that, the last time I had sex with Lucy, in all likelihood, transpired during the summer, around eight months before what I call The Shit Show, which you will read about soon.

Chapter Thirty-Two

Hanky-Panky

Hanky-panky sounds like a cartoonish word for a kid's show, yet it construes unethical behavior, deceit, and illicit sexual relations.

Upon reflection, I realized Lucija's circle of friends contained many who were themselves engaged in affairs. She also had some friends with marital problems, whom she would coach on how to leave their spouse. It appears she surrounded herself with these troubled people.

I found pictures of a party Lucy attended. It was difficult to determine the number of people who participated. However, I assumed between fifty and a hundred. Everyone wore extremely revealing and suggestive costumes during a different time of year than Halloween. I never thought my wife would be part of an orgy, despite the fact it looked to me as though she attended a lecherous party designed to later turn into a sex fest. At best, these photos gave the appearance of being inappropriate.

I spoke with Lucy to let her know I did not want her involved with these events or hanging out with any of those people. She never admitted or denied the party was a celebration devoted to sexual enjoyment. However, Lucy agreed to cut ties with those people. I only knew of one other time she involved herself with members of the group. It was about a month later, under the countenance of selling some MLM health products.

Lucy went on several business trips with DeShawn and Janet to Los Angeles, Las Vegas, and Hawaii. After her Hawaiian business trip, she told me, "DeShawn slept in her bed one night."

This announcement was a jaw-dropping, "What the heck?" moment for me. Holy moly—I don't remember Lucy's exact reasons for DeShawn sleeping in her bed.

Yet she told me, "DeShawn had nowhere else to sleep that night."

"He should have slept on a couch or the floor," I argued.

Instead, she calmly assured me, "I slept under the sheets while he stayed on top of the covers."

"Ahh, that doesn't make it any better."

Months later, I found out Janet and DeShawn were engrossed in an affair at the time of the trip. Janet left her husband for DeShawn shortly after their jaunt to Hawaii. Janet went on the same getaway. So why didn't DeShawn sleep with Janet that night?

Let me state that Lucy has not worn a bikini around me since our marriage. I never understood this. She was a stunning and attractive woman. I saw pictures of her in bikinis from before we met, and I can only remember seeing her wearing a bikini once or twice before our marriage. She always told me, "I feel very uncomfortable wearing bikinis."

To my bewildered amazement, or was it to my amazed bewilderment? I found photos from some of her business trips that I considered way beyond inappropriate. She wore skimpy bikinis in these images, from Las Vegas pools, Hawaii, and Los Angeles in the ocean. She looked incredibly hot, except she was often much too close and cozy with DeShawn for my comfort zone. If DeShawn maintained an affair with Janet, why did he snuggle up with Lucy and not Janet in all the pictures?

Then, I found a set of three images from Los Angeles. DeShawn stood knee-deep in the ocean carrying Lucy. I mean, he held her like in a husband's embrace, walking his wife over the threshold on their wedding night–in her shiny gold skimpy bikini. She was in his arms with her arms around his neck. The last picture showed DeShawn curled his arms up and buried his nose directly in Lucy's private area. I confronted Lucy with these pictures and told her what I thought of DeShawn.

She argued, "It's alright. Nothing happened."

"I know exactly what his intentions are, and I can see what he desires," I said, and I would not fall for any more of her malarkey.

Soon afterwards, Lucy's personal and business relationships with these two miscreants ended.

Chapter Thirty-Three

Organic Farming

I felt as though our relationship and marriage degraded as we continued to grow apart. I thought a family-owned business and working together could help us redevelop our oneness again. Did I view my life as a simile or a metaphor in which I wanted to start farming and growing plants as a means to mend and grow my marriage so it could flourish once again?

Full disclosure: I wanted to be a farmer before the age of twelve. I worked on a dairy farm milking a hundred head of cattle one summer when I was twelve or thirteen years old. You must remember I come from a family of lawyers and judges. I guess having me work the summer on a friend's farm was my father's way of trying to cure me of my farming dream and placing me on a path of higher education. I loved the long hours and hard work. When I learned the value of the property and the business was over £20 million, that was in 1970s currency. I thought, where would I ever get that kind of money? It was these startup costs that cured or at least dampened my dreams of farming.

I looked at properties on and off over the past fifteen to twenty years. I started an earnest exploration into farming when I felt my marriage slipping away.

Lucy and I spent years talking about and looking at farms. She wanted to build a retreat on the farm to complement her health businesses. So, in 2014, I bought an affordable yet rundown apple farm in Walden, New York. I performed the tasks to clear up the land and nurse the trees back to a healthy, productive state.

I fertilized the trees with organic seabird guano from Peru and sprayed beneficial insect eggs. There were no pesticides, herbicides, or chemical fertilizers, and we knocked[5] all the trees by hand. Of course, going organic is much more work compared to traditional farming. Nevertheless, the health, financial, and self-satisfaction benefits outweighed the extra effort by a long shot.

I set up my organic plan, found a local organic certifier, and applied. Because the farm was inoperative for several years, I passed the certification process with relative ease.

All the clean air, songbirds, birds of prey, and various other wildlife made the experience worth the change in lifestyle and the extra work. I performed most of the work by myself, learning as I went.

---

5 Knocking an apple tree is the act of thinning fruit clusters so that only one choice apple remains per bunch.

Chapter Thirty-Four

A Wedding and a Funeral

My daughter Cassandra and I picked a song by Israel Kamakawiwo'Ole, also known as Bruddah Iz. The song was a mix of Over the Rainbow / What a Wonderful World for her father-daughter dance.

Six short days before Cassandra's wedding, my father suddenly and peacefully succumbed to emphysema during an afternoon nap at home. It made an already emotional event so much more significant. My mother canceled her trip from England for the wedding, and my sisters decided to stay back in England with my mother.

I cannot tell you how much more meaning the song we chose affected me after my father passed away. My daughter had a beautiful outdoor wedding at a local New York vineyard and winery. It went by all too fast.

Lucy tried to blame my parent's stubbornness for my father's death. My parents did not subscribe to or believe in her health products. She complained about my family's lack of interest in her health products often throughout the years. However, during the period leading up to my daughter's wedding and my father's funeral. Lucy cranked her complaint dial all the way up to on a mission, and it was jarring. It was aberrant behavior and incalculably poor timing.

Lucy did not dance with me once at the wedding, and we have not danced together since we got married.

We had problems getting back to England for the funeral. So much so that I thought I would miss my father's funeral. I cannot describe how devastating it felt to me. Our Green Cards had all expired. These cards are only valid for ten years, even though your permanent residency status in the United States never expires. So, I took the entire family to the local Immigration and Naturalization Services (INS) office in New York, arriving half an hour before the office opened without an appointment. I explained our circumstances to the managing officer, and after some thought, he decided they could process new cards for us. I observed everyone working at the immigration office to be exceptional, accommodating, and courteous. They went out of their way to process my family first. Without a scheduled appointment, I think they could have turned us away had they wanted to—I love our first responders.

The next problem to overcome was our passports' expiry dates approached. Airline rules oppose international transportation of people while they carry expired or soon-to-expire credentials. They did not have to take us. I argued with their management for special permission. All the extra stress, passports, green cards, and airlines during a time of great sadness and grief. We pulled through it and arrived in England just in the nick of time for my father's funeral.

Lucy and I fought about something while in England. I cannot remember the topic of these arguments. Although, it was bad enough, and I would not hold her hand during the burial while we were at the graveside. Lucy crept beside me like some lurking stranger attempting to hold my hand and make herself relevant in the ceremony. Without making a scene, I shook her hand away. It seemed as though Lucy was ceaseless at pushing my buttons to my limits. Most of the time, she tried to keep me hovering in a position close to my threshold.

Lucy's immediate and incessant campaign about returning to the United States for some meetings began the evening of the funeral. Within two days of my father's burial, Lucy left with Fannie. She abandoned us, and with the funeral over, did family and feelings no longer mean anything?

I stayed with my mother for over a month, and we enjoyed a quiet break. We sat and watched TV most of the time. Anything Mum needed, I was there to help. I think we both enjoyed it. While I stayed with Mum, we received newly issued passports for Maggie, the twins, and me.

My theory on life, the universe, and everything[6] is that you need to find a hobby. To help you pass the time and deal with your feelings of grief and sadness. I discovered genealogy dealt with my feelings of loss at my father's passing.

I must caution you genealogy can also bring about fresh feelings of sorrow. In the beginning, you are not gathering the stories of your ancestors' past. Instead, you are most likely limited to collecting names, birth dates, marriage dates, and death dates, leading to thoughts of our mortality. After our demise, are we wholly forgotten in two or three generations? Please stop for a minute to think about it. Do you know the names of your eight great-grandparents? Do your kids know their names?

Is all we leave behind a tombstone with a name, birth date, and death date? Such a painful pill to swallow. In time, you find more information on individuals, and their stories begin to crystallize. Anyhow, genealogy became of great importance to me, almost to the point of an obsession.

"Oh, all right, I am thoroughly obsessed with it, completely!"

My family tree now contains over six thousand individuals. I have proven half of these individuals with copies of baptism, marriage, and burial records dating back to the 1500s. I also possess pictures of many ancestors, photos, drawings, and paintings going back over two hundred years.

---

6 I quoted The Hitchhiker's Guide to the Galaxy by Douglas Adam. His answer to the question was Forty-Two. However, in contrast, my answer is to find a hobby and keep busy.

I tried to add Lucy's ancestors to the family tree, and it was next to impossible. I could not read Croatian or find any information on the internet. Lucy gave me different names for her grandparents several times, and some of her grandparents were still alive when we married. I found the changing identities and lack of information about her family quite perplexing. Yet, I was overly busy researching my own family tree to give much heed to her vagaries.

Chapter Thirty-Five

Christmas Before the Final Move

This year, my entire family made plans to celebrate Christmas and New Year's at my oldest daughter Cassandra's home in White Plains, New York. My three University students, Maggie, Gilbert, and Clifford, flew in from London to spend their winter break with us. In addition, Lucy and our youngest daughter, Fannie, flew in from Florida. I was excited to have the entire family together.

Why was it so challenging to get my wife to do something with me on all occasions? I took Lucy out to an expensive restaurant for New Year's dinner. Trying to persuade Lucy to go with me became a bizarre predicament. She and Fannie were all dressed up, and Lucy talked about visiting some local friends.

I had dinner reservations at a fancy restaurant for us. But Lucy was not interested. It took all five of my children's pressure to convince Lucy to spend New Year's Eve with me for dinner at this posh establishment.

When we arrived at the restaurant, Lucy criticized everything. Her litany of complaints included our children obliging her to attend, the modest menu, the mediocre food, and the expense. She felt we could have saved money eating elsewhere. Her grievances began on our drive to the restaurant and continued all night long.

She ruined what I had arranged as a memorable evening.

In October, Lucy and I decided to move her and Fannie to the farm in December. It almost occurred, yet Lucy ran out of time to pack everything because of the Christmas break plans. So, moving them to the farm was postponed until after New Year's.

During the holiday period, all seven of us discussed the logistics and the need to move Lucy and Fannie to the farm. We had already transferred most of the contents from our home in Florida to the farm the previous summer. We used a moving company and filled the tractor-trailer with most of the items from our house. Then, we agreed that after four years of delays, it was finally time to complete the relocation. We decided that I would fly back to Florida in late January to pack the remaining items from the house into a rental moving truck, and we would drive back to the farm in early February. After four years of living apart, it felt exhilarating to finalize our plans for the move. At long last, Lucy and Fannie were moving to the farm.

Sometime after New Year's and before I flew to Florida to move, a terrible round of gout consumed me. The flare-up included pain and swelling in the knuckles of all five toes and my ankle.

Chapter Thirty-Six

An Interlude Regarding Sam

Several people who reviewed or edited my book have asked similar questions concerning me. They did not feel I wrote enough about what I thought or felt at the time, pertaining to many of the events so far.

My story, to this point, covers an almost thirty-year duration, in which I chose to share many adverse circumstances relevant to the book's second half. To be fair, I also experienced many good times with Lucy, or at least I perceived them as so. However, those so-called good times were not germane to the story.

I was politely asked, "What's wrong with you?" or "Why weren't you more upset?"

They wanted a more profound introspection from me in my storytelling.

"What did I have to be upset about?" was the only answer I could marshal.

Her wit was exceptional, and she was quick at spinning convincing lies. I perceived Lucy as an innocent and believed that her naïveté often put her in compromising situations. I envisioned these scenarios as other people trying to take advantage of my wife, and I never viewed her as an active participant. I even accepted her account of the one-time affair with Rifah as a mistake and forgave her.

It seemed like I was similar to a weapon of war, a missile where the pilot can "Fire and Forget." I was her thrall that would "Forgive and Forget."

I returned several times to the previous chapters and attempted to add more of my thoughts and feelings as things occurred. However, I was careful not to taint those events with anything beyond my cluelessness about Lucy's deceptions. I believe anyone previously tormented by a narcissist can sympathize with the not-knowing that which should be abundantly clear. It is unfortunate that we do not have a built-in robot to tell us, "Danger, Will Robinson, Danger."[7]

I always trusted her and discerned no reason to presume otherwise.

Was it denial? Not really, perhaps a little. However, I would fall back to my prologue's dense analogy and say I only saw the surface and was unaware of any deeper implications. My trust and broad shoulders made me the perfect gullible candidate as a narcissist's thrall.

I will also say that my life spun out of control for the next three-plus years, and you may observe that lost sense of composure reflected in my storytelling at times.

The turbulence in my life was about to begin with a gale-forced fury. I became mindful of her artifice in the next part of my disturbing story, starting with the following chapter. However, turbulence does not adequately begin to describe how chaotic my life would become. Tumultuous better characterizes the state of affairs in which I lived. I always viewed my life through a lens and believed in the clear picture I thought I saw. Afterwards, with the turmoil I found myself mired in, things were no longer straightforward.

Think of it as I viewed a well-focused picture up until this point. Then, this impression of my life was Photoshopped using a swirl filter that modified my perception with a lollipop or whirlpool

---

7 The robot B-9 (Benign), from the 1960s science fiction television series Lost In Space.

effect until the image I had of my life was no longer recognizable. Another way to think of it is that I started to view my shattered life through a kaleidoscopic lens. However, kaleidoscopes display things of beauty, something my marriage to Lucy did not share.

My life can never be the same. It was forever changed.

I hope to satisfy these questions regarding my thoughts and feelings with an increased reflective contemplation as my comprehension progressed.

PART 2
Memoirs of a Divorce

Chapter Thirty-Seven

The Shit Show

I titled this chapter The Shit Show, not because it is the best choice of words. I chose this title because, when all the following occurred, I verbally referred to it as such in real life with Fannie, Cassandra, and my son-in-law Laurence. In the months to follow, I continued referring to this era of my life as The Shit Show while describing these events to my family, lawyer, therapists, and anyone else to whom I spoke. While possibly not the best choice of words, it accurately represented how I felt about what I discovered and underwent.

Standing at the Precipice, Staring into the Abyss

I flew into Florida on a Wednesday night about ten days before our drive to New York. Lucy picked me up from the airport. I put my suitcase into our SUV's back seat beside a baby's car seat with a large baby doll strapped in.

I commented, "Oh, Fannie is now doing the school parenting exercise her sisters previously did?"

"Uh-huh." Lucy agreed.

When we arrived at our house from the airport, Lucy was already asking for more time to pack. I entered our home to find nothing packed or ready. It was a letdown, and I do not honestly remember how I felt.

The next ten days of insights placed my mind in a state similar to vertigo. It was like having tunnel vision, yet not through a smooth, straight tube. It was as though the tunnel walls kept vacillating in diameter, and it slowly snaked and meandered as my mind's eye traveled through it without any sense of which way was up. It was very disquieting to learn so many disturbing things. All I could focus on was completing the move.

I drove Fannie to high school in the morning and then went back to start packing. When I returned home, Lucy said, "I have some errands to run."

So, she disappeared for the entire day in a car she borrowed from her friend and business partner, Loqueesha. Later in the day, I picked Fannie up from school. When we returned home, she began telling me a whirlwind of stories about Lucy and what had happened in the past.

The Sixteen-Year Affair

"So, what do you know about Rifah?" Fannie asked.

Her intense gaze locked on me with an expression of fear or perhaps apprehension etched on her face. This question was an unexpected and out-of-the-blue circumstance for me.

I must have exhibited a surprised look as I shot back, "What do you know?"

It all started in this way: a question answered with a question. Picture us fencing in a delicate dance to poke and prod answers from each other, to determine how much each of us knew and what was safe to share.

Fannie began by explaining how Lucy often declared to her that I was not her biological father. Fannie lived under a dome of distress. Her mother's persistent assertions to Fannie that if I or any of her siblings ever found out about Rifah being her biological father, she would be disowned by the rest of us. She convinced Fannie of it and used these tactics to keep her obedient and fearful.

Fannie told me the three of them (Lucy, Rifah, and Fannie) often stayed at hotels and motels for as long as she could remember.

Once, Fannie saw them smoking drugs together in the bathroom of a hotel room. The bathroom door was left open while Fannie sat in plain view of their conduct.

She also told me, "They had sex together in a hotel room in the bed right next to my bed."

"Did they think Fannie slept through their appalling behavior?" I thought to myself, "Yeah. Like that makes it all right."

Time and again, Lucy requested an engagement ring from Rifah. She also always compelled Fannie to beg Rifah to offer Lucy one. I believe she hoped he would give in to her requests.

The thought, "What is it with Lucy and rings?" crossed my mind.

It sounded as though she remained in a perpetual state of preparedness to drop me like a lead balloon at the first opportunity. Yet, my youngest daughter, Fannie, believed Lucy would not leave me because she enjoyed the lavish appearance of stability, family, and wealth I brought into her life. She enjoyed the luxuries that I provided to her. "Why would she want to leave that type of comfort behind?" Fannie queried.

Fannie told me, "Rifah slept in your bed the weekend you took my brothers for an out-of-town hockey tournament."

Upon hearing this, I went deaf while watching Fannie's lips move in silence as she continued to talk.

The solitary thing my mind contemplated— "They had sex in my bed?[8]"

Time slowed, and through my nostrils, I exhaled the noxious fumes of a putrid unease emanating from the pit of my stomach. Call it the cootie creeps or something akin to that. I felt gross all over—a sensation of bugs and spiders crawling down my back,

---

[8] The interrobang ‽ punctuation mark, like me, is a product of the sixties. It is used to impart an exclamatory and often rhetorical question. Prior to its creation in 1967, writers used standard keystrokes such as !?, ?!, !?!, or ?!? to convey its meaning.

in my hair, and trousers. It was utterly disgusting, not just their actions but the audacity that came with it. I perceived my bed as an immense fungal sandwich. These visuals I described are not remotely comparable to the depths of anguish battering my conscience that day.

Fannie's Attempted Suicide

Our daughter, Fannie, was a mere fifteen years old when she told me, "I tried to kill myself two years ago."

She was only thirteen years of age when she attempted to commit suicide while I was living on the farm.

"I swallowed a bottle of Ibuprofen pills," she said, "I wanted to escape from Mom."

Shock and awful horror began to grip my innards. I could not fathom a thirteen-year-old child wanting to attempt suicide. My poor daughter endured so much pain.

"I spent a week recovering in the hospital."

I felt a silent scream begin to escape from deep inside. "I NEVER knew this."

"HOW is it possible I never knew?"

"WHY has nobody ever told me?"

According to Fannie, both Lucy and Rifah came to her hospital room. Fannie demanded the hospital staff remove him. She did not want him there.

My mind screamed, "Oh my God, Lucy called Rifah when this happened and never told me!"

Rifah showed up from out of state. Both Lucy and Rifah did not return for a few days. I arrived at the distinct conviction that they must have enjoyed a delightful time together filled with adultery, debauchery, drugs, and partying. Yet, I am only a stupid, clueless husband. What do I know?

I have since learned Fannie battled depression for what I estimate to be about ten years. It appears her depression grew as her elder brothers and sisters left home. Then, her depression swelled in magnitude after I moved to the farm in New York, leaving Fannie alone with her mother, Lucy.

Child Protective Services (CPS) conducted an investigation comprising a paltry set of two individual interviews with Fannie. One consultation in the hospital while she was drugged up and not entirely coherent. And a follow-up interview at home about a week later.

I cannot find a suitable approach to express how disappointed, pissed off, and angry I am with the hospital and Child Protective Services. In my view, they botched the handling of my daughter's case. No wonder the high rate of teenage suicide is extraordinarily unacceptable in our country.

The parents or the teenager must say nothing more than, "I feel better now," and CPS will close the case—Inconceivable.

Isn't CPS's mission to be there to protect these vulnerable children? I will leave it at that and won't expound anymore on this rabbit hole comprised of my thoughts and feelings.

As I drove Fannie to school the following morning, I broke down into a sobbing mess of tears. I pulled the car over and stopped. I tried to say something to Fannie but could not. I had lost my voice through my constricted throat.

When I finally regained my ability to talk, I told Fannie, through choked tears, "Never hurt yourself again," I let her know, "You are too important to me."

How do you find the right words to describe your love? My explanation continued, "You should get help or come to me for support."

As I thought of what-ifs, I told her, "If your problems are with me for some reason, you can go to your sisters. They would stand up to help and protect you with a passion, even from me, if needed."

I finished my speech by saying, "Just don't ever do it again," I did not want to lose her.

Child Abuse

Upon hearing of Lucy's scandalous conduct, Pam, from the cartoon Archer, jumped to the forefront of my psyche and said, "What the shit snacks."

Then the bad news continued to pile on and kept rolling in, getting worse and worse and more mind-numbing with each crashing wave in an unrelenting dirge of distressful information.

I do not want to use labels here, except this disgusting, almost ghoulish individual I once loved and called my wife—abused all my children. My daughters took the brunt of her offensive behavior.

My shoulders sank when Fannie said, "Mom used to make Maggie take diet pills when she was seven or eight [years old]."

My mind howled in pain, "WTF! She gave diet pills to a seven-year-old."

I do not know how many years Lucy forced Maggie to take these pills. I never knew about it and only found out while Fannie recounted these horrible things. I do not even know what brand of diet pills she forced my daughter to take or their side effects.

Then Fannie told me, "Mom gave me drugs for my weight."

My arms went limp like strings attached to my shoulders as I felt a nervous pang build in the pit of my stomach. Fannie was slim and slender and did not need to lose weight.

"The diet supplements she gave me were liquid drops," Fannie continued, "But I stopped taking them when I was eight [years old]."

I do not know how old Fannie was when Lucy began giving her these drugs that Fannie refused to take around the age of eight. However, I know Lucy's undaunted persistence well enough to presume she continued by sneaking the drops into Fannie's drinks.

Lucy constantly weight-shamed Fannie. So much so that Fannie felt insecure and self-conscious enough to place herself on a secretive sugar-free gum and tea diet; she lost fifteen pounds in ten days. This was not healthy for a young twelve-year-old girl.

And this revelation made my body feel sick. It felt like poison coursed through my veins, and tar or liquid cement filled my muscles, weighing me down.

Fannie believes in the importance of knowing that Lucy's unkind verbal abuse made her feel bad enough to do something like this at such a young age.

My daughter, Maggie, a gorgeous young woman, was also beautiful as a young girl. However, she had a weight problem that started in her teens. In my opinion, her weight problem reached unhealthy proportions after high school. Concerned for her health, I now believe, or should I say, I know, I became an unwitting accomplice to her struggles. I do not know when Lucy started fat-shaming Maggie. I didn't even know she did this to our daughter. From the stories Maggie has since told me, it was terrible, ugly, and often. According to Maggie, she felt humiliated by her mother's reproach. When Lucy had friends or clients over, she required Maggie to stay hidden upstairs, as Lucy did not want to be embarrassed.

I only remember one episode when I saw Lucy pummeling and striking one of my children. It was the time she attacked Clifford for slamming the bedroom door on Fannie's finger. However, according to my children's stories, Lucy's enraged attacks against them occurred often and on a somewhat regular basis.

Of my daughters, Maggie took the most and the worst of Lucy's aggression. Her weight held as a serious matter of contention for Lucy. Fannie and Maggie told me about one of the worst beatings for Maggie. The slugfest occurred while they drove in the car to a professional sports arena for a religious convention. Lucy started hitting Maggie on the head while driving on the highway. Maggie sat in the back seat behind her, and Lucy quickly pulled the car over. Once stopped on the shoulder of a six-lane highway, she turned around and beat Maggie in the head and across her face with both hands. Because of her horrible beating, Maggie refused to leave the car or participate when they arrived at the religious event.

When I talk about these psychopathic episodes, Lucy enters. She would become enraged, lose all control, and mete out savage beatings on my children. I am talking about repeated and uncontrolled roundhouse slaps and forearm strikes on my children's heads and faces. I cannot describe how appalled I am by what I learned from my children.

Gilbert said, "You know, Mom hit me in the head with a hairdryer once." Then, he tried to blame himself for the incident.

With a burdened heart, I explained to him, "There is never any excuse for a parent to treat their child like this, not under any circumstance."

Fannie told me, "Mom would pinch and hit me to make me cry for Rifah on the phone." Lucy did it often for various reasons. The most common was to solicit money, travel expenses, gifts, or other things from Rifah.

She forced all three of my daughters to clean the house, not like chores, more like slavery. Lucy wrote page-long lists of tasks for them to do and demanded things be spotless. Lucy would punish them if they did not complete every single item on the list. Threats like being grounded for a week, a month, or even a year. Punishments like canceling the prom. Lucy went so overboard with her penalties that it was ridiculous. I would always revoke the groundings after a day or two. The few times I saw these lists, I would tell the girls to get two or three things done, and they were good to go. I saw these lists a few times and thought they seldom took place. But, according to all my daughters now, it was an almost daily event. Each of my daughters thought I knew about it, and they thought I stood with Lucy. I apologized to them often for being oblivious and not seeing what happened. To this day, all my daughters despise the word spotless and only use it jokingly as a sharp rebuke.

Thievery

Even after I caught Lucy's friend stealing and kicked her out of our lives, things continued to go missing unbeknownst to me. Mum recently told me that money, jewelry, and art continued to disappear from my parent's home until we moved to the United States. My parents perceived a wedge driven between them and me. They did not want to further distance me by bringing up their suspicions regarding Lucy.

Lucy tried to indoctrinate my daughters into her thieving ways.

Cassandra told me how Lucy involved the twins in the theft of toys. While they sat in their stroller in the checkout lines at stores, Lucy would hand them toys from the store to play with and not pay for them. Eventually, Cassandra started taking the toys from the boys by placing them on the conveyor belt for the cashier.

Lucy taught Maggie to steal clothes from stores by wearing them under her clothes in the fitting room. Maggie began to refuse to do this around the age of nine.

Sophie told me she used to disappear from Lucy while shopping in any store. Otherwise, Lucy would force her to change the price tags on merchandise with lower-cost stickers from similar items.

Remember the piano lessons story, in which Lucy's friend Iva accused Lucy of stealing money from her purse?

Fannie explained the entire situation to me, saying, "Oh yes, she stole from Iva."

Lucy's scheme employed a method I now call "Tea to Pee."

Lucy had some monster-sized teacups. In essence, these cups were soup bowls with tea handles. Lucy would fill Iva's cup with tea to induce the need for a bathroom break before leaving our home.

"When Iva was in the bathroom from drinking too much tea, Mom would take money out of Iva's purse and pay her for the piano lessons with it," Fannie told me.

So, while Iva was in the bathroom, Lucy snatched enough cash from Iva's purse and used that stolen money to pay Iva for the piano lessons. What kind of friend was Lucy?

Lucy had a friend named Fay, who accused Lucy of stealing clothes from her home. Well, the friendship ended right away. Fay was petite, and Lucy explained, "Fay's clothes are too small for me. This is crazy. I couldn't use them. They wouldn't even fit me."

I accepted Lucy's story over Fay's because it made the most sense. I now do not doubt Lucy stole her clothes.

Then my thoughts turned to, "Why was Lucy even at their home with only Fay's husband present?"

According to Fay, Lucy took the clothes from her bedroom. Did Lucy also have an affair with Fay's husband? I believe she did. Perhaps the stolen clothes were a trophy, or a more credible contrivance, a gift for some other friend of Lucy's.

She is a Stalker

Rifah remarried. Nonetheless, the "Lucy and Rifah" affair continued. Fannie told me about one of Lucy and Rifah's many rendezvouses with Fannie in tow. After the meetup, Lucy covertly followed Rifah back to his home. Lucy parked down the street to observe him and drove off after he went inside.

She stalked her previous husband while she and I first dated, and she fought with his new girlfriend. He died years ago in England, and somehow, Lucy has his urn with his ashes, the ultimate stalker's trophy. His brother lived in England, and his mother in Croatia. So why did his ashes come to Lucy in the United States? And not to his mother or brother.

Lies and Other Inappropriate Things

When I flew to Florida, Lucy picked me up at the airport. I placed my things in the back seat, next to a baby's car seat with a large doll strapped in. Fannie confirmed that the car seat and manikin were in the SUV to give the appearance Lucy could use the carpool lane anytime she wanted. Does her sense of privilege know no bounds?

I found an official plastic Handicap parking pass meant to hang from the rearview mirror in the glove compartment of Lucy's SUV after moving it to the farm.

Fannie told me, "When Mom was a caregiver, she got it from the disabled lady she helped and never gave it back."

"She helped herself to the parking pass from this lady. She stole it," I thought.

"Mom uses it all the time so she can park closer, in the handicap spots."

She fed pork, chicken, and other meats to vegans. She claimed to them the food was vegan. Apart from being a practice of tremendous unethical import, it could cause physical harm to someone with food allergies or cause emotional distress to a vegan person upon discovering the deception.

For years, Lucy often told Fannie, "Sam is hung like a horse, and I like it small."

Lucy told Fannie many times, "Sam is too large," or "Sex with Sam hurts me, and that is rape."

These zingers were entirely inappropriate on a scope that left me speechless, and I am a talker. It is a rare day to catch me dumbstruck. Hearing these statements mortified me, and I found it all the more atrocious to hear coming from my fifteen-year-old daughter. After seconds of uncomfortable silence, in an automatic knee-jerk reaction, my unorthodox sense of humor kicked in.

Without thinking, I pawed the ground with my right foot and whinnied like a horse, "Wur, huh, huh, huh, huh," increasing that awkward moment of unpleasantness a thousandfold.

A few seconds later, the ice broke, and we both burst out in laughter at the ridiculousness of it all.

Lucy even lied to Fannie about the story of her birth. On many occasions, Lucy explained to Fannie how she drove herself to the hospital and remained all alone while she gave birth to Fannie. How untrue. I drove her to the hospital, and I held Lucy's hand as she gave birth to Fannie. I took pictures of Fannie right after her birth, some before they had cleaned her up. I followed and stayed with Fannie in the hospital while they washed, measured, weighed, and attached the hospital identification bracelet to her ankle. I carried her back, in my arms, to Lucy's room after it all transpired. I also took an entire month off work to help at home.

My brain was numb from all the things Fannie told me. Have you ever hit your thumb with a hammer? It hurts a lot, and then you smash your thumb a second and third time. That digit still hurts, but it is numb. And it is no longer the pain that registers. Instead, the numbness only allows you to feel a massive throbbing sensation pulsating with every beat of your heart.

It seems the same thing happened to my mind when hit by each new revelation from Fannie. Call it information overload or lost in profound thought. Most of the things Fannie told me were lost in a blur after I heard she tried to kill herself by attempting suicide around two years earlier. Fannie had to recount many of these things two, three, or even four times in the following months. Without a doubt, my mind could not absorb all this disturbing information at once.

I learned much more later on, as each of my children opened up to me about past traumatic events they endured with Lucy.

Guns, Guns, and a Ton of Ammo

Let me give you a little backstory for this section. I was trained in the use of rifles before I was ten years old. I believe I fired my first 12-gauge shotgun before I could legally drive a car. Before I met Lucy, I had an antique 1902 Dumoulin 12-gauge double-barreled shotgun and a Ruger .22 caliber rifle. I always knew of Lucy's absolute hostility towards guns and her vehement opposition to keeping any of my rifles. I used them for target practice or skeet shooting at our summer country lodge. Because of Lucy's intense aversion to these weapons, they remained at my parents' home in England. I never kept them in our marital home and did not bring these guns to the United States, and as far as I know, they continue to remain stored to this day at my parents' place.

On the second day of packing, Lucy again left early for a day of errands. So, I started to pack the master bedroom closet. It was a large closet, roughly fourteen feet deep and eight feet wide, filled with mostly Lucy's clothes, shoes, and purses. There was enough room for the door to swing open, and then a mountain of Lucy's clothes began, five to six feet tall, going all the way to the back wall.

I found an unfamiliar and hefty bag on the floor of the large walk-in closet right behind the door. When I opened the bag, I discovered a shotgun cleaning kit. Curiosity got the better of me, and I dug into the duffle a little further, where I found a large cache of various caliber boxed munitions. Closer to the bottom of the bag, I found plenty of loose ammo, a target ball, a gun I did not detect at the time, and a white sock with something in it. As I peeled the white sock off its contents, I became flabbergasted, discovering it concealed a large handgun in a sturdy leather holster.

While I may have an active imagination, I am not prone to flights of fantasy, and in general, I am not a paranoid person. However, many sequential questions flooded my head, beginning with, "Why was this gun in my house?"

"Was the bag stolen?" The questions continued.

Then my thoughts turned to motive, "Does this weapon belong to Rifah?"

There was an oversized tennis ball with many shot marks on it. "Was Lucy practicing shooting guns with her boyfriend?" My mind inquired.

"Why was there easy access to the gun bag from the bedroom?" As speculation turned to alarm.

My thoughts climaxed in a thunderous panic, "Was Lucy planning to kill me while I slept?"

Then, all of a sudden, the chill of a terrible fear ran down my spine. I quickly put everything back in the bag, sealed it up, and placed it right where it had been. I left the closet as though it were untouched. I did not gather up the courage to return to the closet and reexamine the bag until the next day after Lucy left the house for yet another full day of errands. And that next day, I took many pictures of the bag's contents.

Did I tell you I get gout flare-ups? A rhetorical question. Of course, I did, and now you will discover how I used it to keep my distance from Lucy and stay relatively safe.

The week before I came to Florida, I experienced another nasty flare-up. After I found the bag of guns and ammo, I pretended that I had not fully recovered from my gout and the flare-up was recurring. I hobbled around and complained about the pain when Lucy was nearby. I stayed awake at night, and either slept or worked during the day while Lucy was away performing her so-called errands.

I used a foot warmer in bed and played up the oh-poor-me syndrome whenever she was home. The warming blanket helped considerably with the joint pain, even though I was no longer in the middle of a flare-up.

This little dog and pony show I put on for Lucy was my method of avoiding her, avoiding conflict, and staying alive.

The bag weighing over fifty pounds contained:

- A shotgun cleaning kit
- Two additional gun-cleaning kits
- One-hundred rounds of .22 long rifle bullets
- Two fully loaded .22 clips, with ten rounds each
- Two full boxes of 7mm ammo
- A full box of fifty .38 special hollow point ammo
- A full box of fifty .357 Magnum ammo
- A full box of 12-gauge rifled slug shotgun ammo
- Three full boxes of 12-gauge trap load ammo
- Lots of loose ammo scattered at the bottom of the bag
- A used and shot-up target ball
- A Smith & Wesson .357 Magnum revolver
- A Ruger semi-automatic .22 long-barrel pistol

Were there other handguns and rifles hidden in the house for all the various caliber ammo she possessed? I had serious questions regarding her apparent intentions for these particular weapons, which were unsecured, hidden, and easily accessible in the master bedroom.

I texted my son-in-law, Laurence, with the pictures I took of the guns and ammo, stating, "If I die, Lucy did it."

The following thought did not occur to me until a month later. I guess I was too numb with information overload and fear at the time. I want you to visualize me raising my voice, almost yelling the following paragraph at you.

"What kind of **RETARD** stores unsecured guns, together with a mountain of ammunition on the floor in the open, and easily accessible when a child lives there, and the child living there had attempted suicide less than two years prior?"

Yes, I know the highlighted word is retired from most people's vocabulary. However, in the current instance, the highlighted word is an absolute requirement. I put it there to offend the reader. To elucidate, within the reader's very marrow, the degree of conscientious abandonment that I felt took place.

I was terrified she would try to kill me. And I was confounded by the extent of her ineptitude surrounding the careless storage of these weapons. It all appeared as sheer madness to me. Lucy and guns, in my mind, did not mix like oil and water. They were diametrically opposed.

The Rot

Lucy is a hoarder. I never knew how bad a hoarder she was until I returned to our house in Florida after four years of being away on the farm. Over the years, while living together, I would pitch out the junk and do the periodic cleaning of rotten food. Which, I guess, kept the appearance of her extreme hoarding tendencies in check and below my radar.

Over the years, Lucy often placed food, including perishable items, in the garage. She made excuses, such as not having room in the kitchen, and many other justifications. Often a contentious topic between us. I wanted it to stop. I was troubled that it would attract pests, rodents, and roaches. I worried about her feeding us diseased or contaminated food.

Nevertheless, she persisted with the practice. I often went through the garage to discard food stored there. At times, the smell emanating from the garage was overwhelming and disgusting. I hunted through the mountains of stuff, usually to find a bag or two of liquefied food. Disposing of this filth was, without fail, a gut-wrenching experience, to the point of wanting to vomit.

In my opinion, cars, tools, and equipment belong in the garage. I see now Lucy was a hoarder, and slowly, over time, she would take over the garage to store tons of junk and food. She left no room to park a single car.

Before I bought the farm, Lucy often made trail mix for me to take to work. It tasted pretty good. However, once I ate from a bowl of trail mix in the kitchen. It smacked of moldy wood, which was hard and felt like chewing sawdust expelled from a chainsaw. Spitting it out and trying to clear my mouth of this debris, I looked closer at the bowl of granola, almonds, and raisins. I saw plenty of potpourris mixed in, not sitting on the top. So, my eating any of her trail mixes came to an abrupt end.

Have you ever watched an episode of *Hoarders*? All the episodes that I watched in the past depicted unfortunate and often decrepit old ladies living in ramshackle homes or apartments. They live in appalling conditions. It is a circumstance that I can only describe as suffering from severe mental issues. How could you not feel empathetic to these people's plight?

And Lucy could compete for the title with most of these extreme accumulators. However, Lucy kept the worst of her tendencies hidden in specific rooms such as the garage, closets, bedrooms, and crawlspace. However, I suspect she would clean or cook the rotten food before serving it to her unsuspecting family and guests. I have no compassion for her. In Lucy's case, I believe it to be both a disease of hoarding and a malignant choice to feed other people the excrements of her labor.

After spending four years on the farm and returning to our house for the first time, I discovered the food rot bloom was in full effect. I found several of the kitchen cabinets loaded with long-expired food.

We had two Side-by-Side style refrigerators, and both were twenty-five cubic feet in approximate size, one in the kitchen and the other out in the garage. Lucy stuffed the kitchen fridge, I mean, packed tight, both front to back and top to bottom with food. Refrigerators require airflow and cannot operate properly or cool items when jam-packed like this. The kitchen fridge contained lots of expired and rotting food towards the back. The refrigerator in the garage revealed a completely different story. Packed tight, like the kitchen fridge. However, all the food appeared rotten to me. Lucy cooked with this refuse.

I found storage and moving boxes throughout the garage filled with rotting food, spoiled juices, and old beverages. It was an utterly disgusting sight. In the middle of the extra-long two-car garage, on the floor, I found a large, five-gallon cooking pot full of homemade moldy brownies. It appeared as though someone had picked through it not so long ago. Then I realized a bowl full of these brownies sat in the center of the kitchen table. Lucy had fed guests and us this rotten waste. Oh, ho, ho, how overly glad I was that I had not eaten any of those brownies. Just the thought of what could have happened sickens me. I do not like to think about it.

I need to quote this: one of Lucy's friends filed a declaration in court a few months later stating, "Lucy participates in various community, volunteer, church and school parent/teacher sponsored programs and activities, usually headed by Lucy offering her renowned home-cooked, organic, vegetarian meals."

I think I barfed in my mouth a little the moment I first read her friend's statement.

Right in front of Fannie and me, she ate some of her refuse. It was chocolates that had expired two years earlier. I threw these candies in a large garbage bag filled with all sorts of slimy, gross, and rotten food. Now, you need to visualize the following scene. Because I threw her stuff out, Lucy became distraught. She angrily screamed at me as she rifled through the bag of soggy, rotten garbage. Still yelling, she pulled many items, including some long-expired chocolates, out of the garbage bag. Lucy wiped them on her hip, threw two of these old, discolored chocolates into her mouth, and ate them directly in front of us. I felt sick to my stomach.

And what's more, her screaming ended while she smacked her lips and made an "Mmhm mmhm" closed-lip sound.

Then, with a completely changed demeanor, she said to us in a young, girlish voice, "See, this is still good."

I saw her dumpster dive to save things before, and now you can gag me with a spoon. I watched her as she ate the shit snacks. How sterling!

I guess Sam I am, and I will not eat her rotten eggs or moldy ham. I do not know what manner of decaying food she fed me in the past, but I swore I would never again eat any food she has made or handled.

Threat of Suicide

Moving day finally arrived, and I loaded her SUV on the car hauler. While I strapped it down, Lucy came outside. Yelling, she demanded I take her car down from the trailer so that she could run some errands.

"Today is not the day for shopping," I told her, "We do not need anything else except to move."

She wanted to disappear for the day and postpone the move yet again. But I saw her deceit for what it was and as it occurred.

Lucy stomped her foot on the ground in a show of theatrics, and then she went back into the house while I finished securing the car. When I entered our place, Fannie warned me that Lucy planned to play sick to delay the move. Soon after, I found Fannie and Lucy sitting beside each other on the couch, and both gave little fake coughs.

Lucy said meekly, "We are both feeling sick. Could you kindly please give us more time to move?"

I told her, "I don't care for these games. We're leaving today."

Then I went upstairs to grab the last of the things. Fannie came upstairs with tears in her eyes. She told me, "Mom pinched and punched my leg. To make it look like I cried. So that you would give her more time."

Then Fannie quietly confided, "Mom said to me, 'I want to kill myself.'"

I gently held Fannie's arm, leaned in close, and whispered, "You stay close to me."

I grabbed the bag of guns and ammo, and we left the house together. I locked the gun bag in the back of the moving truck, and we drove off to the local police station. On the way to the police station, I called 911 and told them about Lucy's suicide threat and the guns she kept hidden.

Fannie's head moved back from her shoulders and tilted slightly. She gave me the strangest inquisitive look and said, "I thought those were your grandfather's old hunting guns that you inherited."

"Ahhh. No," I replied, "I have never seen these guns before."

I will add a little background on the gun story here. Months after this incident, Fannie explained the following: The summer earlier, a tractor-trailer transported a full load of furniture and boxes of things from our house in Florida to the farm in New York. Lucy recruited a group of friends to help with the packing and loading. According to Fannie, one of these friends found the bag of guns and brought it to Lucy's attention. Fannie heard Lucy's explanation to her friends. Lucy claimed that these weapons were my grandfather's old hunting guns, which I inherited.

Let me start with an unequivocal statement, "All handguns are illegal in England—unless they are the muzzle-loading black powder variant."

My grandfather was a prominent lawyer, and I do not believe he ever owned any handguns. He may have possessed a rifle. However, I was never aware that he had any firearms. He would never do something as stupid as possessing illegal handguns, being a man of the law. However, I found the story intriguing and amusing in an absurd manner.

After a short delay, the 911 operator told me, "Officers are en route to your house. You should return to file the report with them."

By the time we arrived back at our place, the officer had already completed his interview with Lucy. He met with me outside. I opened the back of the truck, pointed to the bag of guns, and took a step away. I did not reach for the pack because we did not need any confusion or misunderstanding between us. I wanted the officer to feel comfortable while he examined the weapons. He inspected and disposed of the two handguns but left the ammunition with me.

The officer told me, "Your wife denied her suicide threat, so there is nothing further I can do."

Lucy came storming down the driveway from the house, yelling, "I'm going to divorce you and take 'MY' daughter."

Everything was swiftly spiraling out of control. The muscles of my face must have completely relaxed, leaving me with a limp look of incredulity.

The officer said, "With the danger of these guns leaving with me, it is now a civil matter, not a police matter," then he returned to his car to write a report.

To my surprise, Lucy climbed into the driver's seat of the moving truck. She locked me out, holding the lock knob down with her hand. As Fannie sat in the passenger seat, Lucy performed a hysterical cry. She only looked straight forward, refused to acknowledge me outside the door, and possibly said things to Fannie through her mumbling tears.

I walked over to the police car and knocked on the window. The officer gave me a "What is it now look" as I asked for assistance.

I pointed at the truck and said, "Look, she has locked herself in the truck and won't let me in. Can you help?"

As he got out of his patrol car and turned towards the truck, Fannie came running around the truck's front towards me, with a terrified look imprinted on her face. She crawled under my arm with my body between her and Lucy.

The officer persuaded Lucy out of the truck. Then, pointing his arm toward the vehicle for emphasis, he reminded her, "Your move was obviously planned for a long time," he paused to let it sink in.

"Your daughter and Sam are leaving as previously agreed and planned," he continued.

Then, speaking over her arguments, he finally told her, "Listen, you have a choice to make. You can either go with them as planned or stay behind."

Lucy tried to argue with the officer, and he would have none of it. He became adamant. "They are leaving with or without you."

With some reluctance, Lucy decided to come with us, asking, "Could I please have just another hour to pack?"

The officer seemed annoyed, "Can you wait another hour," he asked me.

"Yes," I agreed without hesitation—I love our first responders.

Her entire outburst that morning made no sense to me. Lucy did not know that Fannie had confided any secrets to me. Her exaggerated behavior was solely due to the moving.

Chapter Thirty-Eight

One Hell of a Trip

Fannie and I waited for Lucy in the truck for over two hours before she came out ready. While in the truck's cabin, still on the driveway of our house, Lucy made some final demands for packing and moving things that were not allowed to cross State lines.

I told her, "No way."

"You're a monster!" She exclaimed in a loud voice.

She turned, facing forward, and sat slouched on the bench with her arms crossed. Then we got on our way to Walden, New York. I drove, Lucy sat on the passenger side, and Fannie sat between us.

The first two and a half hours were quiet and uneventful. We drove in silence while Lucy kept to herself, red-faced and brooding. The uneasy calm shattered when I saw Lucy say something to Fannie, and then suddenly, Fannie turned towards me and away from Lucy. Tears streamed down her cheeks, and she held onto and squeezed my knee. I pulled over at the next gas stop to fill up the truck.

While Lucy bought drinks and snacks from inside, Fannie cautiously approached the gas pump and told me, "I cried a little earlier because Mom said, 'I have a gun, and if I have to die, I am taking the two of you with me.'"

My mind screamed out, "Yo, yo, yo! What kind of crazy is this?"

It was not a rational sentence. What was the exact meaning? She talked about killing me, Fannie, and herself. She threatened to commit murder-suicide! My mind raced with "What if" scenarios.

I even considered driving away with Fannie and abandoning Lucy at the gas station. However, that would lead to an Amber Alert, worsening the entire situation. We were in the middle of nowhere, no longer in Florida, and a twenty-hour drive to New York remained. I was stranded in this horrible situation until we arrived in New York. Fannie asked me if I thought Lucy had another gun. I did not know. I did not believe she did, but it was possible. There was no telling what this woman was capable of. She was unhinged and unpredictable.

I found two handguns in the bag. However, the bag also contained ammunition for a shotgun, high-powered rifles, and multiple other caliber handguns. Lucy also could be hiding a knife. At that moment, I felt like I stood in a parched and desolate tundra, helplessly watching the thunderous approach of a tsunami's five-hundred-foot-high wall of water in the midst of broadsiding me. Overwhelmed and beaten, I resolved to continue driving on this long and arduous trek.

I sent my son-in-law, Laurence, the following text, "Lucy said a moment ago, 'I have a gun, and if I have to die, I am taking the two of you with me.'"

I also repeated my fears of not making it home alive. Laurence and I spoke on the phone in more detail at the next stop.

Lucy's agitation and brooding continued over the next couple of hours when I espied her again, saying something to Fannie. This time, when Fannie turned away from Lucy, I remember her eyes squeezed tight with an expression of severe pain on her face, and even through her tightly sealed eyes, the tears still bubbled out from the corner of her eyes and flowed down her cheeks. Fannie ducked under my arm, and I pulled her closer to me to console her as best I could.

I turned to Lucy and asked her, "Why are you doing this? What did you say to Fannie?"

Never before have I witnessed the face of a crazed and insane person. This lunacy was nothing like a cheap jump scare in a movie. Her antics were actually happening in my presence, right before my very eyes! All I could think was, "Egads! Man, that was frightening," as the alarm bells of my soul drowned out other thoughts.

Ever since then, I have referred to it as The Full Psycho.

An indelible vision of that moment was ingrained in my mind. Lucy's head turned to face me. Her head appeared lower than her shoulders like a hunchback, her face all beet red, and her jaw twisted, off-center, and ajar.

As she spat out at me in a raspy voice, "It's none — of your business — what I say — to 'MY' daughter!" taking a short breath or pause between some words.

Her outburst was the scary stuff you've come to expect from a horror movie. Unfortunately, this played out in real life, right there, on the bench seat beside me. I half expected her head to spin around while she spewed green pea soup. I did not need gas for the truck, and there was no way I would wait for the next gas station. So, I pulled into the first rest stop.

Repeating what I wrote in a previous paragraph. I can say, "Never before had I witnessed the face of an insane person before this moment," ever since I called this episode The Full Psycho.

As Lucy went to the restroom at the rest stop, Fannie came over to me and whispered, "I cried because Mom said, 'I am going to kill your father.'"

I could tell Fannie feared our lives were in danger. Heck, I also believed it with every fiber of my being. The officer took the two guns I found. Could there be more guns? Could she have a knife? I came up with a quick plan and shared it with Fannie. I would try to drive straight through the night all the way to the farm in New York.

In case I could not make it all the way and was required to take a nap, I told Fannie, "You try to get some sleep early. Then, if I need to take a catnap along the way, you could be awake to stand guard."

What kind of a father was I, asking my fifteen-year-old daughter to watch over me? But what choice did I wield?

Fannie told me, "I know what to do to calm Mom down."

I did not know what she meant at the time. I did not think I would live through the night to see another day.

As evening approached, Lucy remained in a state of brooding, all tense and edgy. I was shocked by what I heard from our daughter as she started talking to Lucy. I could not hear everything over the sounds of the truck. However, during the hours Fannie spent placating Lucy, I distinctly remember hearing two odd statements.

Firstly, Fannie apologized to Lucy, saying, "Mom, I am sorry for betraying your trust."

A little later, I heard her say, "We should pray to God for forgiveness."

Fannie continued to say things Lucy visibly wanted to hear. I continued to drive, saddened at how our daughter assumed responsibility for Lucy's actions with the sole purpose of getting her to calm down. I have no doubt that Fannie has been subjected to and dealt with these types of situations many times before.

For the rest of the trip, I made sure not to leave Fannie alone at any point. I watched Lucy like a hawk to ensure she did not reach into her bag for a gun or other weapon. Fannie clung to me and was even scared to go to the bathroom unless I stood guard outside the door.

Shortly after midnight, I could no longer continue driving without some rest. So, I pulled into a truck stop, woke Fannie, and left Lucy sleeping while I got some rest. About four hours later, I woke up and took Fannie to the restroom.

Fannie told me, "Mom slept the entire night," then she informed me, "I went through both of Mom's purses and didn't find a gun."

An Evening at the Overlook Hotel?

The heading of this section is a reference to Steven King's *The Shining*. How do you spell relief? r-e-d-r-u-m thwarted!

The next day's ride seemed a much less eventful ordeal. Lucy appeared to be in better spirits, and the brooding appeared to be more or less over. When we were two hours away from the farm, Lucy began to crave a hotel room for the night. She wanted a shower and a good rest before arriving at the farm. I would not pay for a hotel, as Lucy had already blown my move budget with all her delays. She got on her cell phone and started calling hotels looking for rooms and reasonable rates, hotels with room for the truck and trailer to park. She found a place, a non-brand hotel chain, and paid for the hotel herself without any problems.

After we got to the hotel, parked, and checked in, we went to the room to discover a well-appointed suite. Lucy became an outright different person. I felt as though we had left the *Twilight Zone* only to begin another separate new episode. Lucy entered the room ahead of me, dropped her bags, and walked through the room with her arms outstretched to the sides, taking it in. Lucy gushed flamboyantly over how marvelous and luxurious a place she found. She flopped down on the couch and propped up on her elbow in an almost laying down stance like some form of a lounge lizard. She planted her foot from her closer leg on the couch, with her leg forming an upside-down V. The leg farther from me crossed over the first leg, and she tapped her foot in the air. The exuberance Lucy exhibited in finding the place struck me as nothing short of irregular. While still fearing for my life, all I could think was, "Was she planning to use this hotel to stage future affairs?"

Each of us took separate showers. Then, when night arrived, I slept in one bed while Lucy and Fannie slept together in the other bed next to me.

On the Farm and Back to Florida

In hindsight, I know continuing to drive to the farm without abandoning Lucy along the way was the right decision. However, when I decided on this course of action, I could not have known there would be a positive outcome, and it often haunted my thoughts.

As a complete aside, I averted injecting my political and religious views into the book. I do not want to talk about my beliefs or lack thereof. I cannot define the following as hedging my bets. It was a natural feeling that overcame me after surviving something entirely out of my control.

So, I must admit that since moving Lucy and Fannie to the farm, I have looked up into the sky several times and said, "Hey man, thanks."

Arriving at the farm alive was one of those occasions. All these events shook my belief system to its core and made me rethink many of my principles. Almost four years later, I still don't know if it will push me further away or reel me in closer. All I can say is that I continue to reevaluate my beliefs.

Upon arrival at the farm, Lucy appeared to calm down. She barked orders at Fannie and me about how to unload the truck into the greenhouse for storage. All the while not offering much help. It seemed to me she clutched a sense of renewed control—control over herself and us.

There are five stages of grief: denial, anger, bargaining, depression, and acceptance. These stages bore almost no pertinence to my current situation. I experienced no denial or bargaining. I am not even sure if I felt much anger or depression. When I say no anger, I mean I was not angry over our relationship ending. However, I assure you I encountered a hint of angry feelings mixed in with a great deal of sadness and fear over what Lucy did and threatened to do to my children and me. I went straight to acceptance, and I intrepidly embraced my trepidations of fear and apprehension— my fears of what I believed she was capable of doing. I willingly put my life on hold for over four years, hiding out locked up on the farm or bouncing homeless from motel to hotel, afraid of what she may do.

After Lucy went to sleep the first night at the farm, I went through her purse and found a red kitchen knife inside. It was not a butter spreader. Instead, the two-inch blade had a pointy tip and a sharp edge. She concealed it, wrapped it in lots of paper towels, in turn, stored it in a transparent Ziplock bag, and buried it at the bottom of her purse. The hidden plastic bag was under a whole lot of old junk that appeared to have been there for years. She carried the concealed knife for the entire trip. It's a good thing that Fannie knew how to calm Lucy down. Otherwise, Lucy may have used that knife two nights before.

While on the farm, Lucy never spent one minute alone with me. She kept Fannie by her side at all times. I slept each night on the couch while they slept together in the bedroom.

One day, while Fannie and I waited in the truck for Lucy before we left to go grocery shopping, Fannie pointed to one of Lucy's old, ratty-looking purses sitting in my pickup truck. Torn vinyl covered this purse, and each small patch of torn pieces peeled and curled at the edges. She picked up the empty bag between her thumb and pointer finger, then held it in front of me while she explained how Lucy used it for shoplifting.

In a matter-of-fact tone, Fannie said, "If you see Mom take this purse into a store, she's going to steal things." Then she opened her grip, dropping the bag back onto the floor.

We went to the local grocery store, which seemed like an uneventful trip. When we arrived and vacated the truck, I saw Lucy grab her ratty old bag, and I watched her place it hidden behind her regular purse of similar shape and size. Lucy disappeared for maybe five minutes down a different aisle from us. I bought about one hundred and eighty dollars' worth of groceries.

Afterwards, while I loaded the groceries into the truck, Lucy declared, "I have to go to the dollar store to look at stuff."

Then she took Fannie with her. It was a little—no, it felt tremendously—upsetting for me as I did not want Fannie to be alone with her. I watched the door to the dollar store from my truck, worried about what could occur. I was terrified Lucy could attempt to abscond with our daughter Fannie. Finally, after about fifteen minutes, they left the store and returned to me in the truck. It was astonishing how many unpalatable scenarios my mind could dream up and worry about in fifteen minutes.

When we returned to the farm, I unloaded the groceries. Then Fannie told me, "Mom stole from the dollar store."

My recollection now is that she told me Lucy stole jewelry. However, in Fannie's memory, her mother pinched decorations, not jewelry. Lucy left her shabby shoplifting bag in the truck's passenger side footwell, which I checked out after I finished unpacking. The bag was no longer empty. It was gorged containing cleaning products and scrubbing pads. I did not go through the entire handbag. I assumed she stole about sixty dollars' worth of products. Why shoplift when I was ready to pay? It made no sense to me, yet this event provided concrete proof to reinforce some of the outlandish stories Fannie told me.

At one point, while on the farm, Lucy asked me, "Why did you call the Police?"

I told her, "I worried about your thoughts of suicide and wanted to get you help."

"Oh, come on, Sam. You have to be smarter than the system. If the Police ask you, 'Are you suicidal?' you never say, 'Yes.'" She expertly replied.

I found the past three weeks mind-numbing. I was incapable of processing the torrent of disturbing information Fannie confided in me. The facts completely conflicted with what I thought I knew of Lucy and our relationship.

It was not until after the insanity of her death threats during this harrowing trip that I entered a state of liminality and approached the Rubicon Roadhouse at the crossroads of my life. There was no deal to ink with this evil one I had called my wife. I could only turn my back and flee from Pinhead's[9] offered pleasure dome.

---

9 A reference to the main supernatural being in Clive Barker's Hellraiser. A story of

After everything that happened since Fannie told me of her attempted suicide, these nascent emotions, feelings, and thoughts finally solidified into a concrete decision to divorce Lucy.

About two weeks after we arrived on the farm, Lucy, without warning, insisted on returning to Florida.

She said, "I have to go back to our home."

"Why? We never planned a return trip."

Her reason for the return travel was, "I need to clean up the house and put it up for sale."

Despite her claims, she never listed it. At the time, I was not altogether sure what she planned. I discovered the precise kind of trouble Lucy committed back in Florida two years later, and I will reveal it later in the book. Her leaving at this moment suited my purposes. I had an urgent desire to get her out of my hair. It gave me the leeway required to seek a lawyer and begin my divorce.

Moments before Lucy left to catch the plane back to Florida. She asked Fannie, "What did your father do with the guns?"

"I'm not sure," Fannie told her and offered, "Maybe the Police took them."

Fannie and I had previously discussed the guns, knives, and threats several times. She knew the officer had taken the guns before we began the trip from hell. Her fear of her mother made her answer in an unsure and placating manner.

"You know, I don't feel very safe," Lucy told Fannie, "I think I need to get a gun and take some lessons."

Who is this person who always had an intense fear and dislike of weapons and suddenly wanted them?

While away, Lucy gave Fannie strict orders to call her twice daily. These were a front for three-way calls with Rifah. In the future, I will find out phone calls between Lucy, Fannie, and Rifah were a daily event since Fannie's earliest memories.

Fannie once questioned me about these phone calls, asking, "How could you not know?"

---

twisted perceptions between pleasure or pain. I projected this pleasure of pain concept onto Lucy. The pleasure she enjoyed from the pain she caused.

"I just didn't. I trusted her," was all that I could say to Fannie.

I was a clueless old man who trusted his wife without reservation. Who would look for subterfuge when they believed they lived in a pristine 1950s type of perfect world?

I do not think most people can comprehend the magnitude of the deceit I felt. Each new bit of negative information seemed like a square peg that could not fit through the round holes in my belief system's walls—it did not compute. In the beginning, I could not even sense these negative square pegs. After my mind allowed me to perceive these packets of information, it took even more time to remold my psyche's rigid barrier. And this new conscientiousness enabled me to reconcile these new morsels of non-conforming knowledge against the deceit I had always misguidedly believed to be authentic.

On our first visit to Cassandra and Laurence after Lucy left, Cassandra bore her soul and told me much of what she knew. Cassandra became aware of Fannie's predicament and much of Lucy's worst behavior at the Christmas reunion two months earlier.

She broke out crying and apologized, "Dad, I'm so sorry that I didn't tell you anything back at New Year's when I found out."

"The timing of how it all happened worked out for the best," I gave her a big hug, "Fannie is safe with me, and now, we are all here to protect her."

Chapter Thirty-Nine

Fannie is Now Sophie

Fannie never liked her name. Why? I don't know. I thought it was such an adorable name. Perhaps she found herself at the butt-end of too many jokes, and I guess I now come to the rear end of my Fannie-butt jokes. Yes, I think I've pushed those a little too far.

However, Fannie lived her life under a very different set of rules, circumstances, and beliefs from the rest of the family. I heard rumors or hints over the past few years while I lived on the farm that she wanted to change her name from Fannie to Sophie. I thought of it as teenagers in search of self-identity. I poked fun at the name Sophie and teased her about it. Unbeknownst to me, I added to the trauma of her grief, pain, and depression.

From this point in the book, I will only refer to my youngest daughter as Sophie. And this change of name is a chronological reflection of what occurred in real life.

While I may have added salt to her naming wounds, her injuries were beyond question caused by Lucy and Rifah. Two of her three middle names comprised alternative meanings, special secret intimations associated with Lucy and Rifah's relationship. To be clear, I am blaming Lucy and Rifah for the middle names. Sophie also hated her first name, and I can only ascribe the choice of her first name to Lucy and myself in memory of Lucy's brother, Franko.

It was not easy for me to stop calling her one name and start calling her another. She was Fannie to me for the past fifteen years, her entire life. I goofed up often, and adjusting to her new name took me months. At first, calling her Sophie seemed foreign, and I found it challenging to roll off my tongue. She would giggle at me when my face contorted, and I said something like "Fanophie" while trying mid-word to auto-correct the beginning mistake. Yet, these were her wishes, and the name Sophie now emerges as natural for me to say.

Sophie and I agreed she should wait until she turns eighteen for an official name change. This way, her mother would not be required for any official paperwork. We could avoid all the drama from the nonsense Lucy would stir up if she were involved.

I felt like such a terrible father, and I felt immensely guilty. I failed to protect my children, and now I was trying to make amends.

Chapter Forty

Fear and Security

There was both the fear of what Lucy had already wreaked upon us and what she may soon commit. She was very unpredictable, and I could never tell what this woman was up to.

Soon after I began the divorce, I realized Lucy's proclivity for unprotected casual sex with many individuals. I also discovered it began before our wedding and continued throughout our marriage. What a sad set of circumstances to learn I had married a trollop. I chose the word "trollop" carefully. Even though it sounds a bit like a tulip, lollipop, or truffle, it is not something of beauty like a tulip, nor is it sweet and tasty like a lollipop, and finally, it is not anything like the delicacy of a truffle.

Based on some of the early stories she shared with me, I suspect her animalistic behavior started long before our wedding, and consequently, I felt obliged to get tested. Frankly, the thought of what variety of infectious diseases she may have conferred upon me necessitated a doctor's visit. I mean, I felt healthy, and I did not think I had anything—but still.

I explained my situation to my doctor, who suggested a couple of blood tests. As I continued to describe her affairs, he looked at me with a sad and empathetic look.

He placed a reassuring hand on my shoulder and said, "I'm sorry man, but we should perform a full spectrum of blood tests. Just to be sure."

As I said, I felt fine, but I became progressively anxious as the day approached for the doctor to reveal all the lab work results. Then the phone call came.

Pacing the kitchen floor with ants in my pants, I answered the phone. A female voice on the other end said, "It's negative," after confirming it was me on the line.

"Wait... what?" I paused, then continued in heartbroken disbelief, "Negative news?"

The voice on the other end responded, "No," like I must have been silly, "All of the tests came back negative for any diseases."

My first celebration: **this—body—is—clean!**

> big sigh of relief <

Terror and Fear of Death

As I have previously stated, I do not consider myself paranoid. Yet, I have to ask, "Was it paranoia?"

Was I delusional with fears of mortal danger? After witnessing the face of The Full Psycho, finding a stash of hidden weapons with a boatload of ammo, and enduring multiple death threats.

I do not know how to suitably convey my feelings of absolute fear and terror. This woman knew where I lived and where Sophie went to school. She could show up at any time of her choosing, day or night. It felt like, "When you least expect it. Expect IT!"

To be frozen in terror was paralyzing in so many ways, on both mental and physical levels. It affects your life and your health. For example, this fear messed with my sleep patterns. Most nights, I often woke up startled with ease. It felt like I heard a Grue[10]

---

10 A Grue is a fictional beast that dwells in the dark. There were two text-based games I used to play in the late 1970s and early 1980s. One was called Zork by Infocom, where a Grue would automatically kill you if you went in the dark without a torch. The other game was a multi-user dungeon (MUD) called Dreamscape, and if you died, the console text would say, "A Grue gently chortles."

chortle at me from a distance. Then, I would get up and check the darkened landscape of the orchard through the windows for shadowy signs of intruders. Finally, I would uneasily snicker at myself as I tried to go back to sleep.

I halted all farm work, and my immobility lasted until after the farm sold two and a half years later. It was not until three years later that I found the gumption within myself to get a job and begin a slow course towards normalcy.

Cell Phone

You must remember how Lucy controlled the cell phone account. I did not want her monitoring my cell phone usage and prematurely figuring out I had started the divorce process. I knew I had to be discreet if I wanted to do this right without her discovering my plans.

So, I bought a new phone and opened my own account. I continued to use my old cell phone for typical day-to-day usage and used the latest cell phone for my covert divorce activities. Wow, I had reduced myself to being sneaky.

I planned to discontinue using the old phone from Lucy's account after I started the divorce proceedings.

Lock Down

For an entire year, we kept the gate to the farm padlocked at all times. After a year passed, we relaxed the rule to nighttime. Like the gate, we locked all of the doors at night.

We were extra vigilant during times of high stress, like court dates, birthdays, et cetera. I did not know what could spark one of Lucy's rages. During these times of potential triggers, we reverted to locking everything and remained especially alert.

Security Cameras

I bought an expensive video security system. It had all the bells and whistles, including night vision, 4K resolution, motion detection, and audio microphones. In addition, this system would send me real-time alerts on my new personal cell phone. She threatened to kill us, and I wanted an advanced warning of her probable impending arrival.

I purchased eight video cameras for the system and only had enough time to install one before Lucy's eventual return. I had to dig a hundred-yard-long trench to bury the conduit that held the cables from the camera at the front gate to the Digital Video Recorder (DVR) in the trailer.

Weapons

I bought a rifle for self-defense, although I should have purchased a handgun instead of a long gun. I took a one-day training course to familiarize myself with this specific weapon. Since Lucy threatened to kill us multiple times, I felt compelled to take her at her word. One thing I have learned is that you should never take threats lightly. You should always take them at face value and prepare yourself.

It was a terrifying prospect. I had no wish to shoot or kill my children's mother. Still, I could not stand idly by and let her harm my children or myself. I often contemplated my concern with respect to how I would feel about myself afterwards, if ever forced into a situation requiring the gun's use.

I had a discussion over the phone with my mother about the rifle I bought to safeguard Sophie and me. Purchasing this firearm upset her. I guess Mum worries about the American way with guns and my choice of weapon she disliked even more.

So, I asked her, "Mum, do you want me to wait here for Lucy to bust a cap in the back of my head some night?"

Her reply was hesitant, "No," she said uneasily, and her objections about the rifle I bought ceased.

At some point, I plan to purchase a handgun and take the training to receive a Concealed Carry Weapon Permit (CCW).

Credit Monitoring

I set up credit monitoring. I fully expected this woman would take out credit cards and even loans in my name at some point in the future. I also warned each of my children to set up credit monitoring for themselves for the same reasons.

In the past, I observed Lucy handle many other people's credit applications for her MLM businesses. In the years since I filed for divorce, Sophie told me how Lucy modified the applications.

"Mom used to change the income on applications if she didn't think they made enough money to get the credit cards," Sophie explained, "And she did it without telling them."

What the Sam Hill—Lucy made unauthorized and fraudulent modifications to her clients' credit applications before she submitted the forms.

I wonder how many people who shared their personal information with Lucy fell victim to credit fraud. It is not beyond her to perpetrate such an action.

"After all, she deserves their wealth, doesn't she?" I concede facetiously.

My little social butterfly has emerged to be a parasite of vampiric proportions.

Chapter Forty-One

Filing for Divorce

My parents lived the kind of special relationship I had strived for all my life and thought I had. Their marriage lasted for over fifty years right up until the day—no—to the moment my father passed away. They did everything together. They worked together. They partied and traveled together. They even did the groceries together. My parents were an inseparable pair. They were each other's Frik and Frak, or Yin and Yang.

I thought I had this sort of relationship with Lucija, except I never noticed how rare it was that we did anything together. I completely trusted her and was totally in love with her. In my eyes, she was beautiful, charming, and intelligent. I had the genuine feeling of being the luckiest man alive to have her in my life. Oh, how I lived in a bubble.

I never thought in a million years I would divorce my wife, Lucija. For me, marriage is a lifetime commitment to your best friend based on true love, and I always assumed she reciprocated those sentiments.

Since my teenage years, I have always looked down on men who divorced their wives. I thought less of them, as, from my perspective, they could not keep their family together. How could I reconcile this long-held belief of mine now I had filed for divorce myself? Basically, three things occurred. First, I continued to look down upon myself for the entire situation. Second, I moved the goalposts of my belief system regarding the husband being one hundred percent responsible for the marriage. I no longer recognize divorce as the clear-cut black-and-white situation I once assumed. The final realization I came to grasp was that my marriage and relationship with Lucy were never genuine. From her point of view, it was always a sham. For her, I was simply some patsy to take advantage of for the long term.

Let me introduce the following with what I thought to be accurate as I sought a lawyer. I thought the divorce process would be six to twelve months long, and my legal fees would be between six and ten thousand dollars. While these may be reasonable expectations for the vast majority of divorces in the United States, nothing in my life ever seems that simple.

When I began to write this book, well over two years after the first filing, my divorce remained incomplete. My marriage to this woman had not yet terminated. Unfortunately, the end of this fiasco was no longer in clear view as the courts fell into an indefinite shutdown for the Coronavirus pandemic. My latest court date was removed from the docket, postponed, no longer scheduled, and placed into pending purgatory. My legal and therapy bills surpassed the $100,000 mark over six months before the pandemic began, and these bills continued to grow.

I mentioned this before. I come from a family of lawyers and judges back in England. Years ago, lawyers in England were not allowed to advertise. Instead, they received clients through referrals, reputation, and word of mouth. I did not have the luxury of those three methods in my search. I scoured through internet web pages searching for a divorce lawyer, an exercise lasting two or three days. I decided on a legal firm based on its website's formal and conservative appearance and avoided the copious amount of flashy websites I found. Their website was reminiscent of my father and grandfather's legal practices, which instilled confidence in my choice. While this approach resembled throwing a dart at a wall map to decide your next travel plans' destination. I got lucky and pulled out one of the county's best and most respected divorce lawyers from the proverbial magic top hat.

Until we served Lucy with the divorce papers, I kept my plans pretty close to my chest. I did not want to tip her off to my actions. Two of my children knew from the beginning. My youngest daughter, Sophie, was involved in the thick of it. My oldest daughter, Cassandra, and her husband, Laurence, who helped me during these early stages, were also in the know.

I am not a secretive person. Keeping all my intentions under wraps ate at my very soul from the inside. I wanted everyone in the family to learn about these circumstances from me and not find out through the grapevine or, worse yet, find out from Lucy. My mother knew early on, as I desperately needed to confide in someone. I told Maggie, Gilbert, and Clifford about one week before my lawyer's office had Lucy served. Last but not least, I brought my brothers and sisters into the circle two days before.

Sophie and I were each awarded Temporary Restraining Orders (TRO) for domestic violence and child abuse. Once issued, we broke all contact with Lucy. Although, the TROs were not enforceable until after physical service occurred.

I remember driving Sophie home from High School one day, shortly after finding a lawyer, probably before acquiring our TROs.

"I would do anything to protect you from your mother," I told her, "I would sell the farm and even sell my cars." Then I continued to explain, "These are all just things. And even though they are things I like. They are not invaluable to me, like family."

I do not remember Sophie saying anything in reply. I think she sat in the passenger seat of my truck in quiet contemplation. I guess words are one thing, and actions are another. Sophie still had to relearn how to trust someone.

The legal system is a rather strange animal. In divorce cases, the parents are not allowed to share legal details with their minor children (non-adult children). I understand the court's reasoning, especially regarding parents using or weaponizing their children against each other. The problem with my situation centered around the fact that my youngest daughter knew more details than I did about what transpired leading up to the divorce.

Up to this point, Sophie made three-way calls every day with Lucy and Rifah. I abided by the legal system's rules and did not tell Sophie we had TROs in place. Instead, I only told her, "We are no longer accepting or making phone calls with Lucy or Rifah."

Sophie looked scared and said, "Mom will be very mad."

"Don't worry. Everything is taken care of," I replied with confidence.

At Sophie's next therapist meeting, I gave her therapist a copy of the TRO and explained that Sophie still did not know about it. I decided to let her therapist tell her about the TRO and present it to her in an unbiased fashion.

Shortly after we broke contact with Lucy, she panicked in a florid display of concern. She called the police, who did a wellness check on the farm. We were visiting with Cassandra and were not on the farm when Lucy's frenzied eruption emerged. Cassandra would not share any information concerning us with Lucy. The police called and left me a voice message. I returned the officer's call and explained our situation to him. He needed proof of identification for his report, and I offered to drive back to show him my ID. It was a Sunday, and we left Cassandra's a few hours earlier than planned to help the officer complete his report.

Chapter Forty-Two

TRO Violations

The Temporary Restraining Order violations began immediately. They were somewhat continuous and persisted even three years later while a Domestic Violence Restraining Order (DVRO) was in effect.

Upon Lucy's return to New York, the process server physically served Lucy with the TRO and divorce papers at a car rental area outside the airport.

I closed and padlocked the gate to the farm. I spoke with my mother, Maggie, and the twins back in England on the speakerphone of my first cell phone and watched the front gate's security video feed on my TV. Not a single car approached or passed the property's front entrance; this was the only entrance that a vehicle could enter the property.

Then, two hours after Lucy's scheduled landing, she suddenly appeared behind me in my trailer's doorway on the farm. The drive from the airport takes roughly an hour and a half. I think I almost broke my neck looking at her behind me, then back to the monitor in front of me to double-check the video feed of the gate, and finally snapping my head back in panicked disbelief to look at her again.

This situation felt like the horror movie *Halloween*, where Michael Myers suddenly manifests out of thin air over your right shoulder.

I got up to my feet, both surprised and bewildered that Lucy stood in the same room as me. She said many things like, "I want to talk," and "I'm sorry, I love you," alternating between a shrill voice and a mumbled voice.

I told her repeatedly, "You should not be here," and to "Please leave."

Lucy ignored my requests and paced through my house, screaming, crying, and waving her arms around with flailing motions. All the while, I asked Lucy to leave and warned her, "I will call 9-1-1 if you don't leave now."

Within the first two minutes of Lucy's arrival, I dialed 911 on my second cell phone. My mother and children, Maggie, Gilbert, and Clifford, continued listening to the fracas on the first phone. Unbeknownst to me, they also began recording the incident. I informed the 911 operator of the circumstances, the TRO, the weapons, her death threats, and now she stood here right this instant.

The operator asked me, "Does she have any weapons?"

"I don't think so," I replied, "She just got off an airplane, so ahh, no."

The operator said, "A sheriff has been dispatched and is on his way."

"You need to leave," I told Lucy, "The police are coming."

What did Lucy do? She plopped down and sat on the couch.

At one point, Lucy approached me, got down on her knees, her hands made a praying gesture as they slid down my arm while she went to her knees, and her face ended up uncomfortably close to my crotch, with me on my tippy toes backed up against a wall. I remember the feeling of my skin crawling as I turned my shoulder away in a slow shudder to remove my limp arm from her touch as she falsely tried to expiate upon me. But I did not realize that I made a small, uneasy, and disgusted moan. Like one would make if they fell into a septic tank. The quivering sound I made was audibly detectable on the 911 recording.

Speaking of the twenty-two-minute 911 recording that I received four months after the incident. It revealed that I remained polite during the entire encounter. And it also demonstrated how awkwardly uncomfortable I found the whole episode. It is challenging to hear Lucy on the recording. Most of the time, she sounded like a distant mumble. This enfeebled recording of Lucy was because the phone used to call 911 was not in speaker mode.

You can hear her say, "I love you."

"NO, no," I responded. Lucy must have been attempting to touch me or hold my hand.

Most of the time, I spoke with the 911 operator. However, it also recorded me talking to Lucy.

I said things like, "NO, don't touch me," "You shouldn't be here, the police are on their way, please leave," "DON'T touch me, don't TOUCH me, don't touch me," and "No, just leave."

At another point, I stood at the entrance, blocking Lucy's access to the area leading to Sophie's bedroom, where she hid. Lucy pushed past me, presumably needing to go to the bathroom. I offered some resistance, then decided not to take the chance of entering into an altercation.

While Lucy occupied the bathroom, Sophie threw open her bedroom door and ran outside. I thought she would follow our bug-out plan and run to the safe place we had previously discussed. Alas, no, in her fear and panic, she hid underneath our trailer in the dirt.

Lucy heard the commotion of Sophie running outside and chased after her shortly afterwards, wailing, "I just want a hug."

Sophie screamed back at her from under the trailer, "No!" as she scrambled as far out of Lucy's reach as possible.

Lucy got on her knees and lunged at Sophie under the trailer. Around this time, the 911 operator informed me the Sheriff was about fifteen minutes away. Sophie escaped from under the trailer out the other side and ran back into the house with fear written all over her face, whimpering indistinguishable sounds of alarm.

I followed immediately behind Sophie and attempted to close the door to lock it, with Sophie and me on the inside and Lucy outside. Unfortunately, Lucy trailed directly behind me and had her hand in the opening. The door opened outwards. To avoid harming Lucy, I gripped the door's edge with my hand in the door frame. Lucy held the door open with one hand while her other arm reached for me through the small opening in the doorway, like in a hospital scene from *The Walking Dead*.

Eventually, Lucy let go of the door and wandered around the trailer. I instantly locked the door. I then watched her through the windows. But soon, I lost sight of her. When the Sheriff arrived, Lucy had already fled the area—I love our first responders.

I can only say, "The best laid plans of mice and men often go astray,[11] and far adrift did they go."

We had video surveillance, but she circumvented it by parking way off in the distance, and she walked to the trailer through the orchard from the side of the property. We had a bug-out plan, with an escape route and a neighbor's place as a safe house. But our approach was foiled again because of Sophie's terror. She forgot it all and, in her panic, hid under the trailer.

Sophie later told me, "I felt like I was frozen in terror when Mom first arrived," she took a deep breath and continued, "I was paralyzed with fear. I couldn't move." Then, without a phone in her hands, Sophie made a texting gesture in the air while saying, "Only my thumbs worked. I texted my friends, 'She's here!' from my bed."

Sophie also tried to apologize for being so scared, saying, "Dad, I am sorry I couldn't think straight and went under the trailer instead of taking our escape route."

"It's okay, that was an unnerving experience," I gave her a big reassuring hug, "Nobody could've predicted this [confrontation]."

Upon reflection on the circumstances surrounding this incident, I realized the video security would not give me the five-

---

11 I loosely quoted a passage from the 1785 poem To A Mouse by the Scottish poet Robert Burns
"The best laid schemes o' Mice an' Men Gang aft agley."

minute warning I thought it would. The real-time alerts had a five-minute delay before reaching my cell phone. Lucy may take an alternate route, avoiding the cameras until she arrives at our door. I would most likely receive the signal after Lucy appears in the doorway. It became apparent the system's purpose would be consigned to recording these events to help with future prosecution.

My rifle was secured using two different methods. I have a cable lock running through the magazine well and coming out of the ejector chamber, and I keep my firearm in a locked armored case. I faced a minimum fifteen-minute interval with receiving an alert, identifying Lucy as the intruder, getting to my rifle, unlocking it, loading it, and then being ready to use it if needed. Unfortunately for me, security was not working out as I had planned.

We felt unsafe living on the farm, as Lucy knew where we lived. We needed to move, and in the meantime, locking doors at all times seemed like our best course of action or possibly our only course of action.

Lucy continuously asked our children in England to pass messages to Sophie and me. She asked all our children to intervene. She wanted them to ask me to cancel the Restraining Order and drop the divorce filings.

During the first year of the divorce, Lucy told my children many times, "I want to be a happy family again."

It was a pressure campaign that went on for a long time, for years.

At the Family Court Services (FCS) Mediation, Lucy enlisted some church marriage counselors to approach me right within the court building—yet another attempt to intervene and save the marriage. I will get into the details of this encounter later.

Phone calls from Croatia. I received a dozen phone calls from Croatia, with voice message recordings on a few of them. I could hear Lucy's mother claiming to be unwell. She does not speak my language.

"Sam, Baka sick, Baka sick," she said in broken English, "Please kawl."

Throughout our entire marriage, Lucy's mother and I were unable to communicate without Lucy present to translate.

Furthermore, Lucy's mother never called me and did not even know my phone number. Additionally, her mother never called us because of the prohibitively expensive long-distance rates. Lucy customarily called her mother. I knew Lucy had given her mother my phone number. She wanted her mother to plead with me to grant Lucy another chance.

In the future, after the Court upgraded our TROs to Domestic Violence Restraining Orders (DVRO), Lucy would continue her violations: texts and phone calls to Sophie. Trying to get information about us from people we knew, and worse things like identity theft.

Chapter Forty-Three

High Conflict Preparation

My lawyer gave me a list of five therapists he recommended as a suggestion for what he called High Conflict Preparation. Even though my lawyer considered this measure optional, he strongly advised that, in my case, I should do it. I come from a family of lawyers and always knew and was taught from childhood to follow my lawyer's advice.

I want you to picture the scene of my first meeting with this therapist. He wore toe-shoes, shoes with individual toes in them. I think I did a lot of staring at those strange shoes, and they became a point of focus for me during most of the session. His old, long-haired golden lab lay on a dog bed in the corner of the room. I sat on his couch, with my buttocks close to the edge. I sat forward, all tense, and rolled up. My elbows remained firmly planted on my knees, and my hands clenched together. I may have even rocked back and forth occasionally. I was the complete antithesis of relaxed.

Like the computer engineer I am, I explained the story of recent events in a methodical, concise, and technical manner. After a few minutes, he stopped me.

He sat back in his chair and crossed his legs with his right ankle on his left knee. Then, with his elbows on the chair's armrests and his hands clenched together with the tips of his pointer fingers touching, forming a triangular shape, he told me, "I want you to think about what you just said these past few minutes," he paused before continuing to ask, "Now tell me your story again, except slower this round. I want you to take your time and think about what you're saying as you say it."

I restarted as he requested and did not even get through half of a sentence. Within seconds, I burst into tears right in front of this gentleman I had met only a half-hour earlier. I mean, my body convulsed with tears in front of him, identical to the morning after I learned of Sophie's suicide attempt, the morning I pulled the car over while driving her to high school because I could not safely drive.

I thought I heard him say, "There it is," or was my memory two years later now playing tricks on me?

You must understand that all of my life, before meeting this High Conflict Preparation therapist, I believed psychiatrists and psychologists were for crazy people. Now that I had been through the wringer these past few months, I began rethinking my beliefs.

I explained to him, "I am taking care of my daughter. She is going for counseling."

But he kept asking me, "What about you?" and, "Are you seeing a therapist? Are you taking care of yourself?"

"I feel fine," I kept telling him, "Maybe I'll consider it later after everything settles down."

Because I am a little dense, I guess I made this fellow work for his money to try to get through my thick skull what he knew to be true. He started his line of questioning and asked, "Well, have you ever flown on an airplane?"

"Why yes, of course, I've flown on airplanes before," I replied, "And I even used to have Elite status with an airline,"

Then he asked, "Okay, so at the beginning of each flight, what do they tell you during the safety instructions?"

I rattled off, "They point out the exits, show you how seat belts work, ahh, seats are also flotation devices, [etc.]."

He interrupted Mr. Dense and pulled me back to where he wanted to go. Then he said, "All right then, in an emergency, when the masks drop from the ceiling, what do you do?"

"I put on my mask."

Now that we were on the right track, his questioning continued, "Right, and if you have a child with you, whose mask do you put on first?"

I don't think I even said "mine," as my mouth remained wide open while an incipient level of comprehension slapped me across the face.

I must tip my hat off to him, such an exquisitely simple example of something I knew was a truth, to show me the truth in something else I required. Something I fought against tooth and nail. Did he slap me with the equivalent of a real-life metaphor?

He referred me to a therapist and insisted, "You need their help to take care of yourself."

I knew I had hired him to prepare me for court. However, I did not realize that he also assessed my emotional state to determine my readiness to take the stand in court. To be honest, looking back on it now, without his help and the help of the therapist he referred me to, I know I was nowhere near ready. I think the emotional state in which I existed at the time resembled something akin to a bag of furious feral felines getting tossed around violently while riding an extreme roller coaster.

He gave me an exercise to write down our marriage history, focusing on recent events and another list of accusations I thought Lucy would make.

During this process, I realized and put down on paper, "I have never felt this magnitude of depression before, and I sought help."

I wrote this passage referencing the time I had suicidal thoughts when I first learned about Lucy's affair with Rifah four years earlier.

I started writing this chapter and including it in the book to show how I did not feel I required counseling. To show how, through this process, this gentleman made it quite clear to me how desperately I needed emotional help and support. For all of you tough guys and strong women out there who lived with a narcissist and considered yourself coping well or can work it out on your own, please reflect a little more on my story and then seek out the help you truly need. Internally, you are messed up in ways you cannot fathom. The veil of deceit in your life shrouds your vision from too many truths. Please do not let your pride get in the way of receiving these helpful resources.

Chapter Forty-Four

Family Court Services Mediation

As I previously mentioned in the TRO violations chapter, I attended our Family Court Services Mediation appointment. Family Court Services (FCS) is a department within the courthouse building. I arrived there before Lucy, and because of my fears about her, I requested separate sessions for us. I then sat in the back corner of the waiting room, adjoined to the reception area through a door.

Shortly afterwards, Lucy entered the waiting room. She sat close to and chatted with two people I did not recognize, a male and a female. They appeared to be Hispanic, both clad in some pieces of black leather attire, and they sported lots of tattoos.

The interview seemed short and lasted only between a half-hour and forty-five minutes. Lucy's meeting followed mine. When I left the conference, I waited in the reception area for the court mediator to return my original copies of the police report detailing the guns I had found. I supplied her with the document to make a copy for her files. While I waited for the return of my report, the male who previously sat with Lucy in the adjoining waiting room approached me. My first impression of this gentleman was that he looked quite gruff. But, to my surprise, he spoke softly and eloquently. Never judge a book by its cover. He introduced himself as Juan, a mediator from his church for marriage counseling. He was from a local Baptist Church here in the area.

I immediately told Juan, "I have a Restraining Order against Lucy. She cannot pass messages to me through other people. And likewise, I cannot send her messages."

"Lucy did not want our marriage to end," Juan told me.

I cannot say for sure because I do not remember. All the trauma I had been through, and now Juan was unwittingly making me relive the ordeal again. But I must have non-verbally answered him with an utterly revolted look.

Yet undaunted, he persisted anyway as he continued asking, "Could I help to facilitate."

"Lucy had a sixteen-year affair," I told Juan in no uncertain terms.

An expression of dumbfounded surprise fell over Juan's face as he said, "I," but it sounded like eye, "Did not know—that."

I finished the minutia of our chat with, "There is nothing to be done that could help save our marriage."

When the court mediator returned the original documents to me, I politely took my leave of Juan and exited the building.

So, Lucy brought two people from some, unknown to me, Baptist Church, to the courthouse. They were there to intervene on her part in the divorce, custody, and Restraining Order matters. Of the two people, only Juan approached me, and I believe he did so with good intentions. But this was organized by Lucy. It was inappropriate, a clear and intentional violation of the TRO.

FCS interviewed Sophie separately from Lucy and me about a week later.

Chapter Forty-Five

The Deposition

Because of the TRO, I did not attend the conference in person. However, I did listen in via a muted phone line. My lawyer made Lucija and her lawyer aware of my presence over the phone, and she could not hear me. I listened to the complete deposition. I emailed my lawyer's office with further questions or responses to Lucy's blatant lies. It felt like pulling teeth during her entire testimony, trying to get Lucy to answer even the most basic questions.

The deposition is almost two hundred pages long, and here in this book, I have less than ten pages of my summarization and highlighting dedicated to it.

You may notice Lucy's answers seem like a circular firing squad of non-answers and lies throughout most of her testimony. As I said, it felt like pulling teeth to get her to answer questions and each of the answers she gave seemed to shoot holes in the previous statements she made. While her stand-alone explanations may seem plausible, nothing she told fit together, and it often contradicted other responses she previously claimed. You read on and see for yourself.

She was highly evasive with memory problems and claimed not to speak or understand English very well when eluding questions she did not want to answer. However, when advancing her fanciful versions of reality, she was rather aggressive, her English was top-notch, and her memory was restored and inventive.

Drugs and Brain Fog

Lucy claimed several times that the medications she took for her anxiety gave her brain fog and made it hard to think clearly.

Lucy does not believe in Western Medicine. She perceives all doctors as quacks unless they subscribe to her nutritional products. She considers all drugs as poison and a money grab by Big Pharma. I do not believe for a single second that she took any of the medications she alleged were prescribed to her.

Her claims of having brain fog were all part of her ploy to answer questions with unclear, ambiguous, and misleading answers.

Her foggy memory was not the only side effect she claimed the drugs gave her. She asked for several bathroom breaks. However, twice, she claimed to be feeling sick to her stomach. Both times, she left my lawyer's office, went down the hall with her lawyer to the bathroom, and began throwing up. People in my lawyer's office could hear her retching. Her gagging so loudly tells me it was a show and that she wanted others to listen to the noise and sympathize with her.

Playing Stupid

Lucy accused me of calling her dumb or stupid multiple times during the divorce. This was to paint me as a horrible individual. During our marriage, she also used this tactic to put me on the defensive during arguments. I never called her stupid. However, I often explained that her actions were dumb or reckless. I draw an obvious distinction between calling out her and her actions. While she always tried to conflate the two.

I have never seen her act in such a fashion. Lucy is intelligent, and she speaks seven languages. Yet, there she sat, claiming not to understand the English language. A language Lucy had spoken for years effectively. Declaring she often required a translator.

In the past, Lucy translated to and from English for other people. She even applied to be an official translator while we lived in England.

Rape

If you recall, as far back as Sophie could remember, Lucy told her I was too big, and sex with me hurt her, and she defined it as I raped her. Sexual molestation has been prominent in many of Lucy's life stories. Prior to the deposition, I made my lawyer aware of Lucy's insinuations so my lawyer could prepare, and the following transpired.

When my lawyer asked directly, "Do you believe my client is a rapist?"

Lucy said, "No."

Then my lawyer followed up and asked, "Did Samuel rape you?"

"No," was Lucy's reply.

At another point during the deposition, he asked, "Is Sam a violent person?"

Lucy said, "No. My husband, he was never a violent person before."

Even when Lucy confirmed I was not violent and had not been violent with her, she had to sling some dirt. Why would she end that sentence with the word before? Was she attempting to say that I may have become violent since I began the divorce? Is this one of her suggestive strategies to let your mind fill in the blanks?

Taking the Fifth

During the deposition, Lucy had to take The Fifth several times over many instances of violating the Restraining Order. Think about it: We were in family court for a divorce and custody case, and she had to assert her rights, to plead her Fifth Amendment

Rights, and not incriminate herself. Her lawyer stopped her many times mid-sentence to remind her of those rights.

I know about Fifth Amendment Rights. Except, I have only ever seen or heard of its use in Senate or House committees.

When somebody like a mobster says, "I am taking the Fifth on that question, the next question, and every other question."

I had the distinct impression that Lucy's stagecraft all played out like a B-rated movie.

Lucy took the Fifth about going to the farm after receiving the TRO. She pleaded the Fifth on where she went and what she did after being served. Essentially, Lucy took the Fifth on everything she did that day after being served with the TRO. Later, she took the Fifth about giving her mother my phone number and asking her mother to call me. Finally, she asserted her Fifth Amendment Rights about asking my older children to pass messages to Sophie and me.

Emotional Breakdown

In a new line of questioning, my lawyer asked Lucy, "Did any of your daughters try to kill themselves?"

"I don't know," she replied.

When he asked her, "Were any of your daughters ever hospitalized for any reason?"

Lucy replied, "Yes."

Then, in an awkward and obtuse manner, she named all three of our daughters. Maybe I am wrong, but for me, being hospitalized means being checked into a room for an extended period and does not include emergency or check-up visits. So, with my definition in mind, excluding maternity stays, only my youngest daughter was ever hospitalized.

So, my lawyer asked her, "Was your youngest daughter ever hospitalized, and why?"

"Yes, because of an emotional breakdown with her boyfriend," Lucy replied.

When my lawyer asked, "How did Sophie try to hurt herself."

"I am not certain. The doctor never specified," Lucy replied.

The questions about suicide and Lucy's evasive answers went on ad nauseam. Until my lawyer finally asked, "I'm unclear whether you're claiming your daughter attempted suicide or not. Is your testimony still that your daughter did not attempt suicide?"

"I phrase it that she had an emotional breakdown," she replied.

Then, in rapid succession, Lucy gushed the following word salad, "Either it was attempted suicide, potentially. We weren't certain if that really was. And it wasn't determined if she took any pills or how many. But that was a possibility, you know, as a result of an emotional breakdown and breakup with the boyfriend at the time."

Lucy's first mention of Rifah in the deposition occurred while she explained his reason for visiting Sophie in her hospital room from out of state.

Her answer occurred over several questions, so I paraphrased, "Her [Sophie's] biological father came to the hospital because he called me to find out."

Yes, you read it right. Lucy's explanation under oath in the deposition, Rifah somehow telepathically knew to call Lucy and find out about Sophie's suicide attempt. Lucy used this fallacy to explain his reason for being there from out of state.

Not the Good Father?

When asked if Sam was neglectful of Fannie, Lucy claimed I never really did much with any of our children. She said I never took them to appointments or helped with their schoolwork. Lucy also charged that I never showed any interest or took the time to participate in sports or church activities with our children.

Yet, this woman testified, "My husband never really did much with the children. I did—did everything," poutingly.

Meaning she did everything, and Sam did nothing. Right, please read on.

Only one statement in all of the above contained a modicum of truth—I did not participate in many church activities. However, I should point out that I took Gilbert and Clifford to most of their Boy Scouts activities managed by the Mormon Church. The Mormon Church was not my church, nor was I a member. But the scouting activities included church-related programs and community services that my boyos and I participated in.

We were a family unit and shared responsibility for our children's extracurricular activities. Lucy handled most of the appointments scheduled during my work hours, and on some occasions, I took time off to help. In addition, I often helped with homework, especially explaining Math. You already know that I did most of the driving for sports, and I coached and refereed for several years.

Perhaps I should mention that I was a single parent for many years before I met or married Lucy.

Virgin Birth

When asked, "Have you had a relationship with Rifah for very long?"

Lucy started to play wordsmithing games with a lawyer, no less. Brilliant! She claimed not to understand the meaning of the word relationship.

Then, with a more direct approach, he asked her, "At some point, did you start having sex with Rifah?"

And Lucy said, "No."

There was confusion in the air. Lucy claimed Rifah was Sophie's biological father a few minutes earlier. Now Lucy said she did not have sex with him. How would she reconcile the baffling contrast between the absence of sex versus the natural father?

My lawyer immediately changed the tact of his questioning, starting with, "So, are you now claiming Rifah is not the biological father?"

"We believe he is," Lucy replied.

Digging further, my lawyer asked, "Do you believe he is because you were having sex with him?"

"No," came out of Lucy's mouth in reply.

Finally, in disbelief or exasperation, my lawyer asked, matter-of-factly, "Okay, so how do you believe Rifah inseminated you if you were not having sex?"

"I don't recall," was how Lucy answered.

From this point on, every question regarding their relationship, sex, and who knew Rifah was the biological father, each answered with, "I don't know" or "I don't recall."

I would also like to point out that later in the deposition, Lucy blurted out, "I have a wonderful relationship with my daughter, and we both love each other dearly."

Wait, what? An hour later, she suddenly knew the meaning of a relationship and how to appropriately use it in a sentence.

During one of the several breaks, while Lucy and her lawyer were out of the room, I overheard some of my lawyer's comments. In an off-the-record statement, I heard my lawyer laughingly state his astonishment, "I have never heard anyone claim the Virgin Birth in a case before," a first in his storied career.

The Fix Is In

My lawyer began a new line of questioning, beginning with: "Did you ever tell Samuel you were raped in Croatia?"

"No," Lucy said.

Then my lawyer followed up with, "Did you ever tell Samuel you were raped at all?"

Lucy again replied, "No."

Finally, he asked, "Do you know of any reason why Samuel believed you were raped?"

"I don't know," she replied softly.

I won't get into the line of questioning and all her foolish answers regarding race that ensued. However, I will openly state that Lucy and I are Caucasian. Rifah is Bangladeshi and not

Caucasian. Nevertheless, Lucy tried to claim she did not know I was not the father until several months after Sophie's birth.

What did I hear her claim? She told me she was raped in Croatia while attending her brother's funeral. At this instant, it suddenly dawned on me how she caught herself in her own web of lies. Yes, I was fifteen years slow, but ding, it finally hit me during the deposition. I could not remember the technical word for the operation performed on me.

I emailed my lawyer's office, stating, "I was fixed after the twins were born twenty years ago. I can no longer have children!"

A little while later, my lawyer began a new line of questioning, starting with, "So when you were pregnant with Sophie, did you believe Samuel was the father?"

"I don't recall," Lucy replied.

Next, my lawyers asked, "Do you remember your husband Samuel had a vasectomy twenty years ago?"

And Lucy said, "I don't recall the time frame."

Then he continued his follow-up and asked, "Do you remember when you became pregnant with Sophie, you knew there was no way in the world Samuel could be the father?"

"No," Lucy shot back in response. "I don't recall that."

With a slightly raised voice, my lawyer asked, "Do you know whether or not Samuel had a vasectomy twenty years ago?"

In a calculated voice, Lucy replied, "I don't remember what he had."

With a frustrated tone, my lawyer asked, "Are you saying you never knew whether or not Samuel had a vasectomy twenty years ago?"

I guess Lucy felt caught as she replied, "I did. But I don't remember when."

My lawyer's expression changed dramatically from exasperated to friendly as he half-stated the question, "Okay, so you knew Sam had a vasectomy?"

"Yes."

He continued his friendly demeanor and asked, "And you knew Sam had a vasectomy before you became pregnant with Sophie?"

"Yes, I believe so," Lucy replied hesitantly.

Putting it all together, my lawyer asked Lucy, "Okay, so when you became pregnant with Sophie, knowing your husband could not have fathered the child, who do you think the father might be?"

Lucy tried to answer with the ridiculous, "There's always a possibility the vasectomy is not accurate."

My lawyer ignored the answer and continued on his roll, "Do you know how many potential fathers there were when you became pregnant with Sophie?"

Lucy reverted to playing simple-mindedness, saying, "I don't understand the question."

So, my lawyer simplified his question by asking, "Well, how many men were you having sex with about the time you became pregnant with Sophie?"

"None to my knowledge," Lucy simply stated.

Undeterred, my lawyer pressed on, asking, "When you became pregnant and knowing your husband had a vasectomy, what was your explanation to him, as to how you became pregnant?"

Lucy's quick wit appeared to run out of steam, and she said, "I don't recall, I don't remember, honestly." I think she gave up while she deceptively tried to claim to be candid.

Finally, my lawyer asked her, "If Sam says you told him you were raped in Croatia, would Samuel be lying to us?"

Lucy said, "I don't know," in a small voice.

Ah, yes, vasectomy was the technical word for the operation I underwent. It was the term that I could not remember for being fixed. There were only two people on God's green Earth who knew I had a vasectomy. Those were Lucy and me (I guess the doctor also knew, aside from that, he is not a part of my life or this story). I had the operation shortly after the twins were born at my wife's insistence. She would not submit to a procedure as she felt it would impact her health later in life. Additionally, she would not take birth control pills as she believed they could also affect her health in the future.

The email I sent to my lawyer's office was the first time information regarding my vasectomy was shared with anyone outside of Lucy and me. I found the operation kind of embarrassing, that it diminished me as a man, even though I knew it did not—it always felt that way to me. I never talked about having a vasectomy with anyone. When someone I knew would vasectomize themselves, I would tease the heck out of them.

Telling them, "I will be all man until the day I die."

To all my friends whom I gave such a hard time: yes, like you, I have mutilated myself.

Of course, Lucy knew I had a vasectomy after the twins were born. She researched and found a doctor to perform the operation. She watched while I shaved the area the night before the procedure. She even checked out the area. She went to the doctor's office with me. To my knowledge, this doctor's office only performed vasectomies, nothing else. She waited in the reception area while the deed was done and drove me home afterwards. She also made fun of me and how I walked for several days—a gentle and delicate walk. It seemed like she chaffed a chafed cowboy who recently got off his horse after several days of hard riding. This vasectomy business took place back in England before we moved to the United States.

Sam's Attempted Suicide?

Remember, I had thoughts of suicide and had the mental wherewithal to call for help. I went to the hospital and was tested for drugs, observed, and released, all on the same day.

Lucy claimed in the deposition, "I went to the hospital, and the doctor told me that Sam had attempted suicide."

When explicitly asked under oath, she could not recall being told or knowing how I attempted suicide.

On the day I had suicidal thoughts, I called Lucy from the hospital to ask her to come to collect me. I sat in the reception area for half an hour with a counselor, waiting for Lucy to arrive. Then, through the windows, I watched Lucy walk through the parking lot and enter the hospital. She never spoke with any doctors.

Lucy said without any problem in the deposition that I attempted suicide. It became rather evident she had told her friends for years I had.

One of her friend's court declarations stated, "Sam exhibits mood swings and has been hospitalized for attempted suicide."

Okay, Sam, who never actually attempted suicide, Lucy said I did. Then, Sophie, who, in fact, swallowed an entire bottle of pills in an attempt to end her life, Lucy said she only had an emotional breakdown and did not attempt suicide.

I mean, her lies are everywhere, and her dubious stories are rather insidious. I always found her stand-alone stories and lies to be believable. However, they all fell apart when strung together while under interrogation in the deposition.

The Castle

Her castle is a short topic despite having played such a massive foundational part in that woman's story since I first met her.

My lawyer asked her, "Do you have any assets in Croatia?"

"No," Lucy replied.

My lawyer continued, asking, "Do you have a family castle in Croatia?"

Again, Lucy said, "No."

"There's no castle?" he asked questioningly, with a smack of skepticism.

And again, Lucy said, "No."

He pressed on and asked, "There's not thousands and thousands of acres in Croatia?"

Lucy answered a little differently this time, "No, not that belongs to me."

Then my lawyer asked, "Does your family have a castle in Croatia?"

"No."

Finally, my lawyer asked her, "Do you know why Samuel believes you have a castle or your family has one in Croatia?"

"Because generations back, my family used to have rights to it," Lucy replied, "We don't own anything."

All I can say is, "Wow. **WOW**, Lucy denied the existence of her castle!"

Should I be surprised? I do not know what to think. After all her stories. And her brother took an entire roll of pictures of the castle for me when he was alive. I was left stunned to discover, without a doubt, it was all a calculated ruse.

It's Not a Knife–It's a Peeler

Lucy threatened to divorce me two hours before we left Florida on The Trip From Hell. I already explained the story in the sub-chapter Threat of Suicide from the chapter The Shit Show.

"Okay, while the police were at your house, you told your husband you wanted a divorce?" my lawyer asked.

"He was very hostile about the whole situation. I had expressed that if he was going to continue this kind of treatment and abuse, I would," then Lucy paused to rethink how to continue, "Perhaps we should divorce."

Pleased with her answer, she finished, "Is how I phrased it. How I mentioned that."

Her explanation was somewhat of an alternate reality from what I experienced that day.

After the trip, I found a knife hidden in her purse when we arrived at the farm. This woman claimed during the deposition, "Never. I never carry a knife." Instead, she insisted, "I only bring a little peeler with me on road trips. It's a peeler-looking thing, whatever a peeler looks like."

Well, the knife with the two-inch blade she hid in her purse in the moving truck while we drove to New York, which she called a peeler. I call it a pig sticker.

I can only imagine how, in her mind, "Sam was the swine to be stuck" that day as we drove across states.

She brought a grocery bag full of fruits, vegetables, and whatnot into the deposition as a prop to show off her eating habits. Who totes support aids to a deposition? Who, in their right mind, brings a grocery bag of food, fruit, and vegetables to an interrogation?

This grocery bag was her lame method of demonstrating she did not possess a knife in the truck during the move to New York while she devolved into her Full Psycho mode. It was a pretty weak refutation of my claim with pictures, proving she did indeed bring a concealed knife.

By the way, this charmer did not bring any fruit or vegetables on the moving trip. There was nothing to peel. Yet, she carried a concealed knife.

Denial of Businesses

All the MLM businesses she operated for years and that I financially supported. She claimed they did not exist. At least the more active and somewhat successful businesses she had, she now claimed, did not exist.

All I could think was, "What a liar."

She ran her most successful MLM business through her friend Loqueesha's corporation. I often helped to deliver and install some of the products she sold. She told me years ago that she was made President of Loqueesha's company. I knew details about the company, such as it was formed and registered in the District of Columbia. However, during the deposition, Lucy denied being the President or having a business run through this company.

According to Lucy, before I started the divorce, she was close to making over $100,000 per year with one of her MLM businesses.

She also said she was only a few sales away from attaining a new level in the business, in which she would also receive a salary and regular bonuses to compensate for her travel.

Sophie told me she and Lucy would pick up several checks every couple of days from Lucy's Post Office Box at Mail Boxes Etc. The value of the payments varied, usually a few hundred dollars each, then sometimes a check for several thousands of dollars would appear. I guess I never mentioned Lucy had her own post office box. She acquired it around the time I found out about the Rifah affair. She said it was for her businesses. I think it also helped to support her secret lives. The cell phone bills probably disappeared from our home to this post office box.

Not all Therapists are Alike

Late in the deposition, Lucy claimed she attended therapy for the debilitating anxiety and depression I had caused her. She was vague with all her answers. Lucy could not recall this therapist's office address or the general area of the office. She could not remember the name of the therapist's office. Lucy could not even supply an estimate of how many times she attended therapy. Under continued questioning, Lucy volunteered her therapist's name.

While the deposition continued, I performed an internet search for her therapist in the surrounding cities. All I could find was a massage therapist with the same name that Lucy supplied. So, I forwarded this information to my lawyer via email.

When my lawyer confronted Lucy with this massage therapist information, she played dumb and attempted to deny it with a litany of imprecise answers.

Then, finally, Lucy awkwardly said in a tiny voice, "Oh, I thought it was my massage therapy."

Chapter Forty-Six

Ascension from Madness

My definition of therapy is to rip it out and let it heal. To rip the Band-Aid off, exposing all the hurt. No physical ripping takes place. Yet, there is an abundance of emotional tearing, all by talking about what happened and how I felt. Simply talking sounds like it should be painless. But do not let me fool you. It was a painful and challenging process. Good thing for me that I am a talker. It helped immensely with unpacking and processing all those emotional knots I found myself tied in.

I realize the following song has nothing to do with what I went through. I often sing it in my head while writing this book. It is a powerful song and reverberates within me. The tune remains the same. But the words in my head are slightly different from the original lyrics. The song is *Lightning Crashes* by Live, and the modified lyrics in my head go like this.

> Lightning crashes as my old life dies
> All my intentions fall to the floor
> The angel opens my eyes
> And confusion sets in
> All my feelings coming back again
> Like a rolling thunder crashing deep within
> Forces pulling from the center of my soul,
> This sin
> I can feel it

Since my little angel Sophie opened up and started telling me about Lucy, I have not shed a single tear for Lucy or the relationship I thought Lucy and I had. I do not care about her. All my tears and anguish are for my children, who suffered greatly at this wicked woman's hands. I guess to remain honest and truthful, some of my tears are for myself in the sense of what she perpetrated against me.

I arrived at an understanding. Lucy is nothing more than another person on the planet whom I do not know. I do not care if she finds someone rich and lives in the lap of luxury, and I do not care if she is a homeless beggar on a street corner. I simply don't care; I don't know this woman, and I do not want to know her or know about her. Let me be extremely clear. This insight was not forgiveness. To forgive is divine. Me, I am only human. I will never forgive her for who she is or what she did. I exorcised her from my life, or as I call it, I have been "narsorssized."

Several therapists said that because they had never met or interviewed Lucija, they could not render a diagnosis of her. However, the same therapists also said based on what happened in the stories and descriptions my children and I told. Those behaviors we described followed a classic narcissistic pattern. Narcissists typically operate as sociopaths, which is not considered dangerous. However, when the world a narcissist constructed for themselves is messed with or falls apart, they can instantly switch to a psychopath mode, which can be dangerous and kill.

Since the first time I met Lucy, everything was a lie, roughly thirty years of lies. It was a painfully complicated procedure that took a long time to reconcile all the falsehoods I once thought were true.

How can I describe how it felt to have a narcissist traipse through my life? I visualize it as similar to being eaten by a boa constrictor. Your demise is a long, drawn-out, and snail-paced process. Yet you do not feel your life force squeezed from you. At least not until close to the end, when all the pain rushes in at once.

The Realization

It took months, maybe even a year, to realize nothing about Lucy struck me as genuine or authentic. With all the lies, and to this day, I continue to learn about more of her deceptions. I do not know this person. She never loved me, and she never cared about me. From the first time we met, I was simply a mark to her. I may say the following several times in the book. She is merely another person on the planet's surface whom I do not care about or know.

She is not an actual person. She is real in the sense of flesh and blood, but not a single thing about her is authentic. It is all charades within charades and lies upon lies. She will present herself to the person she is talking to only within a framework of how she perceives they want her to be. She is a succubus shrouded in a chameleon's clothing. And to top it off, she is remorseless about all the pain and suffering she caused.

Do not ask me why. Throughout my life, I perceived it as the man's responsibility to keep his marriage together. I also believed the man pursued and seduced the woman into the relationship during affairs. As I said, I do not know why I had such a one-sided view regarding divorce and extra-marital relations.

Since The Shit Show, I came to realize the old adage, "It takes two to Tango," were the precise actions that transpired between Lucy and each of the men she chased.

I thought all these sleazy individuals pursued my beautiful wife. I fully believed in her faithfulness to our family and me. I presumed she put an end to all their advances. However, I have since recognized Lucy actively sought out and instigated many of these depraved relationships and affairs.

It took me a while to wrap my head around this new understanding. This new belief was that, generally speaking, women are equally responsible as men for the failure of their marriage or any affairs in which they found themselves involved.

Family and Friends

Clifford decided to drop out of university and return to the farm to help me. He had not adjusted well to life in England, unhappy with his grades and homesick for quite some time. Everything Clifford learned regarding the treatment of his sisters affected him deeply. He continues to deal with the guilt he harbors for not seeing more or intervening to protect his sisters. Which only added to his longing to come home. While I wanted Clifford to remain enrolled in university and finish his studies, I knew he had to do what was right for him.

I am not angry with Lucy's friends for thinking, "Sam is the monster," as she portrayed me.

How could I be offended or even upset with them for her pulling the wool over their eyes? After all, she had the same woolen wig held firmly over my eyes for almost thirty years, and I lived with her full-time. If I could not see through her veil of deceit, how could I expect her friends to see through it?

The way I see it, Lucy does not have any friends, well, not any real friends. There are three types or categories of people in her life: marks, props, and enablers. All along, she targeted me as one of her marks, and our marriage was one of her props. Our children were all props to her. Most of her friends were more of her marks. Some of her longer-term friends and her business partners were props who eventually became her enablers. All people in her life are disposable. She would throw anyone under the bus to save her skin or validate her perspective.

Church Shopping

Lucy did what I now call church shopping. These kind-hearted people of various faiths and denominations provided an easy crowd for her to take advantage of and prey upon. We are Catholic. Before all of the information regarding her behavior exploded in my face, Lucy attended several Catholic churches. She went to some Mormon churches and tried to get Maggie to join. She also participated in Christian services. I knew of those places of worship, and I'm sure there were others.

Since I filed for divorce, I knew Lucy went to a Baptist church to recruit them for mediation purposes in her effort to get things back to her normal. I also knew she enlisted at least one Christian church for support in court. Undoubtedly, she targeted other churches and faiths to take advantage of, yet I have no direct knowledge of it.

Keep this in mind: I no longer care about Lucy one way or the other. I find it noble of the people out there who will support and help the unfortunate, yet I am also sad for those same people who will get burned by her.

Chapter Forty-Seven

Revelations

This entire chapter may come across as Sam airing his dirty laundry or as Sam spewing out his grievances, and it feels as such each time I read it. However, this was not my intention, nor was it the purpose of this chapter. I have rewritten this chapter several times and remain unhappy with it. It started as a bulleted list of events, and I attempted to add more to the story surrounding each topic. Are my negative feelings towards this chapter because of my lack of writing sophistication? Or could it be the distasteful discoveries my mind pieced together?

The following consolidates the accumulation of over three years of insights and new understandings into roughly a dozen pages of text. I now suspect the worst with practically everything regarding Lucy. Of course, I could be wrong about some things. Yet, I believe I am spot on for the most part.

There were many other instances and slightly off situations throughout our relationship, and I now question or consider the involvement of some form of foul play existed.

Revelations—Of my Children

Gilbert and Clifford, my twin sons, were born three months premature. Lucy's water broke, and later, her amniotic sac resealed, all due to the fact the rupture developed at the top of the fetal membrane. I believe Lucy tried to self-abort the twins by hitting herself on the top of her belly.

Since I began my divorce, Maggie has struggled with her identity. My use of the word struggle could be a bit of an exaggeration. However, she once asked me, "Do you think I am genetically your daughter?"

Our conversation was a little awkward at first. However, the more we talked, the easier it became to discuss.

"I am uncertain and always had suspicions about your mother and her ex-husband," I said, "It never mattered to me; you are my daughter, and I've always loved you."

Maggie asked, "Do you think I should get a DNA test to find out?"

Again, I emphasized, "You're my daughter. I love you," as I thought about it a little more, I added, "You don't need to get a test done for me. But, if you feel you need to know for yourself, you can do a DNA test at any time you choose." Then I finished my thoughts, saying, "And you don't even need to tell me any results one way or the other."

I know Lucy enjoyed casual sex with multiple partners during our marriage. She was also opposed to using any form of birth control. All were leading me to questionable thoughts about my children's parentage. Were they genetically mine? My children now had these same questions and doubts, which augmented my sadness to new heights.

I can state with indisputable certainty, "It is not a matter of concern for me because they are my children, and nothing could ever change that."

The question of my children's genetics is more out of curiosity and from my morose perspective of Lucy.

Revelations—Of Sam

I had several epiphanies regarding Lucija's lurid behavior surrounding many past events. I realize now that Lucy always got in front of a story. She told her rendition of a story's events before I heard about it from others. So, if something happened, and she thought I could find out about it, Lucy told me first, and of course, she gave her personal spin. She would frame the story in such a way it would be acceptable or passable to me, and if I heard about it from others later, I would discard their account. I can now see how this happened often, and it worked.

When I think about the meth head and his statements about Lucy immediately before he assaulted me, I reckon he spoke the truth. Lucy lurked at the bikini bar, picking up strangers for sex, as he had alleged, before attacking me. I think Lucy triggered his anger and hatred, which caused him to attack me. Did she care I got hurt? Nope, seemingly not. It also dawned on me that Lucy's lurking in the bikini bar must be how she initially met the single mother who worked there and rented a room in our home. They did not meet in the organic section of some grocery store, as Lucy had told me.

I have not danced for around the past twenty-five years. I already told you Lucy made fun of my dancing. Maybe my dancing style was a little off. Be that as it may, who cares? Dancing is all about having fun with family, friends, and especially the one special person in your life. All through High School, University, College, and my early working life, a part of my life included going out on the town and dancing. Then I met Lucy, and slowly, over time, her ridicule of my dancing became a refusal to dance with me. Yet another thing she stole from me.

Before we married, life with Lucy was romantic. We often kissed passionately, and Lucy would say, "You take my breath away."

We went for many strolls, holding hands or in each other's arms, along downtown streets, by the river, or in parks. After we married, walking in each other's arms quickly became a thing of the past. Holding hands ever so slowly became a rare event. To kiss my wife became a labored contest.

Over the years, she complained, "I cannot breathe while kissing you," as she feigned gasping for air and waved her hand in front of her face.

Then our kisses became shorter in duration until, eventually, we no longer kissed. In the end, all that remained were little pecks on the cheek.

Since Lucy never cared about me, why was there a concern that her friend Iva, the piano teacher, could accuse me of stealing? While editing the book, it dawned on me that Lucy wanted me upstairs and out of the way while Iva taught piano and shared tea in our house, not out of any consideration for me. She wanted me out of the way to perform her thievery schemes unimpeded. She did not want me interfering with or witnessing her in the act of stealing. Having me downstairs would only complicate her machinations.

Money always seemed to disappear. Initially, I appeared to lose the loose change in my pockets. Later, it escalated to my bank accounts continuously emptying and eventually all the crushing revolving credit debt. Lucy always bought my clothes, and most of the time, one pocket in each of the pants she bought for me would have a hole along the bottom seam the size of a quarter. I now have no doubt that Lucy opened these holes in the seams in my pants pockets to keep me thinking and believing I lost money on my own to cover her stealing.

My life, my marriage, was an ethereal stage composed solely of a cold, dank miasmatic mist. It was a place where I found warmth in her lies. When my daughter Sophie opened the blinds and shed sunlight on the illusions Lucy spun, the haze burnt away, and I realized I had nothing. There was never anything real between us except meaningless lies.

My marriage to Lucy was phony. There was nothing to save or rebuild. I had no need for mediators or marriage counselors. Our marriage was never authentic, and my only desire was to terminate it through a divorce.

My relationship with Lucy was artificial. She was never my best friend, let alone any sort of friend. Her companionship was never sincere, and I crave for the day I can no longer recall her.

On her stage, she played me as Shakespeare's ruddy fool, as it were. I did not know what an imbecile I was, yet I played the part well. And now that I am wise to her, I perceive myself as more capable and have acquired a solid resolve to rid her from my life.

Revelations—Of Lucy

Lucy claimed to be an accomplished piano player and vowed never to play again in her dead boyfriend's memory. I always thought it was strange, yet I was impressed by it. Now, I call it out as baloney. She never knew how to play piano, merely another deception in a long string of unnecessary lies.

In the deposition, under oath, Lucy stated there was no Castle. Does this also mean her family never had an oil painting, and there was no theft by the Germans? While we lived in England, Lucy recounted her story of the stolen painting residing in some German museum. It was around the same time works of art disappeared from my parent's home. Was it a smokescreen for the thefts? Or to make her appear as my family's equal vis-à-vis art, a mechanism to affirm her image of self-importance?

Lucy is a narcissist, and nothing about a narcissist occurs by happenstance. Everything they do is premeditated and contrived; a deliberate purpose exists for everything they do, and they never forget their schemes. So, what was the reason for those guns, easily accessible, in the open on the floor of the master bedroom closet for roughly eight months? I can only think of two dreadfully unpleasant scenarios.

The first scenario adhered to my original worries that she planned to bust a cap in the back of my head. This scenario would require Lucy to play an active role. It would place her at risk of jail time. She would have to concoct a story and feign herself the victim.

A second and much more nefariously plausible scenario, she was willing to forfeit a pawn in her life. Her sacrificial lamb could give Lucy the appearance of true victimhood. Was Lucy thinking of leaving the guns out for her suicidal daughter's use as an easy and decisive method to finish the job this time? In my opinion, this synopsis seems to conform to Lucy's style, set up the dominoes, sit back in the shadows, and take a non-active role. I can also envision Lucy dreaming that a sorrowful Rifah would leave his current wife for Lucy. That is precisely one more reason why this woman scares me altogether. She terrorizes my thoughts.

During my ten-day ocean cruise through the Caribbean, Lucy disappeared for over twelve hours while I sat in our cabin seasick. She returned sometime around 4 a.m. the following day. I believe that she had a one-nighter with the piano bar singer, probably in his room. Why else would he be so bold as to call on her months later? And she even gave him her phone number.

Think back to the ring story with the real estate agent. I do not know who pursued who, and it does not matter. They were both equally involved. I presume they joined in sexual relations, and Lucy asked him for a ring. Not the other way around. I do not believe he offered her a ring in exchange for sex. The stories of this guy faded away after he married. Recall the bathroom story with the same real estate agent. I believe they shagged in the bathroom while my children and I attended the same party in the same house. Lucy merely got in front of the story in case anyone heard anything. With her approach, I would not suspect her.

I wrote about this earlier in the book, yet there is merit in bringing it up again and repeating it here. Lucy assisted her clients with credit applications. She often modified their declared income without their knowledge or permission. Could Lucy now be applying for credit using her customers' personal information? Did she sell her customers' personal information? I suspect the worst. If it has not happened yet, it will occur sometime in the future.

Revelations—Of Lucy's Family

I wrote about the "It's Not Butter" comment earlier in the book when Lucy claimed that a thug raped her in Croatia. Now that I am writing the book and thinking about it, new visions of conceivable events from long before I met Lucy come to mind. She moved to England around the age of nineteen as a teenager.

Why would her mother say, "It's not butter, and your private parts won't melt away from having sex," to Lucy as a teenager or younger? Before she immigrated to England.

Was her mother a prostitute? Years ago, Lucy told me stories about the desperate circumstances of living under communist rule.

She told me, "I used to see all the women who lined the muddy streets for prostitution. Because times were tough, and they had no money. It was the only way they could put food on the table."

I don't know, and I don't care. I am merely thinking aloud in my book—I believe Lucy's mother engaged in prostitution, and she kept her kids close by while performing these acts.

I derive no pleasure from speaking ill of the dead. However, I now suspect that, like Lucy, her brother also exemplified narcissistic behavior. He had a stolen car, was involved in thievery and possibly organized crime, got caught, and lost his job. I think he lied about many things, fooled around, got caught, and his wife barred him and his family from her life.

Revelations—Of Lucy's Cohorts

Lucy told me that she and DeShawn slept in the same bed on the Hawaii business trip, with him sleeping on top of the sheets. I think they fooled around that night. Connecting those dots left a rancorous, vile, and rancid taste in my mouth, which stank to high heaven.

Regarding the California business trip, in which I found a picture of DeShawn's nose buried deep in Lucy's honeypot. Sophie confirmed the travels involved no business whatsoever.

The California trip was exclusively a vacation. Sophie overheard DeShawn asking Lucy to leave me as he wanted Lucy to join him and Janet as a threesome, and she would bear his babies. There is absolutely no way he would ask Lucy to join them like this out of the blue. No, there must have already been an encounter or affair with him, or worse, with the two of them.

I told you the story of Lucy stealing clothes from her friend. Well, why was Lucy alone at her friend's house with her friend's husband? The more I think of it now, the more I am convinced they two-timed against Fay and me, and I naturally believe she stole his wife's clothes from their bedroom.

Revelations—Of Deception

Many years ago, our family joined the Facebook wave. I could never find Lucy's profile to add her as a friend. I would always see her on her laptop, adding thousands of people, who she did not know, as friends to her Facebook profile. At the time, I brushed it off and decided since she resided in the same house as me, although it was a big home. I could still easily walk over and talk to her instead of texting her.

"Mom blocked you from her Facebook profile the very first week she set up her account," Sophie confirmed, "She used Facebook to make it look like she was single." Then, he finally added, "And Rifah is on her friend's list."

Lucy presented her narrative of being a swinging single using her social media accounts.

Lucy's deceit went right to the contacts on her phone. Sophie explained the display on Lucy's phone showed my number as the name of one of her business partners. She did not want to arouse Rifah's suspicions or upset him. She kept me in the dark for the exact same reasons. Rifah's phone number showed up as one of her good friend's names. In both cases, Lucy used the pluralized version of a friend's first name and set the last name as "Phone."

Five of my grandfather's brothers fought in WWII. Three of his brothers fought in the Artillery, two working on gun crews and one as a spotter behind enemy lines. One of his brothers was a ship's pharmacist in the US Navy, and another a bombardier in the RAF. After the war, one of his brothers brought home a German harbor patrol ceremonial dagger. I inherited the blade and scabbard before I married Lucy.

Sometime after our marriage, I showed Lucy my war memorabilia, including the dagger. I guess not to appear outdone. She told a story of two German daggers that her father had. She further spun the tale that one of those daggers was special and made of platinum. When I asked how he came to possess such treasures, her story became a little less substantive. From what I recall of her story, they came from German officers in some concentration camp.

I always wondered if her family was involved with the Germans and these camps. Or if they were straight-up gypsies who happened to find the daggers in the rubble of war. Now, I think she was lying. She concocted the story, and her family never had German WWII daggers.

Roughly five years into our marriage, Lucy no longer wore her wedding band. At one point, she claimed to have lost it, and at another time, she claimed it no longer fit her finger, which hurt her. This story made sense to me at the time. However, Lucy has the skinniest of fingers, and neither Lucy nor her fingers at any time grew bulkier. I am without doubt that her ring would have fit her properly throughout our marriage.

While we lived in Florida, pictures of me slowly disappeared from view in our home. Eventually, when I lived on the farm, not a single picture of us together or of me could be found displayed anywhere in our home. It was as if she had erased my existence. Even the framed professional photos of us on the bedside tables vanished. Instead, I found them hidden in the bedside table drawers.

Here is an example of how I honestly could not connect the dots between red flag events due to all the time that passed by. Lucy claimed a rapist attacked, struck her in the head, and raped her while in Croatia for her brother's funeral. She came home with a mark on her forehead. Almost ten years later, I found out she engaged in an affair, and no rape occurred. Not until writing this section of the book, nearly another ten years after discovering her infidelity and eighteen years after first observing the mark on her face. It finally registered with me. No rape or attack took place against Lucy. Ergo, she never received a hit to the head. So, what made the strange mark on her forehead? Remember, it did not exhibit the characteristics of a real bruise: no swelling, no breaks in the skin, no blood, and no scabbing.

At first, I thought, "Could it be henna?"

But henna stains the skin much too orange in color. The mark on Lucy's forehead appeared as a deep reddish-brown color. Then I thought back to some of Lucy's Croatian cuisine, and I think she used the juice from red beetroots to stain her skin. Beet-stained skin matches exactly my recollections of the color of the mark on her forehead. My hands appeared the same color when peeling beets for her. She must have been reapplying the beet stain weekly and then covering it up with lots of makeup. Think about the required extent of effort she expended over a year-long timespan to successfully achieve the façade of her ruse.

According to Sophie, since I bought the farm and moved, Lucy told Rifah she and I were separated/divorced, and I farmed somewhere out West.

One day, months after I filed for divorce, Sophie told me the story of being in some church reception hall. Lucy stood in the center of a circle of people, and she gyrated with their hands on her while she spoke in tongues. Then Lucy seized as she passed out into someone's arms.

Sophie cried out and tried to run to her mother. To see if Lucy was all right or needed help. But someone participating in the circle yelled at Sophie, "No. You stay away."

I sat at the kitchen table and listened to Sophie's story. Picture this: I had my elbows on the table and kept my jaw cupped in both palms of my hands. I tried to keep my slack jaw from falling agape on the table, like in a scene from the movie The Mask.

I do not know. Maybe for some people, talking in tongues is an acceptable or standard practice. Although, for me, her rubbish amounted to cultish lunacy. Especially knowing Lucy duped those believers with some erotic trance-like dance of hers.

I can only imagine how Sophie's young mind processed the events of this macabre scenario involving her mother, who appeared to be in pain. Then, someone yelled at Sophie for wanting to help her mother. It had to be a traumatic day for her.

A year or two later, I inquired with Sophie for confirmation and more details regarding this outlandish story. Sophie reaffirmed the specifics of that day at the church reception hall.

Then she told me, "That wasn't the only time. Mom did this [routine] with smaller groups of two to four people at our house."

Lucy also performed her spasmodic spectacle in our home—for Pete's sake!

I can only say, "I don't know this person I called my wife. I don't know her. I do not know who she is."

Chapter Forty-Eight

Tattoos

I never had any tattoos, and my body remains a blank canvas to this day. On the other hand, my father had a tattoo on his shoulder that depicted an anchor with a scroll-like ribbon-type flag. His tattoo was primarily blue ink with some green and a little bit of faded red. There was some writing or initials either on the banner or the anchor. Sorry, Dad, I cannot remember what the script was or represented.

When I was a teenager in High School, I considered getting my own tattoo. But unfortunately, I was not very imaginative and did not put much thought into it. I probably would have got an anchor, just like Dad. But my father convinced me not to get one. He explained how much he regretted getting his own, and once tattooed, you are stuck with an irreversible, lifetime decision to sustain.

Many years later, when I found out Lucy had an affair and no rape occurred in Croatia, I fell into despair and thought of suicide. Then, the thought of getting tattooed crossed my mind once again. I did not know what I wanted, but I wanted something to remind me of my pain and recovery. Again, I did not pull the trigger and get tattooed.

During the first few months after I started my divorce, I seriously considered getting a tattoo. I researched some of the local tattoo artists, and I had a specific design in mind. First, I wanted the tattoo placed on my back and all the images inverted as if seen in a mirror. Next, I wanted a lifelike heart drawn on the anatomically wrong side of my back. The heart was to have a dagger wound in it. Then, I wanted a dagger displayed close to the heart with one drop of blood dripping from the knife's edge. The blade was to have a backwards and mirrored inscription "BETRAYER." Finally, I wanted my tattoo to be primarily dark blue ink. Only the blood was to be brightly colored.

After a while, I came to realize I did not want to mark my body with something that would remind me of her. I yearned to erase this woman from my life, not memorialize her on my skin, and I am so glad I did not get this tattoo.

If I ever chose to have ink done, I decided it would appear as a pair, one tattoo on each calf. These tattoos would represent who I am in my genealogical family tree: paternal on the left and maternal on the right. A Celtic design on my left calf would symbolize my father's Irish roots. The French crown's fleur-de-lis insignia on my right calf would depict my mother's French heritage.

Chapter Forty-Nine

Therapy

I discussed therapy and therapists several times in this book for various reasons. I cannot emphasize enough how important it is for your mental health if you have lived with a narcissist in your life.

I knew Maggie went to therapy for several years before I began the divorce. Lucy led me to believe it was due to her weight problems. However, I found out Maggie suffers anxiety and panic attacks because of the physical and mental trauma of child abuse she sustained at her mother's hands. From all accounts, Maggie is still unwell but doing much better. Yet, she still suffers from the attacks and continues to visit her therapist.

I found a therapist for Sophie the first month she moved to the farm. She enjoys her sessions and has a great rapport with her therapist. However, I cannot fathom all the feelings and emotions that Sophie has dealt with throughout her life. The secrets and lies Lucy and Rifah forced her to keep. The physical and mental abuse Lucy imposed on her. The depths of her anguish and her attempt to take her life. Then, risking her life as she knew it. She was betraying her biological parents, Lucy and Rifah, for me, her siblings' father. She did not know if I would accept or reject her. That took immense courage.

I think Sophie stopped being a victim and became a survivor after she attempted suicide. She planned to run away from Lucy once she turned eighteen years old. These plans stayed with her even after we received the custody and Restraining Orders to protect her. She wanted to take extra classes in high school to skip a grade and move out sooner. I convinced her to take her time and enjoy her high school years.

As a side note, enjoying her high school years did not work out as planned due to the COVID pandemic. But that is another "best laid plans" story that is not for this book.

Sophie has a "thing" in which she does not like to be touched. I have always given my children hugs and reassuring pats on the shoulder, making her no-touch wish very difficult for me. Almost three years later, Sophie still had her do-not-touch twitch. However, it was no longer as extreme, and she started giving me hugs. When we talked about her little twitch, she told me that I often failed to respect her boundaries and wishes. At the end of each of these conversations, I apologized, told her I loved her, and gave her a big hug.

When she read the previous paragraph, Sophie giggled, saying, "Dad, that's exactly what you do every time you say sorry."

And she finished her point of view with, "It's enough for me when you say you love me. You don't also need to hug me."

So, I said, "I'm sorry, I love you so much," and gave her a big hug.

I cannot help being the way I am. This old dog cannot unlearn that old trick. I love my children and automatically give them hugs when I think they need them.

After living a life fraught with deceit in actions and words, I can only imagine her fears and mistrust of the things she hears and feels after gaining her freedom.

Gilbert reached out to a school therapist at his university in London and spent less than six months in sessions. He told me that he is done with his mother and does not wish to see or speak with her. He does not even talk about her.

Clifford spent over a year in weekly sessions. He remains reclusive and introverted. Afraid of what people think of him. However, he is much better now compared to three years ago. He often makes an effort to get out of his comfort zone, confront his fears, and talk to people. Clifford remains angry with his mother and often wants to tell her off and curse at her. I have counseled him not to act in anger. I do not want him to harbor additional feelings of guilt later.

Lucy treated my children as wickedly as Gothel[12] or Claude Frollo[13] treated their wards. First, like Gothel, she used all my children to maintain her image of herself, and then, like Claude Frollo, Lucy used Sophie as a tool to advance and sustain her lustful relationship with Rifah.

I spent a year and a half visiting my therapist, weekly sessions at first. Knowing I fell prey to a lifetime of Lucy's sugary sweet lies coated in her softly spoken voice. I carried the weight of guilt and shame for not sheltering my children from her scurrilous treatment. I was dismayed with myself for not noticing her appalling and abusive behavior. I held the sorrow of knowing that I allowed what happened to my children and for my separation from my parents and siblings.

There were many times that I cried and required tissues. Discussing the horrible things Lucy did and expressing my feelings from the past as things occurred or as I currently understood was, well it was painful. A few times, I saw my therapist wipe her eyes.

Once, while telling a story about something traumatic, I do not remember what it was. What I do remember is that I was kind of detached and emotionless in my storytelling. Not that I was unfeeling, but I narrated the incident matter-of-factly while I gazed off into the distance. When I noticed my therapist, she was crying.

---

12 The ogress witch from the 1634 fairy tale Petrosinella by Giambattista Basile. Then re-imagined in the 1812 Brothers Grimm fairy tale Rapunzel as Dame Gothel.
13 Monseigneur Claude Frollo was the Archdeacon of Notre-Dame cathedral in Victor Hugo's 1831 novel Notre-Dame de Paris or, as we know it, The Hunchback of Notre-Dame.

I said, "Here you go," and handed her my box of tissues.

She wiped her ruddied eyes and then her nose. Then, looking at me, she said, "I'm sorry, I'm human too. I have emotions just like anyone else."

I sat there for a moment, expressionless, thinking about what I had been through and how my story impacted others.

Cassandra, as far as I know, is my only child who has not required therapy.

Chapter Fifty

Sophie's Story

Portions of the following may be repeated in other places within the book, either with more or less detail, as Sophie told me about her circumstances.

On many occasions, Sophie expressed all the adversities she endured while living with Lucy. She described how Lucy always lied, the secrets her mother forced her to keep, and the lies her mother forced her to make. Some of her earliest memories involved the secret trips and vacations with Lucy and Rifah.

Lucy had Sophie believing that her brothers, sisters, and I were unaware she was not my biological child. So, she understood the situation as "Dad did not know."

Lucy often told Sophie not to tell anyone that I was not her biological father, and Lucy reinforced this with, "The entire family will disown you if they ever find out."

As a result, Sophie held on to this uncomfortably painful secret for most of her life. She wanted to tell us but feared the consequences should the truth be revealed.

Lucy and Sophie regularly traveled to visit Rifah. Unfortunately, the other kids and I were kept in the dark and unaware of these travel destinations, as Lucy would lie to us with tales of going on business trips.

Sophie felt as though Lucy used her to get to Rifah. This cloak-and-dagger life had Sophie feeling like Lucy's pawn. Lucy used her to exploit Rifah for money, gifts, trips, and other things. The manipulation process required Sophie to cry over the phone to Rifah.

"Mom would tell me things to make me sad and cry," Sophie told me, "And if that did not work, she would hit and pinch my legs until I started crying. That's when I had to ask Rifah for things."

Sophie said, "I felt like a puppet," held on Lucy's taut strings.

Sophie often spoke about feeling like a puppet on her mother's strings. She explained how she did not like that feeling and did not want me to bring it up as it depressed her.

Sophie believed that her mother was deeply in love with Rifah and that Sophie was the only real connection between them.

During the first few weeks Sophie had moved to the farm, she told me, "Mom usually treated me like a child," complaining Lucy coddled her like a baby and kept her on a tight leash.

"Sometimes she treated me like her forty-year-old girlfriend," Sophie told me. Citing examples like Lucy being highly inappropriate with Sophie by sharing her personal explicit sexual preferences or complaining I was too large.

When Sophie was younger, she and Lucy stayed in a hotel with Rifah. During this visit, Sophie heard them making strange noises in the bed next to hers. She did not know what they were doing at the time. Then, as Sophie grew older and became more aware, she knew exactly what they did.

"They had sex in the bed next to me," Sophie told me in disgust.

Lucy and Rifah's aberrant behavior appalled me, and because they did this in Sophie's presence, it intensified my emotions a thousandfold.

When Sophie was eleven years old, her brothers and sisters had all left the house, either married or away in college. I was also gone, living on the farm. She told me she became depressed and felt trapped living alone with Lucy. So, she began to cut herself. She cut into her wrists and arms, yet Lucy never noticed.

Sophie told me, "I walked around the house with dried blood on my arms and wearing bloodstained T-shirts. Mom never cared enough to notice."

Immediately upon hearing this cutting story, I wanted to inspect her arms. There were no welts like the girl Lucy once rented a bedroom. I found that Sophie's scars had faded and were barely visible. Only then did my sudden fears of mutilation slowly diminish. In the following days, I asked to check her arms several times to soothe my unease and as confirmation that she was all right.

Whenever I asked to check Sophie's arms, with a smile, she would tell me, "Dad, it was a long time ago. I'm alright."

Sophie's feelings of ensnarement only grew while she continued to live alone with Lucy. Eventually, she became so hopeless that she tried to take her own life. She swallowed a bottle of pills, hoping to overdose and escape her mother. Sophie messaged her boyfriend about her attempt soon afterwards. Her boyfriend's father contacted Lucy regarding the message, and Lucy took her to the hospital.

On the way to the hospital, Lucy asked Sophie accusatorial questions analogous to, "How could you do this to me?"

Lucy never inquired if Sophie was all right or why she tried to harm herself. It is evident to me that Lucy always found a way to make things about herself and showed no concern for Sophie's welfare.

Sophie told me, "I had a plan to run away when I turn eighteen. And Mom would never see me again." Then she looked at me apologetically and continued, "And I thought I wouldn't see you anymore because I thought you would stay with Mom and take her side."

She did not feel safe around Lucy and, as you already know, was terrified of her mother.

One thing that gets Sophie all bent out of shape is how Lucy continuously explains that she had an emotional breakdown from her breakup with her boyfriend. Sophie insists that she broke up with him after her attempt. This particular lie differed from all the others, as it was directed at Sophie.

Sophie has shared many of her insights with me. For example, one of her beliefs was that I provided a base of stability in Lucy's life and a source of constant income. Sophie presumed these were essential for Lucy. Whereas I think it was crucial in helping Lucy maintain and project her cooked-up image.

Chapter Fifty-One

Breathe

Is it just me? Or do many other people dislike advice on how to perform menial things? I perceived it as condescending when someone told me how or when to breathe correctly. I have inhaled and exhaled with great success since the day I was born. Thank you very much. Duh! Yeah, I agree with you. I have an attitude problem with the things I felt were unwarranted.

Jiu-Jitsu and Tai Chi have breathing techniques to increase your body's inner power or Chi. I never understood, saw the benefit, or made use of them. I was more focused and interested in learning their movement, holds, and combat techniques.

A UNIX saying comes to mind, "More is less, and less is more."

One of my sisters was driving me nuts. I knew she meant well, and I appreciated her thoughts and concerns. She loved and cared about me. She was trying to help her ailing brother.

Because of the state I was in at the time, I was not receptive to her text messages and emojis to "just breathe" or pictures of sunsets, which only increased my stress levels. It felt like a constant barrage that only added to my frustrations. Yet, I allowed my sister to continue with her way of trying to help me and never told her it had the opposite effect.

My therapist often made me perform breathing exercises. She knew I had a "Whatever" attitude towards these activities. It was not until my therapist pointed out that I took a deep, involuntary breath of my body's own volition. It was in response to recounting some traumatic experiences with Lucy. And so, I began to realize when my body required a deep breath or two.

Early on, my therapist suggested I try the app Headspace. I used this app diligently for roughly ten days. However, coerced meditation and breathing techniques from a pretentious voice over my phone using this app irritated me beyond belief. I tried the app and made an honest attempt to stick with the program, but it simply was not my cup of tea.

While Headspace may be the perfect tool for some people, for me, it only served to exacerbate my condition. One of my sisters swore by Headspace, which did wonders for her. My therapist highly recommended it, which must have helped many of her clients.

I do not subscribe to spending some prescribed amount of time each day to meditate with breathing exercises. I found it to be a waste of time for me. We are all unique individuals, and everyone is different. When dealing with these toxic feelings and emotions, you must find what works best for you.

I will not patronize you with "You have to breathe in deep" stuff.

However, may I suggest that you pay attention to your body and your body's needs. My telltale signs were severe butterflies in the pit of my stomach or my left pinky finger to my wrist going tingly and numb. Try to learn how your body reacts when you feel caught in the grips of agitation, tension, terror, or any other devastating emotions. It could be beneficial to be aware of and sense your body's reactions, pausing and taking a deep breath, followed by a brisk exhale as your body requires. Try it to see if it helps you. I hope it does.

But for me, it works! Inhaling a deep breath and then letting it all out helps relieve my stress and toxic feelings when they build up.

Chapter Fifty-Two

Narcissists

You think you would know someone after thirty years of being together. With most people, you most likely do recognize them for who they are. However, evil has an aptitude to conceal itself very well and could easily lurk undetected within your circle of friends. I was not cognizant of the Himalayan misconduct of my narcissist. I did not even begin to scratch the surface of the numerous platitudes of her paltry behavior.

A relationship with a narcissist does not involve love. Although, to me, it felt like love. Meaning I was genuinely in love with the person I thought she was. However, it was all a deception. She deceived me, and my emotions misled me. It is not love. Rather, it is simply their meat hooks twisted into a particular position to give their victim the appearance of love.

Two questions that people should want to have answered. What is a narcissist? And are there degrees or levels of narcissism? Hopefully, this chapter can help to begin to answer those questions.

I wanted to quote Joe Rogan, but I can only paraphrase him here with, "I am not an expert on narcissism. I'm just a dope with a lot of poppycock to write about."

Please do not take this chapter as gospel. It reflects the "Samuel Frearson Experience," matriculated in the school of narcissistic hard knocks for twenty-some years of living with my special little charmer. And I never graduated—as I continued to discover more unpleasantries.

I liken the writing of my ordeal to someone who survived COVID-19 in an ICU on a respirator and then writing a white paper on the coronavirus. I lack the authority to offer an expert opinion or clinical judgment. Based on what I endured, what I gleaned from various therapists, and reading published articles, videos, and online, I can only convey my personal views.

I cannot even put my finger on the point that I began to realize Lucy was a narcissist. One of my sisters was the first to paste the narcissist label on Lucy. It was only weeks after we served Lucy with the divorce and TRO papers. But I dismissed her claim, thinking, "Just about everyone says that about their ex!"

I know that I was not thinking of Lucy in terms of narcissism during her deposition or FSC interview. By then, I had only concluded that she was a liar, cheater, philanderer, and thief. However, I may have begun researching narcissism on the internet around her deposition. The truth was that I did not know what I was dealing with until after I started therapy. So, six to eight months after the Full Psycho event, the realization that Lucy was an extreme narcissist finally sank into my thick skull.

First off, all the information found on the internet, in publications, and from your therapist can be downright overwhelming, especially if you recently hit the proverbial emotional concrete wall. There are volumes of information available, and most of it either did not apply to my situation or delved much too profoundly to keep my attention. As I had no interest whatsoever in helping cure her, I was not concerned about getting even with her and was not interested in trying to cope with living with her. I merely wanted to understand what I had endured. I yearned to have this woman out of my life, and I wanted to help my children heal and to restore myself.

My sister, who was irritating me with too many messages, was also responsible for introducing me to a set of wonderful videos that she found helpful. I thought of saying the best internet resource I found. Instead, I will change my statement. The internet resources that best connected with my needs were my sister's recommended videos on YouTube by Melanie Tonia Evans.[14] While Melanie talked about narcissists and narcissistic relationships, the videos I watched were focused on the victims and accounted for the victims' recovery. None of it from a clinical type of standpoint, all presented from a layman's point of view, which I could legitimately relate to with ease. Her videos gave amazing insights and helped me begin my journey of understanding and healing. I cannot thank my sister enough for suggesting these videos to me.

Then later, while writing this book, friends suggested several online self-help services. I found other helpful video resources on YouTube, some by Kim Saeed[15] and others by Meredith Miller.[16] Indeed, there are plenty of other suitable resources available online. I listed the three that I found helpful.

The following may be harsh, yet it is what I think of a narcissist. Lucy is a soulless husk, an empty shell that looks like a person. She is unable to empathize with other people's feelings. I think she is socially inept on any real or meaningful level yet socially adept on a manipulative level. Despite the already stated, I also understand that narcissists learn how to react to situations without comprehending others' feelings. They become proficient at reading circumstances and then respond with their mimicry in a practiced fashion, choosing the reaction they think is correct for the given situation. I gather this is why rational people with empathy and ordinary social skills have a great deal of trouble spotting this elephant in the room.

The flip side of their practiced reactions to familiar situations is that they do not know how to react to new conditions appropriately, and they either underreact or overreact.

---

14 https://www.melanietoniaevans.com
15 https://www.kimsaeed.com
16 https://www.innerintegration.com

There are no cures or treatments for their recidivistic tendencies. They are bereft of empathy. It is the narcissist's nature to be what they are, so aptly described in the fable *The Scorpion and the Frog*. Maybe they could be taught to be or appear to be a better person. But, in my opinion, this would only be another charade. You cannot teach someone to feel that which they cannot perceive.

How can someone spot a narcissist in a crowd of people? They cannot. It is impossible. A litmus test for narcissism does not exist. You cannot make a determination based on their temperature, intelligence quotient (IQ), blood-borne pathogens, or other physical diagnoses. The symptoms of narcissism are, in essence, behavioral patterns.

I believe the only way to detect a narcissist is to observe their actions over time. Even then, it can be difficult to render an assessment, as their lies and changes in conduct can be subtle.

In a battle between the deceitful and the honest, how does someone on the outside sift through the details? I cannot speak about other people's situations. Since filing for divorce, I had not talked to any of Lucy's friends, our mutual friends, or past neighbors. I had only shared, in droves, with my family, relatives, childhood friends from before I met Lucy, and co-workers who did not know Lucy. Hopefully, you have a good lawyer for a divorce or other legal action against a narcissist. The best possible outcome materializes when an adequate amount of your narcissist's web of lies comes to light with sufficient contradictions so that the Judge can see the truth through all the mud.

I have read that narcissists will attend therapy under the guise they are there to help you. Their purpose for attending is to help them further manipulate you and restore their perceived loss of control. They do not participate with any intention to improve your condition or their own. They usually stop their sessions once they have attained their goal of resetting their meat hooks in you, long before the therapist can provide a diagnosis of their narcissism. From what I understand, even a therapist treating a narcissist requires several months of sessions to determine or diagnose narcissism.

There is a saying, "It is like putting lipstick on a pig.[17]"

Where Lucy's physical appearance and charades are the lipstick. Her personality and machinations form the other part of the phrase's equation.

So, I have manufactured my own saying, "It does not matter if you dress this swine in her finest knee-high boots and mini skirt. She is still nothing but a boar.[18]"

She has a ravenous and insatiable appetite for the self-aggrandizement of her appearance, wealth, and importance. And then, she catapults herself and her image into other people's lives.

A certain[19] avariciousness exists in a narcissist's behavior, which will burn up all the oxygen in your life, leaving you to gasp for breath, like a fish out of water.

It appears Lucy is adept at playing the victim and equally accomplished at making her victims believe they are the villains. Is this a truism with most or all narcissists?

When Lucy plans to perform some dubious operation against you, she may do these in twos. One is the hand she shows you so she can monitor your awareness of the hand she kept hidden. It is the hidden hand that does the actual manipulation and damage. I do not know if this bait-and-switch technique can be attributable to other narcissists or if I am giving Lucy too much credit. We know she will drug people. She used diet pills on my preadolescent daughters. So, it is not a stretch to infer she used other drugs or drugged other people? To illustrate this, I offer the Dream Catcher episode in my life. I think Lucy began to drug

---

17 It appears as though this phrase was first coined around 2002 by the Charles Schwab firm.
18 I got caught up in the etymology of these hog expressions. I made my own variation, based on the original phrase, "A hog in armour is still but a hog" by Thomas Fuller in 1732 and explained in Francis Grose's 1785 book A Classical Dictionary of the Vulgar Tongue and a later variation, "A hog in a silk waistcoat is still a hog" from Charles Spurgeon's 1887 book The Salt-Cellars.
19 I chose the word certain for a double entendre. There is an inevitability to a narcissist's greed, and it embodies a particular style or technique.

me with sleeping pills, roufies, or something similar. At the same time, she introduced the dream catchers to our bedroom. My little charmer used the dream catchers as the proverbial canary in the coal mine. When I started complaining about the effects of the drugs, either she or I misdirected the blame to the dream catchers. I removed the dream catchers, and then she stopped drugging me. It is ingeniously deceitful and appears to bear successful results. Again, am I giving her too much credit? Do other narcissists do this?

Regrettably, I continue to have an aversion to these beautiful Native American works of art. Even though intellectually, I recently figured out the true reason for my temporary loss of dreams from years ago, my phobia of dream catchers persists.

Like having a thief in your midst, the sleight of hand has you searching in the wrong direction for the culprit. My loss of dreams and weary sleep years ago may not have been due to the dream catchers. I suspect Lucy added something to my food or drink. Drugging people seems to be a recurring theme in Lucy's bag of tricks.

During the first year of our marriage, before the Dream Catcher episode ended, I often used to talk in my sleep. At times, it would wake me, leaving me to question myself if I had just spoken aloud. One night, I went to bed before Lucy and was close to drifting off while she was in the master bedroom. I made some kind of noise, and Lucy immediately went to the bed, her face inches from mine as she intently listened for me to say something. So, I made a couple of semi-passionate moaning noises and then mumbled my ex-girlfriend's name.

As Lucy continued to listen in, I heard from beside me her quiet voice exclaim, "Oh shit."

I could not help myself and then burst out laughing while exclaiming, "You see, this is why you shouldn't listen in on other people's dreams."

When this happened, I found it amusing. However, this little talking in my sleep story makes me think of three sinister possibilities. Firstly, did Lucy listen in to the things I said while dreaming so that she could use them as ammo against me in her efforts to control me? Is this a tactic that narcissists generally use against their victims? The second thought was, did Lucy spike my dinner with something to make me drowsy and talkative? She often joked that she would slip something into my tea to give me less sex drive. Finally, I only suffered from this talking in my sleep syndrome for a couple of years. I had never had this problem before I met Lucy, and it subsided after our first few years of marriage. I guess it lasted long enough for Lucy to sink her narcissistic meat hooks into me.

Two thoughts recently came to me that had more to do with us victims. The first was our ability to adapt to adverse conditions is a characteristic which is one of human nature's most significant accomplishments. But, it is also our greatest weakness when involved with a narcissist. Narcissists take advantage of our capacity to adapt as they slowly modify our behavioral patterns to their twisted needs. And they do indeed thrive based on this adaptability.

The second, because I believe narcissists are soulless husks, it becomes easy for their victims to project and see their own moral values in their oppressors.

I am a talker. I am naturally inclined to make small talk with strangers and share too much information with friends and acquaintances. Over time, Lucy isolated me from my friends, most neighbors, and co-workers. I was not kept locked up or anything like that. However, to avoid upsetting Lucy, I spoke with family and friends less often and kept my conversations short with them. It appears everyone we knew were her newfound friends and partners.

I began avoiding phone calls because of all the debt that Lucy accrued and her strange business dealings. Too many creditors, scammers, and salesmen were calling, adding to my isolation.

I still find it remarkably difficult to understand how she held me, somewhat of an extrovert, so introverted. And to this day, I continue to avoid or reject unknown phone calls.

I genuinely dislike wasting such an elegant and lovely word as panache on the likes of a narcissist. Yet it is true. They have a very well-manicured, glamorous air or style about them. It is a practiced ruse with a superficial, colorful flair.

Lucy is a master manipulator. Until now, I have not explicitly described her machinations as manipulation. She is very skillful with social engineering. For example, she knows how to exploit and trick people into giving up personal or confidential information. From many of the past events I recounted, you should see and understand precisely how accomplished she is at this. She is well versed in influencing people and events, shaping them to her needs. She knows how to exploit people and situations to her benefit. I cannot comprehend how she kept all her differing sets of lies straight. It appears to me that she operated these schemes as a game on a three-dimensional chessboard, where she plays the black queen, and everyone else in her world participates as a white pawn. I do not know if all narcissists operate at the level she does. However, I do believe they all conduct themselves in a similar fashion.

Narcissists are storytellers, well, braggarts, in fact. They weave impressive tales regarding some rather specific topics. However, the details are often vague or ambiguous and left to your imagination to complete the picture. When questioning their stories, their answers become uncertain, evasive, and possibly conflicting. The entire deposition was a workshop in equivocation.

Eventually, they will refuse to answer with devolving statements like, "I don't know" or "I don't remember."

Narcissists are offensive when pushing their own narratives, and I suggest offensive in all forms of its definitions. They will become verbally and possibly physically aggressive with their attacks to make their views sink in. Their attitude will develop into disrespect for your opinion, and they will insult you with all kinds of frivolous accusations. It is reasonable to infer that they will do anything to get their way.

If misleading or disruptive behavior becomes a recurring theme over the discussion of an assorted number of subjects, be aware that you may be dealing with a narcissist.

While I worked in the aerospace industry, we had a rhetorical saying for bad ideas, inadequate equipment, and lousy software being imposed upon us, "How do you polish a turd?"

Unfortunately, when it came to my little narcissist, I never realized the other aspects of her personality. I now perceive her as a multi-faceted turd gem, each facet a phony disguise to a disparate charade. During our marriage, I only saw the pretense she devised for me. She kept all of her other aspects obscured from my view. Nothing about her was ever genuine. I spent nearly twenty-five years of my life married to this woman, and I still do not know who she is. We were, without exception, perfect strangers with nothing in common.

I am not sure if the following applies to narcissists in general or only to Lucy. However, I observed some themes in her life. Suicide was the first. According to Lucy, her high school boyfriend had committed suicide before she immigrated to England. She drove me to the brink with thoughts of suicide, and she forced Sophie to the point of attempting to take her own life. Other commodities she peddled and spread over the years were accusations of abuse, sexual assault, and rape. When I first met her, she accused her then-estranged husband of having sex with a minor. When she became pregnant with Sophie, she told me she was raped while in Croatia for her brother's funeral. Lucy told Sophie many times that sex with me hurt her and was rape. Spoiler alert that I will explain in more detail later in the book: after I filed for divorce, Lucy filed a police report containing a statement that I raped her almost every day for twenty years. In the future, when my oldest daughter Cassandra confronted Lucy about her affair with Rifah.

Lucy denied their liaison and threw Rifah under the bus, accusing him of sexually assaulting her.

Are narcissists unmoral or immoral? It is more of an academic question for me. I do not care one way or the other, but you can color me curious. Are they unmoral beasts with no perception of right versus wrong or good versus evil? Or are they immoral scoundrels that willfully and without regret choose to perform their wrongdoings?

Luckily, Restraining Orders have been in effect since the day I filed for divorce. The TRO and subsequent DVRO provided me with an immense benefit to help keep Lucy away and irrelevant in my life. I have completely broken contact with her, and the Restraining Order allows me to implement the no-contact more easily.

However, even with the Restraining Order, Lucy kept messaging my older children, saying, "All I want is the family back together again," and other similar statements.

The following depends on your circumstances. If you pulled away from a narcissist and suffered past abuse, or they will not leave you alone to the point you feel harassed. Consider the courts and a Restraining Order. If applicable to your predicament, it can be a crucial tool for us abused souls.

Everything about her has been callous treachery, and I feel as though I have been narsorssized!

Chapter Fifty-Three

Custody

Fighting for the custody and well-being of your children is stressful and nerve-wracking under any circumstances. Right, wrong, or indifferent, I firmly believe that courts usually favor the mother in these proceedings. I was a ball of nerves and terrified for my daughter.

Family Court Services Report

The report provided by Family Court Services (FCS) was a ten-page document, and it was very damning against Lucy.

Originally, I had intended to copy some portions of the report verbatim. Eventually, I became aware of the report's Confidential nature. Since I could not go out and receive approval from all parties to include portions of the brief in my book, I decided to remove and replace those excerpts with my prehensions.

The report had a small section regarding my interview and another small portion dedicated to Lucy's interview. Both sections contained some background information and nothing special beyond that. Most of the report centered around Sophie's interview, which was explosive.

The report finished with some extreme recommendations, including full legal custody for me, no court-ordered visitation for Lucy, and no contact with Rifah.

"We could not have hoped for a better report," my lawyer said.

Then he explained, "It is uncommon for recommendations like this to be handed out, and then, only under the most grievous circumstances."

Sophie's Interview

My youngest daughter, Sophie, was only fifteen years old at the time of her interview. The mediator commented on Sophie's maturity and how she found Sophie to be confident, intelligent, and eloquent.

The mediator's report detailed many of the same concerns Sophie expressed to me. The difficulties and oppression she endured while living with her mother, Lucy. The document contained no additional events or information beyond what I have already recounted elsewhere in this book. The only distinction was how the report told Sophie's story as Sophie told the mediator herself and in her own words.

Each time I read the report, the one thing that always catches my eye is that Sophie told the mediator that she has never been happier in her life. She smiles more and feels like a new person.

Her Lawyers

Up to this point in time, seven months into the divorce proceedings, Lucy was already on her third lawyer. Initially, she applied for free legal help and received free legal counsel for the custody and Restraining Order proceedings. However, at some point, her legal counsel transferred to another lawyer within the legal aid system. Eventually, her second lawyer formally requested that the court withdraw her as Lucy's legal representative.

I will probably never know the actual reason that her second lawyer wanted to dissolve her relationship with Lucy. I understand there are only two main reasons for lawyers to terminate their representation of a client. The first was for financial reasons when their client was not paying them. The first reason did not fit the circumstances as I knew them because her lawyer took the case through legal aid's free services. The second reason to terminate their representation was if lawyers find themselves placed in an illegal or unethical position. I could completely sympathize with her lawyer's situation, especially considering Lucy.

What I do know is that her second lawyer asked the court for a separate hearing to have the courts formally terminate her representation of Lucy.

Her lawyer told the court, "Your Honor, I need a court order from you terminating my representation of my client. I am afraid that if I withdraw myself on my own, my client may not understand and could sue me in the future."

All I could think was, "Something is going on under those bedsheets."

I surmise the court granted her second lawyer's request, and Lucy appeared at the custody and Restraining Order hearing with her third lawyer.

Courthouse Security Checkpoint

The day of the Custody hearing finally arrived. Sophie, Clifford, and I entered the courthouse and lined up for the security checkpoint. We did not notice Lucy directly in front of us in the line. Sophie stood only inches behind her at the checkpoint. It was not until Lucy turned around to look at us with a forced, wide-eyed, phony, sad stare that I saw her standing there. I put my hand on Sophie's shoulder. She had not seen Lucy in front of her. I pulled her back several paces. We continued to back away from the checkpoint until we reached the front entry doors. After Lucy cleared security, we waited a few minutes before passing the security checkpoint ourselves. While passing through the security screening with my two youngest children, I explained our strange behavior to the Sheriffs working the security checkpoint and showed them the TRO.

Circus and a Translator

Lucy had her entourage of church support people. She also brought a translator and a single-day lawyer. This new lawyer was her third, who Lucy apparently paid for this one day. What an awkward joke. She brought a translator to court. Lucija is fluent in English. English has been her primary language since around 1990. Just read the language she used in her deposition.

I had the distinct impression that going to court was nothing more than a game to her. All of this fanfare and pageantry were for show.

"Lucy is playing games. She doesn't need a Translator," I told my lawyer in a hushed voice.

He replied quietly in a hushed tone, "Oh, believe me, I know," and he seemed sure the court knew. I guess because of the deposition.

This business about a translator consumes less than half a page, but it speaks volumes to the hypocritical dishonesty I witnessed this woman carry out.

Antics and Weird Looks

While my two youngest children and I sat on a bench in the courthouse hallway, Lucy exited a conference room directly across the hall from us with her lawyer and church support people in tow. She looked shocked to see us there, and I know I was surprised to see her and wished we had sat somewhere else.

The next thing that happened was equivalent to the most bizarre Kabuki theater. Lucy first looked surprised at seeing us sitting there, and then she spun around, doing a complete three-sixty. She did not turn on her toes. No, she took three or four steps to complete the three-hundred-and-sixty degrees. Her head also did a bob. I mean, while she twirled around, she got lower to an almost crouched-like stance and finished popping up tall. Her surprised expression disappeared. Now, she stared at us, giving us "the look." It was a wide-eyed, sad, and pouty stare. With each dejected breath she took, she renewed her pout. The sound she made each time was a quick "sniff" in, followed by a slow "huh" out.

I do not know how long she sustained her awkwardly forced and exaggerated performance right in front of us. However, she continued long enough for her lawyer to take notice and interrupt her little skit.

Her lawyer grasped Lucy by the shoulder, tugged at her, and told her, "C'mon, we have to move to the far end of the hallway."

As Lucy spoke with her entourage, roughly thirty feet away from us down the hallway, she stepped away from them and began to stare us down. It was unnatural, obviously conspicuous, and uncomfortable for us. When Sophie's lawyer observed her charade, he stood between Lucy and us. And he let us know he would stay there and block her from view to help us through it. Lucy readjusted her position several times to continue her annoying spectacle. This look Lucy gave us appeared rehearsed.

Later at home, Sophie told me, "Oh yes, that stare of hers is practiced. And she forced me to learn it."

Sophie demonstrated the look and explained the various circumstances in which she had to perform it.

I can now see Lucy's charm was all a well-rehearsed, deceitful routine she honed over the years.

Restraining Orders

The court awarded me sole and full custody of our youngest daughter. In addition, the court issued a nineteen-page Restraining Order for domestic violence and child abuse, also called a Domestic Violence Restraining Order (DVRO). It had an expiry date set towards the end of 2020 and included a no-contact order and a hundred-yard stay-away order.

In the days before going to court, my mother told me to stand up straight and look Lucy in the eye to let her and the Judge know I was strong. I could not do this and did not want to look at Lucy.

Throughout the DVRO court hearing and all future hearings, I looked straight ahead and rarely towards her. The few times I mistakenly looked at her made me feel uneasy and anxious. Maybe I gave the appearance of weakness? I do not know, but I instinctively felt it was appropriate for me. Years later, I watched another video by Melanie Tonia Evans,[20] who coached us, victims of narcissism, not to make eye contact with them in court and to ignore them completely. According to Melanie, looking at them validates their existence and feeds their narcissistic battery. Ignoring them is a form of rejection that ostensibly drives them crazy.

When we stepped from the courtroom into the hallway, I watched in astonishment as my lawyer performed a hop and a skip. Then he turned to me, all smiles, saying, "It could not have gone any better. We achieved everything we wanted."

I felt freezing cold during the entire time in court, I think, due to nerves. I felt sick, not like I would throw up; I felt just "Ill." Looking at me, and I must have looked mousy, my lawyer asked out of concern, "Are you alright? You look like crap."

I am generally not a nervous person. Except when my daughter's life hangs in the balance of the Judge's decision, I guess I become an overly tense bag of nerves. It took a full twenty-four hours to calm down and emotionally realize the meaning of this achievement.

> big sigh of relief <

The Kids Are All Right

Even though I called this section, the Kids Are All Right. Please don't be fooled by the title. The reality was my children were messed up. However, since the proverbial feral cat came outta the bag, my children began receiving the help they needed. It was an uphill climb, but they will be all right.

My four youngest children are in therapy. My three youngest children have not spoken to their mother since I let them know I

---

20 https://www.melanietoniaevans.com

would file for divorce. Like me, they have entirely broken contact with her. The two oldest of my children still talk to her and occasionally see her, but they try to keep it to a minimum.

Since what I call The Shit Show began, I told all my kids several times, "In my opinion, the best thing you can do for yourself is to completely break all contact with your mother." I also told them, "But you need to decide to do what you think is right for yourself. I won't be upset, and my feelings won't be hurt if you choose to talk to or see your mother."

I was careful not to demean, express my negative feelings about, or place vulgar labels on Lucy, especially around my children. However, one of my children's therapists called Lucy a Wack-a-doodle, and for a while, my two children, Sophie and Clifford, who were living with me, often referred to Lucy as such. The only thing I had consistently done, which may not have been the preferred thing to do, was whenever the children called her mom, I corrected them and called her Lucy—no labels, good or bad.

During the period between Lucy heading back to Florida and the TRO issuance, I let Sophie know that if she ever wanted to see or speak with Lucy or Rifah, I would help make it happen. I offered this to Sophie before I knew or understood the totality of Lucy's abysmal behavior. Knowing what I know now, I would not lift a finger to help with such an endeavor. However, I would not stand in the way of any of my children's decisions.

Months Later

The custody issue was settled months later, around a year after Lucy's deposition. While in court for a check-in process. A simple five-minute appearance to report the progress or hindrances in the divorce. As a matter of procedure, the Judge could decide to intervene to help the situation move along. Sophie's court-appointed lawyer complained to the Judge that Lucy and Rifah repeatedly violated the Restraining Orders.

He sent separate letters to each of them explaining the violations and to "knock it off."

The latest occurrences being within the same month of our current court hearing, in which:

1. Lucy sent a text message to Sophie,
2. Lucy posted text messages to one of our other children asking them to tell Sophie to do something, and
3. Rifah usually attempts to call Sophie once a month and has tried twice in the past month.

Lucy started explaining to the Judge why she sent the text message. During her long-winded explanation, she talked about several things, attempting to explain her reasoning for doing it, including why she came to the farm once served with the TRO.

The Judge's first words after Lucy's explanation are memorable to me.

The Judge leaned forward, eyebrows lowered, looking directly at her, and said, "Oh no, those are violations."

The Judge went on to explain the Restraining Order to Lucy and what she must not do. When the Judge finished her explanation, my lawyer stood up and asked the Judge to include these admissions in the record, as the proceeding did not have a court recorder present. The Judge did make a note of Lucy's confessions.

Think about how her first lawyer went to great lengths during her deposition to insulate Lucy from legal repercussions by pleading with the Fifth for her Restraining Order violations. Well, Lucy is a narcissist who believes her silk-lined tongue can persuade anyone. So, on this day, while she represented herself in court, she tried to appeal to the Judge's sensibilities and convince the Judge to take her side on these actions. It only backfired on her.

Typically, when people do not know what they are dealing with, Lucy's stories and quick wit work like magic to influence them. Now that my family knew what we were dealing with, her charm was no longer persuasive for us. The courts were more interested in technical details, and a bright spotlight was already shining on Lucy's misdeeds. The courts are not prone to such excuses.

Chapter Fifty-Four

Barging In for Rubbish

We had lots of Lucy's stuff stored in a greenhouse on the farm from Lucy and Sophie's final move. The lawyers arranged one specific day for Lucy to come to pick it up. Sophie could not be at the farm on this day. She had a sleepover at a high school friend's home. My lawyer contacted the local Sheriff to facilitate the peaceful turnover of her things. Technically speaking, it would be a violation for her to come to pick up her items because of the Restraining Order. Not to violate the DVRO, she was only allowed at the farm this once and only under the Sheriff's supervision.

In the days before, Clifford and I organized and collected her stuff. We put together everything she requested and almost another fifty boxes worth of her junk. Clifford and I placed everything neatly organized outside the locked gate to the farm the same morning she came to pick them up. Then, I waited for the Sheriff to arrive. He arrived about a half-hour before Lucy and her crew.

I explained the situation to the Sheriff's deputy, then handed him a copy of the Restraining Order to read. He was impressed with the amount of stuff I put out for Lucy. The Sheriff stated that usually, the husband did the pickup, and most of the time, he only got one or two garbage bags of things during these events. He also told me she would probably be unable to take everything and

I should not throw out the leftovers. Instead, I should continue storing it to avoid suffering the court's wrath later.

The Sheriff told me he could have to leave at a moment's notice if he got a call. Likewise, Lucy and her crew would have to leave immediately with the Sheriff. He then instructed me to re-lock the gate and go back inside. He saw no need for her and me to interact.

I will add a little dig at Lucy of my own here. She had over a hundred and fifty pairs of shoes I bagged up and put out for her. Of those, over fifty pairs were high-heeled boots that go over the knees. These boots look pretty on women, but I know Lucy used them for trolling. I do not know the proper name for their specific style, but I call them hooker boots.

Inside, I watched the events unfold on my video security system. There was one car and two pickup trucks full of junk. Over the system, I heard Lucy telling the Sheriff she had more belongings and wanted to rummage through the greenhouse and the trailers. Over her arguments, he told her to focus on the things outside the gate by the road.

Lucy prepared to leave while her crew continued to pack. On the security system, I heard the Sheriff call out for me. Clifford and I went to the gate. Lucy saw Clifford from her car and shouted to him through the window. The Sheriff told her to move on and leave.

She pleaded with the Sheriff from her car window, "But I only want to talk to my son."

He firmly told her to "Move on" two more times and finally said, "You need to leave now."

The Sheriff did a fantastic job of keeping us separated and kept Lucy focused on the stuff outside the gate—I love our first responders.

Chapter Fifty-Five

Becoming my Mother

My mother is an emotional individual, and she cries often. For the past forty years, I regularly poked fun at her little emotional outbursts every chance I could. But now that the birds have come home to roost, I am becoming my mother, like those funny insurance commercials.

I do not know if the metamorphosis I found myself undergoing was because I grew older, because of my life's experiences, or because I slowly evolved into a soft little marshmallow. I cried a lot, and I cried often. Sometimes, tears only welled up in my eyes. But frequently, they streamed down my cheeks in torrents; other times, I sobbed uncontrollably. So many things could trigger these episodes, from internal thoughts to external events.

Mum repeatedly asked me to move back home with her in London. Whenever she asked me to move, I told her I did not want to leave.

There was one time that I replied to her with, "Mum, that would make me the fifty-some-year-old living in his mother's basement, and I really don't want to be that guy."

Mum got a chuckle from the humor in the visual. Still, she didn't care and wanted me to move back home to England. I am not ready to give up on my life here. I love this country I adopted, or that adopted me. I still feel I have a viable chance at gainful employment and to continue contributing to my family.

Chapter Fifty-Six

The Kavanaugh Hearings

Well, here I go again. I swear I am trying to keep politics and religion out of my book. However, some events have a natural fit within my story.

I had a phone conversation with my mother, in which she was distraught with Brett Kavanaugh. She thought he was a disgusting rapist, and you ought to believe this, Christine Blasey Ford.

I said, "Mum, you can't immediately jump to a guilty conclusion because Christine Blasey Ford alleged." Then I continued saying, "Lucy repeatedly claimed to Sophie that I had raped her. Are you going to jump to I am guilty?"

My mother's response was, "Well, Lucy is crazy. Nobody will believe her."

I am afraid that I disagree entirely with the MeToo movement's position that we must believe every woman's sexual abuse claim. This stance is much too extreme, dangerous, and unfair to the accused. Nonetheless, please understand my position. In my opinion, rape is serious and utterly abhorrent. But, on the other hand, I also consider false accusations leveled at someone for rape equally loathsome.

I rely on a more principled approach, where every woman's— no, every person's—sexual abuse claim should be listened to, given serious consideration, and investigated. You cannot destroy a person's life and reputation based solely on another's accusations, especially when the allegations are from the distant past or used as ammo in some current event.

I also firmly believe that false accusers should be held to account and punished accordingly. There should be no free pass given to false accusers as a form of consolation prize.

Chapter Fifty-Seven

Divorce Settlement

I believe Lucy is chaotic, focused, and unrelenting. You would assume that chaotic and focused are mutually exclusive from each other. When I expressed that she exhibits both of these attributes simultaneously, I opined that she remains intensely focused on some particular goal, which may or may not be evident. At the same time, in a tirade, she hurls dozens of unrelated accusations, attacks, and demands. I held zero confidence she would settle on anything at the Mandatory Settlement Conference.

Pre-Settlement

The following is the second most painful lifetime revelation I have endured. The single most painful experience in my life was listening to Sophie describe her suicide attempt and learning it occurred two years prior to her telling me.

Remember earlier in this book, Sophie's account that Lucy repeatedly claimed I had raped her.

Then, in the deposition, when directly asked if I raped her, she said, "No."

Well, nine months after the Kavanaugh Hearings, Lucy's pre-settlement documentation included a one-and-a-half-year-old police report for rape! She filed her statement with the police one month before the deposition. As you may recall, when asked directly in the deposition, Lucy specifically testified that I was not a rapist and did not rape her.

In this police report, she claimed I raped her hundreds of times over the last twenty years, and the most recent rape she charged took place while she stayed at the farm after the move. On this most recent claim, I would like to point out that since what I call The Shit Show, Lucy utterly and thoroughly disgusts me. Her touch makes my skin crawl. Try to remember the moaning noise I described making on the 911 call when she touched my arm during her TRO violation at the farm.

At another point in the police report, she claimed I raped her almost daily for twenty years. She also gave some salaciously graphic details, which I will not repeat. I will only say her aspersions are all false and completely fabricated.

In the report, she stated her belief that I filed for divorce and Restraining Orders due to an accumulation of years of sexual abuse I perpetrated against her. Really? I mean, take a minute to think about that one. It was some pretty backwards logic. The perpetrator leaving the victim because of years of sustained and successful abuse? Some people may choose to believe her. However, in real life, I think it is the victim who eventually leaves their abuser upon discovering the abuse or upon surpassing their threshold to tolerate such abuse.

The only time I ever felt hatred for this woman followed my reading of her police report accusing me of rape. It took me weeks to traverse and process the turbulence of these feelings, mentally and emotionally. However, to this day, it remains a shadowy stain on my soul. I always felt compelled to tell people who I am and about these accusations.

The discovery of her report and the details of her accusations were all painful and hurtful for me. All I can say is, "I never raped her. On the contrary, I adored her, completely trusted her, and thought of myself to be lucky to have her in my life." That is, I felt this way up until Sophie started telling me the lifetime of secrets Lucy forced her to keep.

For one-and-a-half years, Lucy kept her rape report hidden in her back pocket. We were in court many times, and she never mentioned it. During her deposition, Lucy's testimony literally contradicted the statements she gave the police. She did not indicate during the Temporary Restraining Order hearings that any rape occurred. Not a single utterance of rape came from her during the Custody hearing. In the multiple Restraining Order Violation hearings, no references to rape ever materialized. Nope, she saved it for the money grab![21] She wanted more than half of the split, and she wanted alimony.

Or as I call it, she wanted "Cash for Life."

She is nothing less than a lucre fiend.

There you go. As onerous as it was, I bared my soul and wrote it down on paper. Like my mother often does, my eyes are welling up yet again. You can judge me as you see fit.

Settlement Agreement

The circus and translator show continued. Once again, Lucy had her entourage of church support people, a single-day lawyer, and a translator.

On paper, she received half, which I would generally consider fair. Except I regard our fifty/fifty asset split as inequitable under the circumstances. In reality, she received much more than half. Due to all her lies, she refused to declare any of her businesses or bank accounts. Hence, for the division of community property, she pocketed half of my assets and all of hers. Well, that pissed me off, yet, if this was the price of getting her out of my hair. Done Deal!

She made a strong bid, demanding Cash for Life from me. She wanted alimony, she wanted money for her education, and

---

[21] I wanted to use the vulgar expression Money Shot here. However, I will take the high road and stick with money grab.

she wanted money for other expenses. The court denied all those requests. The victim of abuse, who is the protected party of a Restraining Order, cannot be compelled to make payments to their abuser. I did not know about this rule until shortly before the settlement. It is indeed an apropos law, making perfect sense.

This charmer refused to pay any child support for Sophie. So, I told my lawyer to drop his request for child support if it would help us to settle.

Post Settlement

How could I be pissed off and happy at the same time? I do not know, yet those were the precise feelings I had.

Good guys finish last. I have remained true to myself. I kept my honesty and integrity as best I could throughout this ordeal, even though Lucy did much to stain and tarnish my reputation. I believed in better days ahead, and I was bound for a much better place than the likes of her.

Why all these happy feelings? It was over and done with; the case was closed, and we settled. I did not believe she would come to an agreement. I had prepared myself for a full five days of court. I was not mentally or emotionally ready for it to resolve!

> big sigh of relief <

I rented two storage units. They were full of our stuff delivered by the tractor-trailer from the summer before I began my divorce. The MSC Settlement Agreement stipulated that Lucy would pick up and remove her stuff from my storage units. Instead, behind my back, she contacted and manipulated people she had no business talking to, with whom I had contracts. She refused to remove her things, and in the end, she took over the leases for the two storage units. I could have written a chapter's worth of her unscrupulous behavior and my frustration, but I decided I would not.

Chapter Fifty-Eight

Online Dating

Years ago, my sons and I would laugh and chuckle at the Senior Citizens Meet commercials. After I bought the farm, my kids often teased me, singing the Farmers Only jingle. It was all fun and games, making fun of my age. I never thought I would get divorced. I never thought that in a million years, I would find myself entangled in this Online Dating stuff. Yet there I was!

When I first got the account, I remember the anxiety of possibly seeing her profile on the site or, worse yet, the fear of Lucy finding my profile.

"Ahhh, why was my life still frozen with this much fear?"

Anyhow, I have moved past it, not past all the fear, only past the dread of her seeing my profile.

I am not good at this stuff, and online dating is so foreign to me. Texting is impersonal, and you cannot read the other person's feelings. Too much room for misinterpretation exists with only the written words of a text. I struggle to write texts because I worry about not choosing the right words or conveying incorrect thoughts.

I said online dating is foreign to me. Well, even dating is unfamiliar territory. Parsing the semantics of love—all those emotions, verbal cues, physical signals, and other undertones during the initial dating stages leaves me amateurishly confused. There are too many subtexts I fail to detect or comprehend.

Talk about Mr. Awkward. I shook hands on my first date in thirty years with the lady as we met for coffee and gelato. It was cartoonishly comical. As we both walked up to each other for the first time to say hello and introduce ourselves, she spread her arms to hug me while, at the exact same time, I extended my arm for a handshake. Then she went for the handshake while I offered a hug. Finally, she crossed the distance, stepped forward, and hugged me.

Was I damaged goods? I considered myself as damaged goods and unworthy of another's affection. I was in financial ruin; who wants that? I was still dealing with the divorce; who wants that? I think I was still emotionally traumatized; who wants that? And finally, she accused me of rape—nobody wants that!

I seldom reach out to anyone or reply to someone. In the first eight months, I texted with maybe six ladies. Of those six, I had only gone out to lunch with two. And one of those two women, I went out for a second date, yet something was amiss for me, and it ended.

There was one lady I dated for a month or two. We both liked each other. However, even though she thought I had better morals than any Christian fellow she had previously dated, she was searching for someone more Christian than myself. So, she moved on.

I am not fond of the idea of being alone; I still believe in marriage, and I am also not in any rush. I want to find someone who accepts me for who I am. If fate has decided I shall remain companionless for the rest of my life, I am all right with it. I would not be entirely alone as my children and grandchildren help fill most of the void.

I miss the simple things, holding hands and looking into someone's eyes while they look back into mine. A heartfelt hug from someone who is genuine and cares. A gift of flowers that makes someone's day. I want to dance again and feel comfortable in my own skin dancing with someone. I want to share my stories with someone who enjoys listening to me and listening to their life's stories with equal appreciation.

I continued to use the dating app and regularly looked through the suggested lists. Yet I did not reach out or reply to anyone, and this was because I felt unworthy of another person's love or respect. I guess I was also afraid to meet another narcissistic robot like Lucy. I did not think I was adequately equipped to detect these flawed people and did not want to fall into the same trap again.

I question whether including someone in my life could put them at risk. Lucy does appear to have a touch of the O.J. Simpson syndrome.

I spent almost thirty years of my life caught in a charade of love and affection. Cripes,[22] I have only recently recognized how out of touch I have been with the semantics of love for these past thirty years. In the future, how will I know if these feelings from others are real?

One thing became clear to me. I underwent a relationship whose intimacy revolved around conduct that was essentially improper. Moving forward in my life, how would I know what was appropriate to say, try, or request? I was so crippled.

Still, I remain both hopeful and fearful of a relationship. I probably question everything too much. Perhaps I should wait until I have completed my divorce and get my life back in order before continuing this quest for friendship and love.

I wish the very best in your pursuit of happiness to everyone out there.

---

22 Cripes and gall-darned are words my grandfather often used to display his disapproval or surprise. He was a very formal gentleman who did not swear or blaspheme. I wish I could have lived up to his standard. But I am only a shadow of the man my grandfather was. I have never once heard anyone else use this word. Until now, I did not realize cripes was an actual word defined in the dictionary. So, I wanted to use it in my book as a nod to my grandfather and used it here to show my astonishment at the lack of my ability to court a lady properly.

Chapter Fifty-Nine

Abusive Relationships

I was a good four inches taller than Lucy and weighed at least sixty pounds more than her. On the other hand, I was stronger and faster than her. So, how could she abuse me? Why should I fear her? Abuse comes in different shapes and sizes. If you trust someone, as I used to love and trust her, it is easy for them to hurt you. Not all misdeeds are physical. Their castigations can also have an emotional component.

Lucy hit me in the family jewels several times over a dozen years towards the end of our marriage. She would typically do this as I tried to hug her. Think of her shoulder being at the fulcrum of a pendulum as she swung her arm to hit me with a cupped open hand. Her attack would drop me to my hands and knees. I felt an electric-like sensation of pain emanating from my testicles and reaching the pinnacle of pain in each side of my rib cage. She even brought me to tears more than once because it hurt so much. Each time Lucy dropped me to my knees, she would stand back and laugh as if it were a joke. She never once apologized or checked to see how badly I was hurt.

The first time Lucy slapped me across the face was over some insignificant argument. It was uncalled for and completely unexpected. I found it insulting and demeaning. She struck me so hard that, to my complete surprise, I immediately slapped her right back. Even though I did not hit her nearly as hard as she did me, I instantly felt guilty and ashamed of myself. I had never struck a woman before, nor have I ever hit a woman since. I suffered the indignation of her slaps to my face many times since that initial strike. I never reacted to any of those slaps; they always ended our argument, and I would walk away in irritated bewilderment.

Lucy used to pull my whiskers, although she never pulled any hairs out. Instead, she would pinch a few hairs and give them a slow, hard tug. Sometimes, she pulled them for a distance, making me walk several steps in a hunched position to avoid the pain. Lucy usually pulled whiskers from the chin or mustache areas. Your lip and upper chin areas are very sensitive, and her method of yanking at my beard caused much pain. Imagine how much it hurts to tweeze out a nose hair. Her approach caused much more pain.

I can only imagine how terrifying the physical abuse could be with a large narcissistic male abusing a much smaller female. It is indeed chilling to envisage.

Many people to whom I have explained my situation have told me, "I have also been there."

They explained that they had a relationship of their own in the past with a narcissist. Unfortunately, I do not usually get their entire story, so I cannot judge their situations. I would listen to what they shared, show empathy for their past circumstances, and share what words of comfort I could.

I do not believe that all abusive relationships are necessarily narcissistic. However, I firmly believe that all narcissistic relationships include an abundance of both physical and mental abuse.

Narcissists commonly divvy out their malevolence with premeditated purpose, the only exception when they enter a psychopathic mode and lose control. The first goal of their misconduct is to mold you into their perfect obedient thrall. After setting their meat hooks into you, they become disdainful towards you. This contempt is because they do not like you and must suffer your presence to drain you financially and emotionally. Finally, they will lose control as a knee-jerk reaction to your non-conformance to their rules or the shattering of the made-up image they have constructed of their life. The abuse is a means to their ultimate goal of control.

I am guessing that non-narcissistic abusers administer their maltreatment on impulse and without the same purpose as narcissists. Maybe they cannot help themselves, or conceivably, they enjoy themselves. They tend to be in the moment when causing pain and suffering. Perhaps they want the rush from a brief sense of control. The abuse is their ultimate goal of abuse.

Chapter Sixty

Fraud

Remember that I set up credit monitoring, expecting Lucy to take out credit cards in my name. Then, almost two years after I filed for divorce and set up the monitoring, I received a credit alert on my phone. I logged in to the monitoring service to check what happened. The report I received stated that I had filed for bankruptcy. Wait, what the what? I did not file for bankruptcy.

This discovery went way beyond credit card fraud. I had not expected to find anything of this nature. Honestly, I should not have been surprised, yet there it was, glaring at me from my computer screen. It completely shocked me and caught me off my emotional guard. All the feelings of being violated once again arose to the surface of my being. This woman's moral consciousness is so thinly weft that it is undetectable.

I had no idea where to go or what to do. Keep in mind that I was financially broken at this time and could not afford more legal expenses. I spent an entire week, about ten to twelve hours a day, researching and trying to resolve this. And to top it off, someone had filed this bankruptcy in another state than where I lived. I have resided in New York for the past six years. Can you guess where the bankruptcy was filed? Of course, Lucy filed it in Florida. I knew this was Lucy as she tried to keep the house in Florida for herself forever.

I spoke on the phone with the court clerk and explained my situation. They checked the online system and confirmed my name and Social Security Number on the bankruptcy case. Then, the clerk gave me a web link to the court's public access portal. I created an account on their system and then searched for and reviewed the documents. There it was: all of my personal information on court documents with a signature entirely dissimilar from mine.

I called the Bankruptcy Trustee's office and tried to explain the situation. They would not connect me to the Trustee in charge of the case. They said I would have to send a written letter explaining the circumstances before they could do anything. It felt like a dead end.

Not knowing where to start filing a complaint, I decided to aim high for what I believed was the top. I called the FBI and spoke with an officer/receptionist. I lodged an Identity Theft/Fraud complaint with them. They advised me that they would forward the charge to investigators, who would decide whether to pursue the case. They would not contact me if they chose not to pursue the case. Towards the end of our conversation, they told me I should file a complaint with the Justice Department, as they oversaw dealing with Identity Theft.

I called the Justice Department—US Office of the Trustee. I explained the story to them and started a complaint on the phone. After that, I had to log in to their system and complete the claim online.

I called the local police in Florida and explained the story to them. They would not make a report, as I did not live in Florida. Instead, they suggested I file a complaint with my local police.

I contacted the local Sheriff's office, and they started a file. However, they wanted to wait until I communicated with the Judge in charge of the case, before they began any investigations. At this point, I felt like nothing was being accomplished. I had the impression of a long string of opening and closing doors, with no feedback, results, or justice.

I wrote a two-page letter to the Judge in charge of the Bankruptcy case, explaining my situation and the steps I took, all listed above. Also included with the message, I attached copies of our DVROs.

I stated in the letter, "I did not file for bankruptcy, nor had I ever filed for bankruptcy, and I froze my credit."

In the letter, I wrote, "I feel violated. Someone has my personal information and is willing to use it against me for their benefit."

I let the Judge know that our divorce settlement stipulated that our house in Florida was supposed to have been listed for sale. However, Lucy contacted a real estate agent before I could, and from what I heard, she would not give the real estate agent access to the house. I also heard from neighbors that renters occupied the place, which Lucija denied in divorce court.

I wrote to the Judge, "I suspect, or rather I should say I know but cannot prove it is my wife, Lucija Pavlovic, is behind this fraudulent filing in your court."

I let the Judge know that, in my opinion, only one reason existed for someone to file for bankruptcy in my name fraudulently, which would be to postpone the pending foreclosure proceedings of our home in Titusville. Only one person could benefit from delaying the foreclosure: my wife, Lucija. I was confident she collected rent money.

I want this house sold as quickly as possible. Alternatively, I would like to allow it to foreclose so I can move on. Again, I stated I did not file this case and asked if it could be thrown out or removed like it never happened.

The contact information supplied in the case filing was not mine, not familiar to me, and equally as fraudulent as the case. I asked the Judge not to use that contact information. I gave him all of my contact information and a copy of my driver's license.

I closed my letter to the Judge, saying, "My children and I fear for our well-being. There is a Domestic Violence Restraining Order in force to protect us from Lucija, and I ask you to please keep my contact information confidential."

I sent the letter and attachments by US Mail. One week later, the court had still not received it. So, I sent a follow-up letter via UPS with new information and included the original letter with all its attachments.

What could the new information I discovered in the week between those two letters be? Only concrete proof that Lucija was unquestionably behind this fraud perpetrated against me. While I reviewed the public access site to the court system for this case, I discovered additional documentation filed in the bankruptcy case, submitted about one month after the original filing. One of these documents was a Certificate of Credit Counseling from an online credit counseling course. In my mind, these things cost money, and an online class must have been paid for online by credit card.

I spent about two hours in online chats and on the phone with this credit counseling company, explained the situation, and waited for their legal department to decide how they could proceed. I provided them with a valid ID, proving that I was me. Because the online course was registered in my name, and I was the actual verifiable me, they determined they could share the transaction receipt with all the billing information.

Glaring at me, in black and white, the transaction receipt displayed the VISA card of Lucija Pavlovic. It included her new local to New York billing address. Lucy paid for the course. I did not expect her subterfuge to be this easy to track, as I thought she would have obscured her trail using a friend's credit card.

Then, while driving alone in my truck, I said aloud to myself, "I've got her."

And I immediately broke down crying, this time possibly a mixture of joy in those tears.

\> big sigh of relief <

After I resent the original set of letters, documents, and attachments with a new letter and the proof it was Lucy to the Judge, using UPS this time. I set off to the local Sheriff's office to file my formal complaint.

Once again, I explained the entire situation to the Sheriff's deputy, and I had a packet of over two hundred pages of documentation. I guess the circumstances are a little confusing to take in all at once. Heck, I wrote an entire book's worth of information about it. Initially, the deputy gave me the impression of underwhelming interest. Eventually, he took some documents to the secured area of the station to make copies for himself. When he returned to the reception area, he told me he had discussed my situation with other investigators in the back offices. They decided he would produce and send a courtesy report to the local Florida police. Aside from the Restraining Order violation, fraud, and bankruptcy fraud charges I contemplated, he also added forgery.

On a side note, I told the deputy about Lucy's rape accusations, and she filed a police report. Then I showed the report to him. I feel obligated to let people know of these accusations against me. He told me that it is somewhat common for the wife to file rape charges in divorce cases. What a sad commentary on today's society.

Around the same time, I filed the report with the local Sheriff's office. I received a phone call from a Justice Department investigator from Florida, requesting more of my story regarding the fraudulent bankruptcy filing. He told me the Bankruptcy Judge on the case contacted him directly to investigate. Again, I explained the entire situation to him.

He did not seem overly interested until I told him, "I now have proof that Lucija filed the bankruptcy."

"Oh," his voice perked up as he exclaimed, "she is still active."

Later in the conversation, he asked, "Do you have a lawyer to represent you in Florida? To have your case expunged."

I did not, and I explained I could not afford yet another lawyer at this time. I asked, "Is there an immediate need to expunge the case?"

His main concern was that it would be harder for me to get credit when a bankruptcy appeared on my credit history.

I offered to send him all the documentation I had sent to the Judge. He thanked me and gave me his email address. To my surprise, his thank-you email contained the following in his signature line.

Trial Attorney
U.S. Department of Justice
Office of the United States Trustee

A Trial Attorney! Now, I may finally be getting somewhere. While I talked to him on the phone, I thought he was some type of investigator for the US DOJ, but no, he was a Trial Attorney. Like all the other agencies, he let me know I would not be kept apprised of the case's progression, and I would not even know if they opened a case.

I need to change my social security number (SSN) and seriously contemplated changing my name. I remember crying to my mother over the phone. This woman even stole my name! Her abuse never ends.

My lawyer told me I could change my SSN at any time, and it would be a good idea. Since I am now the victim of both identity theft and domestic violence with a Restraining Order, I should not have any problem receiving a new SSN. If I ultimately decided to change my name, which my lawyer believed was also a good idea, I should wait until after the divorce. This way, the new name would not appear on any divorce documents. He also believed the name change proceedings conceivably could be sealed and not part of the public record because of the circumstances.

Chapter Sixty-One

Foreclosure

This winter, around December 2019, I received several alerts on my credit monitoring service. Some of these alerts were about credit cards in my name, which I did not know about, being closed and written off because of the fraudulent bankruptcy Lucy filed in my name. However, one of the alerts regarded the mortgage in Florida as being written off because of the default. I was incredulous. It meant I could sell the house and be able to pay off all my debts. I could walk away from this mess, free and clear of my past with Lucy. It felt too good to be true.

Then, in the spring of 2020, in early March, I decided to stop waiting for Lucy to place the house in Florida up for sale. I finally became a little proactive for the first time. Naturally, the story was not straightforward and took some strange twists. While my real estate agent here in New York presented the farm to prospective buyers, I asked her to contact the real estate agent she recommended in Florida. To find out any recent news about the house.

The return message from the Florida real estate agent, who works for the same agency, was, "[She] did not feel comfortable sharing any information."

She also said, "It was not Sam's house and registered only in Lucy's name."

"WHAT?" I howled upon hearing this.

My real estate agent, who also knows Lucy, then told me, "I remember Lucy saying, 'I filed a Grant Deed to transfer ownership of the property from Sam to me.'"

Lucy's story also spun a tale that I gave her the Grant Deed, including it when served with the divorce papers. This story was nuts. I never did such a thing.

Who says, "I want a Restraining Order and divorce? Oh, and by the way, I would like to give you the house as a gift."

I thought this was yet another one of Lucy's lies, except she specifically used the valid legal term Grant Deed to transfer ownership. So, my real estate agent pulled a title search for me to review. And I discovered the following. First, the house foreclosed in December, and the bank took it. Then, finally, Lucy changed the title on the property from my name to hers the same week I filed for divorce while she was back in Florida before we served her with the TRO and divorce papers.

"How could she do this?" I asked.

A few days later, my real estate agent had copies of all the notarized documents for the ownership transfer. Five months before Lucy transferred ownership, I signed a Grant Deed. I do not remember signing it. However, I remember years of Lucy's pressure campaigns to do so. Now, I know why Lucy did this at that time: to steal the house. Not for any original intention, I may have perceived. Unfortunately, nothing can be done about it now, as the property has already completed foreclosure.

That was in the order I found out about things. Now, let me recap this cesspool of a mess in chronological order to assist in highlighting Lucy's deviant conduct.

- Lucy had possession/control of the house in Florida since I moved to the farm four years before I started the divorce. I went to Florida only once during those four years, and it was to move Lucy and Sophie to New York.
- Over several years, she pressured me to transfer the house to her name. Under the guise, she could more easily sell it.

- Four months earlier, she tricked/pressured me into signing a "Grant Deed" to her for the house in Florida. Which, for some reason, to this day, I do not remember doing. Except it unquestionably had my signature and the date in my handwriting. I did it.
- She did nothing with the Grant Deed for four months.
- She went full psycho on Sophie and me during the move to New York.
- She returned to Florida for some urgent business. Under the pretense of listing the house for sale.
- Upon arrival in Florida, she immediately transferred ownership of the house to herself. Let me say that at this point, I am pretty sure she decided she would divorce me, which is fine. However, I also know she thought she could steal the home from under my feet and keep it all for herself, which is all sorts of wrong.
- After two years of custody and divorce court, she never mentioned transferring the house solely to her name.
- After two years of custody and divorce court, she never listed the house for sale.
- After two years of custody and divorce court, she had renters in the house. Which, by the way, she continually denied in court. Unfortunately, no one ever asked her while she was under oath.
- Six months before the house foreclosure, we reached a divorce settlement. We agreed to sell the house, and the net profits split equally. She did not list the property for sale, yet she told the agent (agreed to in the court settlement) not to share information with me or my real estate agent here in New York.
- The house foreclosed in December, and we lost around $200,000 in equity.
- March, I discovered the house foreclosed, and the bank took possession.

- Later in March, I found out Lucy tried to steal the house from me through malfeasance. As much as I want to call this event a fraud, I cannot. For some unknown reason, I did sign the documents.

She is wicked. She is dishonest. She is untrustworthy. She is treacherous. She is devious. I could go on, but why waste my breath? She is simply everything unseemly.

Chapter Sixty-Two

Coronavirus

I started preparing in January when I first heard China had quarantined over fifty million people. By the time the United States fell under quarantine, I had twenty cases of bottled water and three months of non-perishable food. Mostly snack-type food, trail mix, granola bars, fig bars, and three weeks' worth of frozen meals. Not nearly enough for what I feared could be coming our way. Luckily, our country did not spiral into as much chaos as I thought it could, and I did not need all the food and water I had stored up.

I stand by the saying, "It is better to have and not need than it is to need and not have."

As the world went into lockdown, I decided to sit down and write this book. I had already mulled over writing something for a year.

I was still not divorced; the courts were closed, and my divorce case was postponed indefinitely.

You need some form of a creative and constructive hobby to pass the time of isolation. It does not matter if your isolation is due to quarantine, seclusion, or remoteness. It does not matter if your solitude is physical or emotional. You need something to keep you busy and engaged in this little thing we call life.

For the quarantine, I took to writing this memoir. Thinking about it, I had already, in essence, been in self-isolation over the past two years since I started the divorce proceedings. I hid from the world in lockdown because of my fear of this woman. I had my family's genealogy to research. I started my family tree shortly after my father passed away to keep myself busy. During the COVID crisis, I began my first foray into the world of publications as a junior author. If you can even call me that–you read my book, I am not a literary genius. I merely had a very sad, sad story to recount.

Chapter Sixty-Three

Sold the Farm

I listed my farm for sale one-and-a-half years before it was sold. It was at risk of foreclosure since early in the divorce. I had to go to court to get permission to sell the farm because Lucy became a roadblock. Claiming she had investors, not to buy the farm, but to invest in it and work with me. I had no interest in working with her or her friends. The Judge granted my request.

Six months after the judgment allowed me to list the farm for sale, Lucy and I settled our divorce at the Mandatory Settlement Conference (MSC). The MSC agreement, signed by Lucy, allowed the farm to remain for sale. The net proceeds split between us.

The market was not favorable for selling land or farms at that moment. A year after the MSC, I found a buyer and sold the farm. On the first day of escrow, my lawyer sent Lucy a letter informing her the farm had been sold and was currently in escrow. He gave her a deadline to pick up her remaining items and car, or I would charge her for their disposal.

The very next day, Lucy sent a Cease and Desist letter copied to my lawyer, real estate agent, the title company, and the escrow company. She claimed she had the right of first refusal and, in addition, alleged she had investors who would buy me out. She also threatened court action if we proceeded with the sale.

I shook and trembled for hours in a state of angry anxiety. My face must have been beet-red. My blood pressure felt elevated. My head and chest felt like they would burst. This woman was going to give me a heart attack. While hiding out on the farm in lockdown these past two-and-a-half years, I lost my will to live. Not to end my life, but I felt barren and spiritless as I took a hiatus from living my life.

She had already played this investor game two years earlier, delaying listing the farm for six months. Now, she was attempting to scuttle the sale, making me want to give up on life. Lucy continues to surprise me with these unexpected controversies. Yet again, I should not be shocked. I should be able to anticipate these outlandish maneuvers of hers.

I must admit that I do not understand her. I thought money and material things were her driving force. If the farm foreclosed, she would get nothing. The house in Florida had foreclosed; we lost it and got nothing for it, yet she did make rent money for two years while her scheme lasted. Lucy has a problem with letting go of things. In Lucy's mind, were Sophie and I lost possessions that she was dumpster diving to recover? Was she acting like a jilted lover? Or was it the exhilaration of the game, being able to screw around with someone at will?

Lucy devised her Cease and Desist letter and probably organized it long before. She sent this prepared letter in response to my lawyer's notice of sale and escrow. In less than twenty-four hours, she purportedly organized the letter on her own and without the help of a lawyer. Her document included legal jargon and Latin terms. It also contained deceptively cropped images of legal documents to obscure the intent of court orders. It was not something she wrote by herself or prepared overnight.

My lawyer had to get involved because both Escrow and the Title company were concerned regarding Lucy's inappropriate correspondence. He sent multiple letters to Lucy, my real estate agent, the title company, and the escrow company. He explained the current situation surrounding our divorce and the court's orders to sell the farm and stated that Lucy's actions to disrupt the sale are potentially sanctionable offenses.

Within a week, all the same organizations received a second Cease and Desist letter. Because this letter was so outrageous and from such a dubious and questionable source, I covered its details in an upcoming chapter.

By the end of the week, Lucy was on the horn again. This time, she was speaking directly to my real estate agent. She tried to arrange a meeting between my real estate agent and Lucy's so-called investors. She told my real estate agent that she wanted to buy the property so I could continue to live on the farm with my kids. Can you believe that? I told my real estate agent not to engage with Lucy and warned her not to become Lucy's go-between to pass me messages.

On the last day of the deadline for Lucy to pick up her stuff, she asked my lawyers for more time, and she wanted me to be gone from the property while my real estate agent watched her. My lawyers wanted to offer her one last chance. Even though I was required to clean up and move, I agreed to give her four more days. However, I did not want my real estate agent caught between us, and I would not leave the farm while Lucy tried to rob me. So, I would be at the farm overseeing what she took, and I required a Sheriff's deputy to be present to keep the peace.

The next day, my lawyer's office let me know that Lucy had filed an *ex-parte*[23] motion in court for relief to save her stuff. Unbelievable! She had over two years to collect her things, and my lawyers sent her eight separate letters over these two years, reminding her to get her possessions. Lucy also wanted to be able to roam the property to search for other items. Her latest additional demands were an absolute non-starter for me.

She also cried on the phone to a legal assistant from my lawyer's office, asking for framed pictures of the family from our

---

23 Ex-parte is a Latin legal term, meaning one party is taking legal action without the presence of the other party.

bedside nightstands. I can picture her crocodile tears. Lucy had all the expensive furniture from our Florida home, and she received most of the contents from my two storage units when I handed those units over to her.

The Judge denied her *ex-parte* motion, and my lawyers reiterated our previous four-day extension, with only one day remaining. Our offer required law enforcement's presence, limiting her to her items in the greenhouse storage, no roaming the property or other buildings, and I would be present at all times.

This chapter regarding the farm's sale runs for several pages in length when it should have only been one page. Lucy's unwarranted behavior cost me time, money, and stress.

Chapter Sixty-Four

Red Flags

My entire relationship and marriage with Lucy were chokkeful[24] of red flags. I feel like a complete imbecile and am ashamed of myself for not figuring out her atrocious behavior earlier. How does one not recognize and dismiss these warning signals? I still do not understand how I missed it all. I have no honest answer other than I trusted her.

While Lucy and I were dating before our marriage, she had me invite her ex-husband to my family's summer country lodge for the weekend. I previously described in this book that I saw his hand down the back of her bikini bottom. His fingers reached or extended between her butt cheeks. Somehow, she convinced me that what I thought I saw was not what happened. How could I let myself not believe what my own eyes saw? How could I completely forget this entire event until long after I began the divorce?

The Child Protective Services complaint filed by a neighbor should have set off warning bells. I learned about the investigation from Lucy only after it was completed and closed. Because I did not believe she ever neglected our children, and I regarded Lucy as a doting mother, I viewed this entire event as a nothing burger.

---

24 Chokkeful is a Middle English word meaning crammed full, forced full, or full until choking. A more modern term would be to use chock-full or chuck-full. Yet, I prefer the imagery of choking on red flags.

Yet, it should have played a part in influencing my reasoning about future red flag events. And it did not.

Her wedding band disappeared twice. The first time, roughly four years into our marriage, she said she lost the ring. Eventually, we located the ring. Lucy said, "One of the kids found it under the kitchen sink."

I remember thinking, "Why would her ring be in the cabinet under the kitchen sink?"

After that, she wore the ring on and off for several months, complaining it was tight and hurt her finger. Ultimately, she stopped wearing the wedding band altogether, and it became permanently lost. Why did I consistently take her word for things during these odd situations?

I can remember two separate events that are most likely related. The first occurred while we lived in Houston. I came home from work one day, and Lucy had a bunch of professional photos. Each of the pictures where of her in leather dominatrix attire. Heavens to Murgatroyd. This attire and behavior were weird and out of character for her.

I guess my "What the hell is this?" attitude made her explain that Macy's photography department had a sale and that they supplied the outfits for her to wear.

One night, years later, while we lived in Titusville. Lucy came into the bedroom wearing black leather and lace. She had a masquerade type of mask and an actual leather whip!

She snapped the whip in the air and said, "Yee ahh."

I immediately sat up in bed and firmly told her, "There is no way anyone is going to whip me."

I never saw the whip again until the week of The Shit Show. While packing to move, I found this torture tool hidden away in our walk-in closet. And later, I found the set of Macy's pictures in a box while I cleared out the storage units before turning the units over to her.

Around the time she pulled out the whip, I thought this may have been her idea of how to add some spice to our lives, but I was definitely not into it. However, I know now that she did not love me and was not "into" me, so the whip must have been her concept of how to punish and hurt me. I also think these two events may tie into the photos of what looked like the prequel to an orgy.

The phone call I received from Sadia, Rifah's wife, should have set off warning bells. She was crying and distraught about her marriage falling apart as she announced to me Lucy and her husband carried on an affair. This news should have been a huge red flag for me. Instead, in my mind, it was a nothing event that I immediately rejected as false and never gave it a second thought. If somebody tells you their spouse was having an affair with yours, I advise that you investigate it. Do not dismiss this information out of hand, simply on trust.

My children complained about excessive chores. I saw some of the lists Lucy prepared for them. I thought the lists were for the month, not for the day. I should have listened more to my children and less to the snake's tongue lodged in my ear.

I was attacked on my front lawn by a guy I called the Meth Head. He accused Lucy of trying to hook up with guys at the bar where Lucy's tenant worked. This guy was a drug addict and wanted to fight with me, even though I helped him move some stuff out of my home. I am probably conflating Lucy's narcissism and his drug usage. However, I should not have been so quick to dismiss his claim of Lucy's foul play.

Lucy called me names. From my perspective, they began in a personal setting. She said them to me in a cute fashion, and I considered them as terms of endearment.

The statements I remember her using most often were, "You're a monster" and "You're such an annoying creature."

Because her method of introducing this name-calling appeared innocuous to me, it is difficult to remember her exact approach. However, I suppose I can piece it together well enough. She regularly said these to me privately before expressing them to me with other people present. I would have considered it innocent. However, in the presence of others, her delivery did not always include that cuteness, and these people would have experienced it differently than I did. Finally, how was she conveying these derogatory names to others when I was not around?

Pictures of me disappearing from view in the house should have been a dead giveaway that an affair was in the works. Anyone experiencing this phenomenon should be aware of the likely extramarital relations that may be occurring. The only reason for the vanishing photos was because your significant other was erasing you from their life, making it look like they were single. While not necessarily a sign of a narcissist, it was definitely the hallmark of a cheater.

Sophie's piano teacher claimed Lucy stole money from her purse. She even hid a camera in her bag in an attempt to catch her thief. I should have spoken with the piano teacher myself. There was a purported video, and I should have asked to watch it. With the hindsight I now possess, I should have equated this event's similarity to the time I caught Lucy's friend on video stealing from us.

I found pictures of Lucy wearing bikinis. She always told me, "I don't feel comfortable wearing a bikini."

She never wore one around me during our entire marriage. But she had no problem wearing various thong bikinis on her business trips with strangers, new acquaintances, and business partners.

I often wondered, "What happened to her modesty and self-consciousness around these other people?"

But I never took that concern to the next step. What was wrong with me?

Ten years after Lucy's brother's funeral, I discovered that nobody had raped her while she was in Croatia and that she had an affair with Rifah. Then, not remembering or realizing the bruise ruse, she played on me. I did not fathom the bruise hoax she pulled on me until another ten years passed, sometime after I sold the farm.

Lucy stopped sleeping with me and set up a bedroom for herself downstairs. She began sleeping in the other bedroom occasionally, under the guise that she did not want to wake me when she was working late. Then, later, using a new excuse, she continued this behavior nightly, saying, "You snore too loud."

Sex became excessively infrequent, and Lucy's main reason was, "We are too old for sex."

She would not move to the farm to be with me, using a multitude of justifications that I have already described in the book. All her excuses were red flags for some form of problem in our marriage. And I remained in oblivious complicity. My state of denial was forbidding the foreboding lurking in the recesses of my heart.

Lucy told me she slept in the same bed with DeShawn while in Hawaii. She made the excuse that she slept under the sheets while he remained on top. But this was a violation of our relationship and marriage. I remember being upset while she assured me nothing had happened. How could I let this slide? How did this not reverberate through my very being as the end?

The pictures I found of a party Lucy attended, they instantly looked to me like the kickoff for an orgy. The warning bells did go off. I assumed, in her innocence, that Lucy did not realize what was going on. I explained to her my concerns about what I thought the gathering involved. I told her I did not want her attending any more of these parties or hanging out with those people. Basically, I forbade Lucy from associating with them. Forbade may be too strong of a word, but I let her know how opposed to and my objection to her consorting with them.

Lucy's friend accused her of stealing clothes from her bedroom. The entire situation was absurd. However, portions of the story were undisputed by all three involved. For example, Lucy was at their home when only her friend's husband was present, and the clothes in question went missing from their bedroom. This tale's circumstances contained multiple signals that should have raised the hackles on my back. Why was Lucy alone with her friend's husband? Why was Lucy in their bedroom? I was left wondering why I was so quick to disregard the warning signs once Lucy had the excuse that the clothes would not fit her.

While living in Houston, I had a good friend and neighbor who lived directly across the street from me. We went to the gym together, participated in paintball tournaments, worked on our cars, and entered car shows. Shortly after I bought a new sports car that was rather loud, this neighbor suddenly became angry with me and no longer waved hello or talked to me. I assumed perhaps my car was too loud or possibly he ran into some personal difficulties. Unfortunately, I never had the chance to speak with him, as we moved to Florida soon afterwards. I am now of the belief that Lucy must have done something. Stole from their family? Did she make sexual advances? Or could she have made disparaging remarks regarding me?

While living in Florida, I stored some of my equipment in the backyard of a friend of Lucy's, and I paid them monthly. This arrangement lasted for roughly six months until, without notice, her friend became angry with me and wanted the equipment removed immediately. Lucy explained that her friend's husband was an alcoholic and could be unpredictable. I am convinced Lucy must have said something about me that upset her friend's husband.

These stories about friends who abruptly became angry with me show how the warning signs are sometimes indirectly linked to a narcissist in your life. If you find a continual dose of craziness in your world, in which friends unexpectedly dislike you. It could signify that a narcissist was pulling their strings against you.

I have a final red flag event to share involving lies, deception, and betrayal. While I was living on the farm, Lucy and Sophie visited for a few days. The son of one of our Croatian friends was getting married. Soon after Lucy arrived at the farm, she told me I was not invited to the wedding reception, supposedly because of the cost. However, Lucy and Sophie went. So, I guess Sophie was the "plus one."

I had to wrack my brains to recall the circumstances surrounding the wedding. Lucy had to leave for the entire day before the wedding to help the bride with her hair. I was not invited to the reception and did not attend. However, I remember introducing myself to the bride in her wedding dress, so I must have been present for the wedding ceremony. It was a strange situation.

I introduced myself to the bride, "Hi, I am Sam, Lucy's husband."

"Who?" this young lady said with a confused look.

"Lucy," I explained, "She helped you with your hair yesterday."

Her face became slightly contorted, and I think she said, "No."

Suffice it to say that was an awkward moment. The bride did not recognize Lucy's name when I said it. This situation all happened quickly outside the church doors. At the time, I thought perhaps the bride was overwhelmed with too many new faces and names, and I promptly forgot the incident.

Did I catch Lucy in several lies? Where did she go for an entire day before the wedding? Was I invited to the wedding, and she chose not to bring me? Or was I not invited because Lucy disparaged me to our friends and other people?

To finish this wedding story. I transported Lucy and Sophie to the reception. Lucy phoned me when it was time to pick them up. I drove back to the reception and then waited for over two hours in the parking lot while Lucy would not answer my calls.

Since the beginning of my divorce, I understood that Lucy had fooled around throughout our marriage, and this behavior began before I met her. However, I remained confused concerning the point at which she started to bad-mouth me to our friends and other people behind my back. I do not have a concrete reference point for when her derision of me to others began.

I shared a multitude of situations that occurred over thirty years. Yet, I remain convinced there were many other circumstances that I either no longer recall or continue my failure to perceive as past red flags.

Was I stupid? No, I am an intelligent person. I frequently question my reasoning abilities regarding adverse situations in this intimate personal relationship with Lucy. I also examine my competence to evaluate adverse circumstances in any future connections I may have.

I am ashamed of and even angry with myself for not catching these warning signs earlier in my life. Some of these indications on their own may not have been sufficient to cause worries. However, other crises and the aggregation of multiple events should have culminated with my realization of her true nature. I feel dense, dumb, and dim-witted for allowing myself to fall prey to Lucy's scandalous conduct. I never thought of myself as a gullible individual. However, I was utterly naive to her nihilistic approach to life. I could not see that my wife possessed a gadfly attitude toward me or that she went gallivanting around the country in all sorts of disreputable relationships and exploits.

Chapter Sixty-Five

More Lies Come to Light

During the commotion of selling the farm and closing escrow, Lucy spouted her organized chaos to my kids and others.

She explained to my real estate agent her reasons for halting the farm's sale and her wanting to buy me out. It was so my two youngest children and I could continue living on the farm. Another portion of her story involved the so-called investor she had. The investor, a friend of hers, owns real estate and a particularly posh shopping mall in Manhattan.

Lucy told my oldest daughter, Cassandra, that she lived in Manhattan as a live-in caregiver for an older individual. The Christian church that supported her made the introduction between them and set up the job.

Lucy's story to Maggie had yet another twist. Lucy claimed she was living with a rock star in Manhattan, and he was her investor. They planned to build and start the wellness center Lucy had always wanted. But, to Maggie, she did not mention any benevolent reason for allowing the children and me to live there, as she had spewed to my real estate agent.

She fabricated four different tales for four separate people. I am sure she has other accounts regarding her living situation for other people. I do not know how she keeps all her differing stories and lies straight.

Chapter Sixty-Six

Creepy Porn Lawyer?

I found pictures on Google of Lucy's so-called rock star who lived in Manhattan. It turns out he is not a rock star. He claimed to own several production companies, yet with no credits to his name that I could find. The photos I discovered of him circulating online show that he is nothing short of freakish and comical. I did not write my first impression of him; it was much too unkind. I will call him Barry Blitter from here on.

He wore a wig in the pictures I found; it had to be a wig, and it looked so wrong. One of the images appeared as though he spread bubblegum-pink lipstick on his lips. He carried a purse, not a fanny pack, out in public and wore what looked like a dress. Lucy was mingling or perhaps living with this bizarre, oddball of a person.

The story of the second Cease and Desist letter I referred to earlier begins here. Mr. Blitter supposedly had an in-house attorney who sent the nasty letter via Mr. Blitter's email. He claimed my lawyer did not know the law and threatened to sue me, my lawyer, my real estate agent, the escrow company, the title company, and anyone else involved in the farm's sale.

While reading his stormy letter, my first impression was, "What a sleazebag."

His letter exudes a flavor similar to the now world-infamous creepy porn lawyer currently residing in prison. From this point on, I will refer to this obnoxious lawyer as Mikhaila Vainglatti.

My lawyer could not find Mr. Vainglatti registered with the State's Bar Website. So he wrote to Mr. Vainglatti and requested immediate clarification, his State Bar Number, and proof that he represented Lucy in this case.

The letter finished with, "I look forward to hearing from you soon, although I suspect I will not hear from you again." How poetic.

Is Mr. Vainglatti a figment of Mr. Blitter's imagination, used as an illegitimate front to harass, coerce, and threaten people? Or is there a real schmuck out there masquerading as a lawyer? As fate would have it, this lawyer, Mr. Vainglatti, never replied.

I would laugh at the folly of these events, except it costs me a fortune. I have previously stated in this book that I do not blame Lucy's friends or acquaintances for their negative thoughts regarding me. I know that Lucy has spun some fantastical tales about me to Barry *et al.*[25] or his alter egos, so he can think what he wants. However, he actively participated in this unethical and fraudulent deception. I can tell you, without reservation, that I hold him entirely accountable for these deplorable activities that were an indefinite number of shades beyond the pale. There is no excuse for his actions, and I maintain no respect for him. He is nothing short of a bottom feeder.

---

25 Et al. Is a Latin acronym for et alia, meaning: and others

Chapter Sixty-Seven

The Greenhouse Rubbish

As I wrote in a previous chapter, my lawyer reiterated my offer with an identical deadline for Lucy to come to collect her stuff from the greenhouse. We made our offer, knowing the closing date for the farm's sale approached fast and that I still had to pack, clean, and move.

Lucy and her three helpers, Larry, Maureen, and Carly, arrived under the Sheriff's supervision around noon. These three are members of the Christian church, which Lucy continues to take advantage of. They came underprepared with only one small pickup truck, one full-sized van, one minivan, and a tow truck.

I gave the tow truck driver the keys to Lucy's SUV, and within ten minutes, he removed that three-year-old eyesore from my property.

It was hot in the burning sun, and the heat and humidity inside the greenhouse were unbearable. When they first arrived, both Maureen and Carly took pictures or videos of the property, my vehicles, my equipment, and me—photos of all sorts of stuff not remotely close to the greenhouse. At one point, while Maureen spoke on her phone, she walked to within ten feet of the trailer where I lived. I had to ask the Sheriff to bring her back. She was at least eighty feet away from the greenhouse.

On this first day, Larry did almost all the work. Lucy did nearly nothing and came attired like she was ready for a night out on the town. She was garishly dressed, wearing all sorts of makeup and a fancy, brightly colored one-piece silky jumpsuit. Maureen conducted herself as an enormous distraction and talked the entire time. Carly spent most of the day in the air-conditioning of Maureen's minivan.

At two separate times, both Maureen and Carly asked me, "Where are you moving to?"

Each time, I responded, "I am not comfortable sharing this information with you, and I do not want Lucy to know where I live."

Maureen was the only lady to press on with, "Oh, I wouldn't share that with Lucy. I don't know her and only met her the other day."

After less than one hour, they complained about the heat, wanted to leave, and asked for another day to get the rest. Reluctantly, I gave in to their pressure and agreed to allow only Larry to return with one vehicle. The two women appeared next to useless.

Lucy was not present on the second day, nor was the Sheriff. Larry arrived early and got to work. He let me know that Maureen and Carly were also on their way. On this day, Maureen proved slightly more useful in helping with the work. I question why Carly was even there. She probably moved a total of four boxes in two days.

While speaking with me, Maureen likes to talk a lot. She mentioned she had a daughter and talked a bit about her daughter.

Then she quickly segued into she wanted to meet Sophie, asking, "Could I go in and chat with your daughter for a bit."

Her question caught me off-guard. It was weird.

I told her, "No,"

And I explained the Restraining Orders for domestic violence and child abuse against Lucy. After that, she made a couple more attempts or excuses to visit Sophie.

After I told her, "Sophie probably would not be comfortable meeting with any of Lucy's friends," she apologized awkwardly.

She never asked to meet or speak with Clifford. Do you find that odd? All of the aforementioned from someone who claimed not to know Lucy the day before!

Maureen and Carly approached me around noon. Maureen complained about the heat. She wanted to leave for the day and asked if they could come again the next day, for a third time, to retrieve the rest. I told them there would be no further extensions, and I had to start packing for my move from the farm. They complained that Carly had cancer in her arm and asked if I could please give them more time. I told them I could not, and Maureen walked away.

Carly continued asking, "Could you show a little compassion for a cancer victim and give one more day?"

When I told her, "No, I can't give you another day. I have little time left for my own packing."

She became irate, turned red-faced, and demanded more time. She started going off on me with, "You are heartless and have no compassion for a cancer victim."

This lady was yelling at me. She read me the riot act and accused me of all sorts of horrible things.

As she began her tirade, I muttered to myself, saying, "Oh, here we go."

Then, I sat silently on a step of my ladder, listening to her entire rant.

The last thing she said to me was, "Even when I am in the hospital dying from cancer, I will pray for you."

Then she stormed off into Maureen's minivan and started video recording me on her phone.

Shaken and upset, I was shocked at her behavior while I remained sitting on the ladder. Then, I wrote a text message to my mother, describing what had just transpired. Writing this text message allowed me to calm down and develop a course of action. Finally, I stood up, walked into the greenhouse, and spoke to the gentleman of their crew.

I told Larry, "I have no problem with you, but one of the ladies just yelled at me, was rude, and insulted me. I want her off my property. Immediately. And never return. I don't want to see her again."

He seemed perhaps a little embarrassed at what I told him as he said, "We are pretty much done here anyways. I'll take care of it, and we'll get on our way."

They departed my property, leaving me to ponder Carly's heightened anger over not getting another day. Since this was a simple moving job for Carly, why was she so empowered or invested on behalf of Lucy's personal business? It did not dawn on me until later that Maureen walked away on cue as Carly started her raving. Maureen did not go back to work in the greenhouse and did not enter her minivan. Maureen pretty much disappeared just out of view behind her minivan. I am convinced she was videoing the altercation they had intended, set up, and planned.

I consider this Larry, Moe, and Curly crew as a team of professional pickers. I believe they have worked together for a very long time. They went through boxes and discussed what they could keep for themselves. They refused to take racks of Lucy's clothes. They refused to take any furniture. They refused to take the old TV belonging to Lucy's friend. It seems they only took what they wanted for themselves and things they could swiftly sell. For example, I stopped Maureen from her attempt to take some of my tools. She dropped them at my feet, roughly twenty feet from the greenhouse where she initially took them. Then she explained the location of the scrap metal recycling yard she planned to take them to.

Telling me, "You can get good money there."

My lawyer had to send Lucy a letter stating the unrestricted access they enjoyed to the greenhouse. Nevertheless, they took some of my property and tried to take my tools. In the letter, he pointed out to Lucy how her agents refused to take many of her personal items, including the furniture she demanded in our MSC settlement. He also described the mess they made outside the greenhouse of her discarded items and things they broke and left strewn across a forty-foot area.

Then, my lawyer's letter described several potential third-party Restraining Order violations. Including they took pictures of my property, asked to meet with Sophie, and asked where I planned to move.

Chapter Sixty-Eight
The Crazy Cat Lady

Throughout my life, I have had horrible allergies. Around the age of twelve, the doctors tested me for allergies. I received sixteen allergy testing shots in my arm and reacted to thirteen. I suffered from most of the typical seasonal allergies, which generally attacked me in the spring and fall of each year.

They say your body chemistry and allergies change every five years. So, some things get worse while others improve.

My throat and sinuses would itch, the insides of my ears would itch, and they could not be scratched. The whites of my eyeballs would swell up, turn yellow, and itch like crazy. I would sneeze so hard and repeatedly for an extended time that the membranes of my throat and sinuses would tear and begin to bleed. These tears would inevitably become infected, requiring antibiotics.

Aside from seasonal allergies, I was also allergic to varying degrees to most perfumes and some animals. So, I used to eat a lot of white bread, attempting to wash down as much of the allergens from my throat as I could.

Department stores were a dangerous place for me. Their perfume section was always on the first floor. I used to hyperventilate, hold my breath, enter the store, and then get to the escalators and the second floor as quickly as possible so I would not get violently ill.

I had a mild allergic reaction to dogs. In the worst bouts with dogs, all I had to do was eat some bread to help clear my throat of allergens.

Cats were like instant death to me. I did not even have to be around the cat. Simply visiting a friend's home who owned a cat would trigger my worst allergy bouts. Out of self-preservation, I regularly had to scare cats away from me.

My allergies to cats bring me to the crazy cat lady part of my story. While we lived in Houston, Lucy rescued a litter of feral kittens from our neighbor's backyard. The word rescue was Lucy's terminology. I considered it as though Lucy stole the kittens from their undomesticated mother, who would have been nearby. You have no idea how much I wish she would have left those kittens undisturbed.

For years, Lucy had no less than nine cats; at times, she had as many as fifteen. These cats suffered four or five generations of inbreeding. It was a daunting task, but I finally persuaded Lucy to get her cats neutered or spayed. I convinced her roughly three years before I bought the farm.

Over a fifteen-year span, the cats brought massive plagues of fleas into our home at least five times. Lucy never seemed to care about the fleas, as they either did not bite her or she would not experience an itching reaction to the flea bites. On the other hand, hundreds of bites covered me below my knees. These bites itched so much that I would scratch them until each was raw and bleeding.

Lucy would laugh at me, saying, "You must have sweet blood."

Each time an infestation occurred, I found myself compelled to buy the flea drops for her cats and the flea powder for the rugs. I did this on my own, as Lucy would not. Lucy never helped administer these drugs to her cats. She did not participate in sanitizing multiple massive loads of laundry and did not help treat our home's carpets or the clean up afterwards.

I do not think Lucy truly liked these cats, and I imagine she kept them for my allergies. She never inquired about the cats for three years during the divorce and refused to retrieve them from the farm since the beginning of the divorce. Her cats were a contrived excuse to make Lucy appear as an animal lover, while her real goal was to keep me weak, suffering, and sick from allergies.

Chapter Sixty-Nine

Life's Doldrums

With the farm sold, we had to move. I placed most of my things in storage, and we stayed in motels for the time being. However, my fear of Lucy stalking us remained. She no longer knew where we lived, yet my angst about her finding us lingered, even with the Restraining Order sheltering us from such actions.

With COVID and all this free time to consider my circumstances, I often found myself thinking of my father. My grandchildren love the movie *The Incredibles II*.

Every time I watched the film on TV with them and heard Mister Incredible say, "I'm rolling with the punches, Baby!"

It reminded me of Dad.

Ever since I was a child, I have memories of my father saying, through his uneven, one-sided smile, "Yeah, Baby!" Or talking about Muhammad Ali, "Using the rope-a-dope and rolling with the punches."

He emphasized many things he talked about by finishing his sentences with "Baby!"

Did I just now compare my father to a superhero? Yes, I did. He was my superhero, with a larger-than-life personality, and I find myself living up to being only a fraction of the man he was. I hope he knew that before he died. One of the greatest regrets in my life was that so much was left unsaid. Words cannot describe how much I miss Dad. I wish he could have been here to help advise me throughout this ordeal. Yet, on the other hand, I am also glad he was not here to see the mess my children and I were dragged through or how far I had fallen. It would have broken his heart. Another one of my chief misgivings was not visiting my parents more often. I wish I could travel to see Mum at least once a year.

Before our Restraining Orders expired in October 2020, we applied to renew them. According to my lawyer, a Restraining Order's successful renewal usually results in non-expiring permanent orders. Because of the frequent and sheer number of Lucy's violations, my lawyer had no doubt our DVROs would renew. Moreover, considering her atrocious behavior and her offenses' severe nature, he was confident the court would order them permanent and without expiry dates.

In court, Lucy demanded more time to prepare her defense and search for yet another lawyer. She was successful in delaying the hearing until March 2021.

The week before Christmas, Laurence, my son-in-law, fell ill with a nasty case of COVID. He suffered through all the coronavirus symptoms except for pneumonia. Laurence quarantined himself alone at one of his father's apartments.

A week later, my grandson tested positive for COVID-19 and joined his father, Laurence, in quarantine.

COVID ruined Christmas 2020 and New Year 2021. Clifford, Sophie, and I remained in a motel for the duration of the holidays. Laurence spent the entire holiday in quarantine at his father's place. Cassandra and my two youngest grandchildren remained at their home in isolation due to their initial exposure to Laurence and, later, to their oldest son.

During Laurence's quarantine period, Lucy re-entered Cassandra's life, helping Cassandra with my two youngest grandkids while Laurence and my eldest grandson remained quarantined. I have repeatedly told all my children they need to do what is right for themselves when it comes to Lucy and that I would not be angry or upset with them if they decided to see her. Now that she had returned to one of my children's lives, it put my statements to the test. I have to admit the degree to which it irked me. I was upset about it, but my unease focused on Lucy, not Cassandra.

Lucy claimed all sorts of rubbish stories while lodging at Cassandra's home. All three of my daughters talk to each other, so I received the following details: second or even third-hand.

While Lucy blamed me for all of our family's problems, Cassandra criticized Lucy for her affair with Rifah.

Lucy declared to Cassandra, "I never had an affair."

Cassandra continued, "Oh, come on, you always took Sophie to visit Rifah. She even looks like him, and you made her call him Dad."

"It was not an affair," Lucy shot back, "Rifah sexually abused me."

"Are you saying that you took my sister, Sophie, to visit a rapist?" Cassandra asked in angry disbelief.

Lucy went on, attempting to explain to Cassandra that I knew Rifah sexually abused her. Furthermore, Lucy claimed she and I did not press charges against him because Rifah and his wife Sadia were good friends of our family. Lucy also asserted I was in complete agreement with her and Sophie visiting him throughout the years.

As the confrontation continued, Cassandra asked Lucy, "Why did you make Sophie call Rifah, Dad."

"I never made Sophie call Rifah Dad," Lucy indignantly spewed in reply, "She called him Baba."

Cassandra argued with her, "But baba is Bengali for father!"

I want to remind you that Cassandra is my daughter from a previous relationship. Lucy helped me raise Cassandra since she was around the age of six.

At one point, while Lucy stayed at Cassandra's, she said to Cassandra, "I don't want to say anything bad about your father." Then, she paused to add emphasis before continuing, "But your mother didn't originally want to keep you because your father sexually abused her."

Cassandra's mother and I endured several years of custody and visitation issues. An animus grew between our families. Their hatred of my family lasted for two decades, but not once did they accuse me of rape or even suggest that rape or sexual abuse ever occurred.

Was this woman I called my wife, this narcissist, out to destroy me? Or did she feel an entitlement to say and do anything in order to get everything she desired? Does her sense of privilege know no bounds?

She claimed the last thing Gilbert said to her three years ago, after I filed for divorce, "I probably won't talk to you for a while."

Lucy then explained to Cassandra how I had forced Gilbert not to talk to her anymore. Gilbert was living in England and free to do as he pleased. All my children have minds of their own, speak to each other, and know her lies. You could say they compare notes when they communicate. Gilbert decided soon after I started the divorce that he wanted nothing to do with his mother. When he found out what she did to his sisters, it made him sick to his stomach. He does not want to talk to his mother and does not want to talk about her. For him, she does not exist.

For two years, I searched for work in my field. Since I sold the farm, I looked for any position. Finally, I swallowed what little pride I had left, found a minimum-wage warehousing job in a nearby city, and we began living in hotels from that point.

Three weeks after beginning my new job, roughly four weeks before the scheduled trial date to finalize our divorce and renew our Restraining Orders, I received a phone call from Croatia on my old cell phone. I did not answer the cell phone, and the caller did not leave a voice message. Nevertheless, I am reasonably sure I knew who it was on the other end of the line, Lucy's mother.

The day after the Croatian phone call, I heard from Sophie that Lucy had called her sister Maggie. Lucy told Maggie she knew about the new job I recently started and knew the city where

I worked. Lucy inquired of Maggie if Microsoft was my new employer. Lucy also told Maggie she had an inside source feeding her this information.

This woman, who has a DVRO (Domestic Violence Restraining Order) against her, prohibiting her from pursuing me, was somehow tracking me. It was a very unsettling development for me to discover she continued to stalk me. What plots and schemes was she conniving against me now?

Three weeks before my court date, I learned from my lawyer's office that our Judge had rotated out from family law court after three-plus years of service to another courtroom. While an accomplished justice, the replacement judge had zero experience with family law matters. My lawyer advised that we ask for a different judge to hear our case while this one gains maturity in family law. The court date remains intact, yet it could change based on the alternate Judge's schedule. More delays, will it never end?

Throughout the divorce, I have been careful not to demean or place vulgar labels on Lucy, especially around any of my children.

Believe me when I say, "I have many crude opinions about this charmer."

But I am trying to be a better man, like my grandfather was, and refrain from uttering unfiltered obscenities.

For the first two years, I was also mindful not to express my negative feelings in my children's presence. However, it is my responsibility to protect my children. It is a complex balancing act to swallow one's pride and trauma, to only share enough of the details of events from the past, to help keep your loved ones safe. My children are all adults now. If they showed interest in learning more, I would open up with them after my divorce is completed.

Chapter Seventy

Delay Tactics

I have already written about some of the methods Lucy employs to delay the inevitable. Yet, something curiously funny occurred in Court, which made me add this chapter.

I will recap many of the Delay Tactics she has engaged in against me over the years. For example, she often said, "I need more time," or "I need more time to pack."

She used these two sayings for cleaning, packing, moving, finding documents, etc.

She deferred moving to the farm for four years with excuses like, "The kids need to finish their school year."

She postponed the scheduling of several court dates with her travel itinerary and usually with travel out of the country. She also delayed the Court's scheduling of dates with excuses like, "I need more time to find a lawyer" or "I need to find a translator."

Business travel, conferences, and meetings were her three most common justifications for prolonging a deadline's activity.

Now we come full circle to an entertaining event that occurred in Court. We were assigned a new Judge, which meant we had to reschedule and delay the dates for our divorce trial and renew the Restraining Orders yet again. During this scheduling hearing in the early fall of 2020, the Judge offered to schedule the Restraining Order trial within the next thirty days.

Without skipping a beat, Lucy stated, "I will be out of town."

"Could you attend remotely?" asked the Judge.

Lucy immediately added, "I will be out of the country, actually. So, it would be difficult."

As a result of this scheduling fiasco, I had to wait an additional five months for the trial instead of the thirty-day offer the Judge had offered. It was not the outcome I wanted.

A little later, my daughter's lawyer informed the Court of her wish not to renew her Restraining Order. Due to the restrictions of the COVID pandemic, the Courts held their hearings remotely via video conference. Consequently, I had to watch the surprised look on Lucy's face from my computer screen, followed by ten seconds of her fake tears, and finally by her phony smiles and repeated praying gestures of thanks to the camera.

The Judge commented, "The Restraining Orders in place are complicated documents, and there is no time today to change them. So, the Restraining Orders for both Samuel and Sophie will remain in effect until the June hearing."

The Judge's statement was when Lucy realized her delay tactics had backfired, and she had shot herself in the foot five minutes earlier. Even with my disappointment from all the delays, I found the befuddled expression on Lucy's face somewhat amusing.

As the conference concluded, Lucy complained to the Judge, "After thirty years of marriage, I have been left destitute and penniless."

The Judge tactfully halted Lucy's tirade by telling her, "These are details we will go over during the trial. They are not topics for today."

I am left confused. Over the past three-and-a-half-years, Lucy has delayed our Court hearings four times, using the excuse she was traveling out of the country. How many other times has she traveled? Is Lucy a jet-setter flush with money? Or is she destitute and lying to the courts about her travel? I may point out this contradictory duality in our upcoming divorce trial.

Oh, and by the way. Did you notice that Lucy did not have or require a translator on this occasion? Her comprehension and use of the English language were well above average.

"Destitute and penniless," now that was pretty good English, don't you agree?

Chapter Seventy-One

Finalizing our Divorce

For two years, Lucy refused to sign the final typed divorce settlement agreement. After one year had passed, my lawyers went to court to ask the Judge to terminate our marriage based on the handwritten MSC agreement both Lucy and I signed.

In October 2020, Lucy hired her fourth or fifth lawyer to represent her in the matter of her refusing to sign the formalized MSC agreement. I omitted Mikhaila Vainglatti from my count of her lawyers since I do not consider him a legitimate attorney or even an actual person. The Judge set a hearing date for four months later, in January 2021.

Then, four months later, in January 2021, Lucy and her lawyer did not attend the hearing.

"Is there any known reason why they have not appeared?" asked the Judge.

My lawyer explained to the court, "Your Honor, her latest lawyer quit."

"Can you submit the request forms for the court to accept the formalized version of the handwritten settlement agreement?" the Judge inquired.

That was the MSC agreement from a year and a half ago. "Of course, your Honor," my lawyer agreed.

Then the Judge said, "I see you have a Restraining Order renewal hearing coming up. I can set the divorce to the same date and hear both at the same time. If that works for you?"

She had postponed it again. How aggravating. It had already been three years, and I was not divorced. I felt as though I would die of old age before the termination of my marriage to this woman. This woman, whom I do not care about or know. Yet, did I catch a glimpse of an inkling of the Judge's frustration with Lucy's games? Maybe there was hope the end was near.

By May 2021, I was no longer sure how many lawyers Lucy had brought into the mix, with her continuously changing lawyers' nonsense. I reckon this final lawyer must be her sixth, seventh, or eighth. He was a personal injury lawyer, and it became blatantly obvious even to me that he was way out of his depth. He was not knowledgeable in Family Law or Divorce Law.

The hearing was held over video conference, as the courthouse was closed to the public due to COVID restrictions. Lucy's latest lawyer managed to postpone the Restraining Order lawsuit for another month, and the Judge set it for the day before our divorce trial.

However, as the Judge set the new DVRO renewal trial date, Lucy attempted her delay tactics yet again, saying: "I have business meetings that day and cannot attend."

The Judge was noticeably agitated while searching for another day to schedule the trial.

After a few minutes on mute, her lawyer returned and asked, "Does Lucy have to attend the trial?"

Without looking up from his calendar to look at the video camera, the Judge said in a very stern voice, "Yes."

After a few more minutes of muted discussion, her lawyer returned once again, "Your Honor, my client was able to juggle her schedule and will be able to attend that day."

I feel as though both Lucy and her lawyer made complete fools of themselves in front of the Judge with this scheduling debacle.

The Restraining Order Renewal Trial

We finally got to the DVRO Renewal trial in late June 2021, and it was scheduled for a half-day to determine the renewal of my DVRO and the duration it would last. Unfortunately, Sophie decided that morning not to attend the trial. She claimed not to be scared, just very anxious. However, her reasoning included being afraid that Lucy or one of her Christian surrogates may follow and confront her in the courthouse bathrooms. I know she wanted to be there. Even her boyfriend wanted to attend and listen in.

Clifford also wanted to go but was terrified of being forced to testify. I assured him that he would not be testifying. And so, he decided to attend court with me.

Ten minutes before the trial began, I discovered that Lucy and her lawyer would not attend in person. Instead, they would participate via video conference call. I called Sophie to let her know about this development. I think she regretted her decision not to be there.

As our trial began, my lawyer told the Judge that he estimated he needed roughly a half-hour. Yet, my DVRO trial lasted a little over an hour. Lucy and her lawyer joined the trial separately from each other, on their own phones and both without video. They each claimed they could not get the video working. Their statements surprised me, as they attended the previous hearing via video conference. I am unsure if they could watch the Court on video or only hear the trial's interactions.

I held my left hand clenched tightly within my right hand during the entire trial.

Weeks earlier, Lucy had entered a new declaration from a friend of hers. I found the document to be quite libelous. Moreover, this new friend of Lucy's who had never met me and could not know me made overtures of expertise in the field of abuse psychology. Yet, she had no credentials.

Regardless of the document's origin, the Judge asked, "Do you have any objections to me reading this declaration?"

"I have no objections, your Honor," my lawyer replied, then he continued, "The declaration is immaterial."

They questioned me first. My lawyer began the questioning, followed by her lawyer. I only remember two questions from my lawyer. The first question was about the bankruptcy fraud, and the second was if I remembered being confronted by Lucy's representatives during the Family Court Services Mediation. After ten to fifteen minutes of explaining the details of those two incidents to the Court, my lawyer had no more questions for me.

Lucy's attorney began with questions and statements, revisiting the original Restraining Order and attempting to put it into question.

My lawyer immediately stood up and said, "Your Honor, I object to this line of questioning."

"I agree," the Judge replied, "Sustained."

Then the Judge explained his duty in the trial, "This Court automatically assumes everything from the original DVRO hearing was valid."

Then he clarified his function, "The purpose of today's trial is not to revisit, question, or undermine the original DVRO. Instead, today's trial is to determine if the DVRO should be renewed."

Her lawyer tried to circle back to this line of questioning several times and argued that it was essential to understand. On each occasion, the Judge stopped him, and on the last occurrence, the Judge finally told him in a firm voice, "That is enough on this topic. Move on."

Her lawyer kept asking me unfounded questions not based on reality. Each time he asked a question or suggested an alternate scenario, not only did I answer him, but I gave the background story leading up to each subject he raised. For example, her lawyer attempted to suggest that the guns I found were in the basement.

I answered, "No! The guns I found were on the second floor of our house, in the master bedroom closet, on the floor right behind the door."

Her lawyer questioned me for thirty to forty-five minutes.

Next was Lucy's chance to explain her side of the story. Her lawyer began her questioning. Lucy's explanation for the bankruptcy fraud boiled down to this, "Sam filed for the bankruptcy, and he is trying to frame me for it."

The rest of the questions and answers revolved around Lucy being destitute and how poor old Lucy had difficulty finding a job because of the DVRO. Lucy and her lawyer's questions and answers lasted roughly ten minutes.

When they finished, the Judge asked my lawyer, "Do you have any questions for the defendant?"

Taking his time, my lawyer slowly sat back in a relaxed pose with his hands behind his head and crossing his outstretched legs at the ankles as he said, "I have no questions, your Honor."

It was not until the end of the trial that I realized I rarely made eye contact with anyone in the courtroom. Instead, I spent most of the time looking down in front of me at my clenched hands on the table. As a result, I felt cold and started shivering during the trial.

There were only two times I remember looking up. The first time I looked up, I saw the court recorder make an "Oh" expression when I talked about the Baptist marriage counselor approaching me during the Family Court Services mediation, right here in the courthouse, and telling him of Lucy's sixteen-year affair. The second time, I looked at the Judge, and we made eye contact while I explained my belief that Lucy cannot help herself when it comes to stalking me. I told the Court how I discovered that Lucy knew I had a new job and the city where I worked. I uncovered she knew within ten days of beginning the new position. She was phishing for more information about the company I worked for from one of my daughters.

It felt like it took an eternity for the Judge to render his ruling regarding the renewal of the DVRO, yet it probably lasted less than five minutes. After he explained the law, he revealed the reasoning for his decision.

Then the Judge said, "Samuel has shown adequate fear and need for the order."

During his entire monologue, I kept saying to myself over and over, "Please renew, please renew it."

"The renewal of the Restraining Order is granted," I heard the Judge say.

Then, he immediately began explaining the next step for determining the duration of the DVRO, with options of either five years or never expire.

During this second portion of his monologue, I kept saying to myself, "Please not five years, please not five years. I do not want to go through this again."

"I believe the evidence shows that Lucy did, in fact, file for Bankruptcy in Samuel's name." Then the Judge rendered his decision, "The Restraining Orders will be made permanent."

And just like that, the trial was over.

We left the courtroom and discussed the trial in the court hallway. My lawyer explained that usually, he must often object to other lawyers' questions. He went on to describe how Lucy's lawyer was weakening her case and, in fact, building my case. So, he let her lawyer go on uninterrupted.

Finally, he stepped in front of me and asked, "Do you understand what just happened in there?"

"I got everything I wanted: a permanent Restraining Order that never expires."

Beaming with a big smile, he said, "You're right."

Clifford thought I did an excellent job in Court explaining the circumstances. On the other hand, I felt upset that I had not talked about so many other things. However, the fraction of events I described was more than enough to convince the Judge of my plight.

Her lawyer made a series of unfortunate *faux pas* for her case during the trial. The morals of my legal experiences that you should take away are. Firstly, there is an old saying, "Only a fool represents himself.[26]"

In other words, when dealing with the courts, and the stakes are high (i.e., not in Small Claims Court), find the best lawyer

---

[26] "He who represents himself, has a fool for a client" —Abraham Lincoln

that you can afford. Because we cannot all afford "The best lawyer money can buy."

Secondly, choose a lawyer who specializes in the field of law which you require. This advice should be a no-brainer. Think of it this way: you would not choose your family doctor to perform open heart surgery. The final lesson I must impart is that your lawyer needs to prepare appropriately. If you only share part of your story, or worse yet, you lie to your lawyer. You will most likely make your lawyer play the fool as he weakens or dismantles your case.

The Divorce Trial

The courts scheduled my divorce trial for the day after my Restraining Order trial. It was planned as a half-day trial to complete my divorce and determine the final terms.

I would have liked to write, "And with the stroke of a pen, the Judge ended this nightmare of a marriage by signing my final divorce papers."

After the renewal of my Restraining Order, Lucy settled out of Court. It appears she signed the divorce papers the night before our divorce trial. However, we did not receive copies of her signed judgment until moments before the litigation would have begun.

After two years of shenanigans since the MSC, she refused to sign the formalized settlement agreement and caused me all sorts of additional legal expenses. She finally signed the original unmodified agreement that my lawyer had submitted almost two years earlier. I assume she feared the Court would award me the legal costs for the past two years since the MSC. However, I also believe it was a game for her, and she played it to the last possible moment.

With my divorce, all but *un fait accompli,* the cannibalization of my net worth had come to an end, and I could finally start, in earnest, to rebuild my life and wealth.

It felt as though Lucy was a cancerous growth in my life. My lawyer was the surgeon who carefully and with prejudice performed the necessary excision to eliminate her from my life.

I had a rose gold necklace. It was a wedding gift from Lucy's father. I never took it off for over twenty-five years, except for surgery or to show someone. The day my divorce papers arrived, I removed this gold necklace. My children commented that it was because it reminded me of her. However, that was incorrect. To me, it was a symbol of our marriage. Removing the necklace was symbolic of my marriage to this charmer coming to an end.

Just When You Think It Is Over

For the last eight months, I thought my book would end with the previous subchapter, The Divorce Trial. But, oh no! Nothing is ever that simple with Lucy around, and my story continues.

Lucy attempted to conflate my sources of retirement money. She alleged that aside from the farm money, there was also the 401k from my previous employer. They were both the same money. I invested the entirety of both my 401k and pension plans in my farm. She tried to make it appear as though there were more sources of money.

Lucy threatened to sue me in court if I did not produce everything the Qualified Domestic Relations Order (QDRO) lawyer required to complete the division of my retirement savings. But the QDRO lawyer had not yet sent out her list of requirements. I mean, Lucy dragged her feet for three years, and now, thirty days after she signed the settlement agreement, she threatened me through the QDRO lawyer unless I met her demands instantly. I still did not have the Judge's signature for the divorce and would probably have to wait another sixty days.

But Lucy wants her money now!

Shortly after Lucy's threats through the QDRO attorney, I received the lawyer's questions, forms, and contract. Within two days, I answered all of the QDRO lawyer's questions and paid for my half of the fees. Then everything went silent. I assume Lucy would not pay her half of the costs.

Another dilemma I have struggled with was what I would do if one of my children had a special event and wanted to invite both Lucy and me. How would I feel? What would I do? The topic recently came up in a conversation. My oldest daughter, Cassandra, began planning for a baptism and suggested that I must deal with it and be civil if Lucy was also there. I resent the idea of making my children decide between Lucy and me. I do not think it is fair to make them choose between us. However, I am also not inclined to devalue my Restraining Order. I decided that I would not, under any circumstance, weaken my Restraining Order. If Lucy shows up at an event while I am there, I will loudly tell her to leave. If she does not immediately leave, I will call the police to arrest and remove her. In Boolean terms, Lucy and I are mutually exclusive. I let my children know of this decision.

Chapter Seventy-Two

Retrospectus

My Quote: *"A narcissist is an anathema to your well-being!"*

This book, my story, is the culmination of over three-and-a-half years of divorce proceedings, preceded by the duplicities of an attractive and charming narcissist during our thirty-year relationship. A narcissist who wrought ruin to the lives of my children, myself, and others. To this woman who brought my youngest daughter and me to the brink of death.

This memoir does not contain a conclusion because, in my life, this mess with my little narcissist will undoubtedly never end. Accordingly, I created this chapter in the conclusion's place. Having said that, my marriage to this woman has concluded, and the divorce denotes the end of my story. Lucy is a narcissist, and I do not believe, not even for an instant, that she is through torturing me. My problems with her will continue, hopefully, less often. However, my worries, concerns, and fears will continue to persist.

To illustrate how a narcissist's abuse never truly ends, I received two suspicious credit reports two years after my divorce. Both were fraudulent credit card applications. They were separate applications for two credit card companies, and the applications were about forty days apart. Then, a week after the second fraudulent credit report, I received a letter from Florida for some unpaid court fines. I had not lived in Florida for nine years and started the divorce five years before this letter. So, how could I suddenly owe court fees over there? I will not include details about these three incidents as part of the story because my story ended with the divorce. I only brought these up to show how it never ends.

I guess I considered myself kind of a tough guy. In the past, I never cried over things or events. I would never consider going to a therapist, psychologist, or psychiatrist as my belief system reserved these treatments to the realm of crazy people. Oh boy, was I wrong!

If you, a family member, or a loved one is going through some traumatic events in their lives, the best thing you or they can do is to see a professional who can help unleash all those pent-up thoughts, feelings, and emotions constructively. They will let you talk as they steer your discussion through the confines of your mental anguish. Then, occasionally, they offer some helpful guidance.

Since I began my divorce, I have not seen or heard from this woman in the past four years. There was no news or interaction other than in court, Restraining Order violations, or when my older children talked about her. With the trauma of my divorce completed, I faced a mound of legal bills and additional costs associated with the divorce, which have left me in financial ruin and further debt.

The year before my divorce was granted, I found out the house in Florida foreclosed before Christmas 2019. Amid this discovery of the foreclosure, I had already listed the farm in New York for sale roughly one year earlier, and at long last, it started to see some genuine interest.

Gripped with thoughts like, "Will the farm sell before it forecloses?"

It felt like a race condition. Sell or foreclose. And the results were out of my control. But we all know the tribulations I went through, and as fortune would have it, the farm did sell.

I went from being employed as a computer engineer to being self-employed as a farmer for four years and then an unemployed hermit once I started my divorce. I spent three years living in hotels, or homeless as I perceived it, hiding from this woman. Finding a job in the tech market has been difficult as my talents are exceedingly specialized. I want nothing more than to continue farming. However, the farm I wish to purchase would require between $3 million and $5 million, and my dream currently remains well out of reach.

From the first time I met Lucy, I thought she was beautiful. And to this day, I still perceive her as an attractive and charming woman. These traits of hers are part of the narcissist's allure. Peel away the thin veneer that consists of her fake outer layers, and you will only find all kinds of ugly. They are sycophants who will say and do practically anything they think you want to see and hear. They will expend a lot of energy in their charade with the sole purpose of hooking you into their life. Once they set their meat hooks into you, the effort they need to exhaust on you diminishes, the time spent with you will lessen, and the quality time allocated to you will disappear. They will only do precisely enough to keep their hooks set.

I have come to learn that all the superficial traits about Lucy are cringe-worthy, and I assume the same goes for all narcissists. Now that I have divorced her, it is time to begin rebuilding my self-confidence, which she has thoroughly sapped from me.

A narcissist's callous approach to your relationship, needs, and emotions can lead to depression, suicidal thoughts, and possibly even lead to attempting suicide.

My father taught me not to be unappreciative of any gifts, using an old saying, "Never look a gift horse in the mouth."

While thinking about the gift horse proverb, I remembered some old black-and-white Western movies I used to watch where the cowboy would check the health of a horse he was purchasing by examining the horse's teeth. The connection between the Western scene and my father's saying dawned on me while thinking about writing this paragraph.

Another expression often used by my family was, "Life is a gift."

Our existence and time on Earth are indeed a present, and you should not try to check out early. You have many adventures yet to experience and do not want to miss out on life's future gifts. I sincerely hope you do not become a narcissist's statistic.

The only way to save yourself from a narcissist is to break contact with them altogether. You must completely and utterly eliminate their existence from your life. Do not let them back into your life for any reason. Because the second time around, their treatment towards you will be much worse than the first time. Breaking contact means no contact whatsoever.

- Do not move back together.
- Do not visit them.
- Do not go to the same parties as them.
- Do not keep the same circle of friends as they do.
- Do not talk to them in person or on the phone.
- Do not exchange messages with them via email, texts, or even through other people.
- No contact means they do not exist in your life–for the rest of your life.

The ultimate truth I unearthed from my misfortunes with this charmer was that even the vestiges of the relationship I thought we had were an illusion. Even though this woman burnt down my life to ruin, our marriage and relationship were essentially nonexistent. There were no ashes of our partnership to pick up or scatter.

If you think you are in or were in a relationship with a narcissist, get help. See a therapist—once, twice, or even fifty times. Get help, even if you think you are well, because you are not all right. You recently read my story, an entire book's worth of unsettling events. I could not see my enfeebled condition and thought I was fit as a fiddle. I wanted to help my kids, and I was not especially worried about myself despite often breaking down into a river of tears. It took a High Conflict Preparation therapist, suggested by my lawyer, to convince me that I was a mess and desperately needed help. There is an ordinary world out there. Get the support to guide your return to your new normal.

It bears repeating, *"A narcissist is an anathema to your well-being!"*

Samuel P. Frearson

EPILOGUE

Lucy's lies and deceit predate the first time I met her over thirty years ago. I have written many unkind words about several people. I also shielded these people through anonymity.

Some of the situations recounted in this book I witnessed first-hand. However, most of the circumstances came from the stories and lies Lucy told me over the years. Then after The Shit Show began, my children informed me of many additional stories and details they recalled.

If anyone depicted in this book feels mischaracterized or believes what I wrote libelous, they can only blame Lucy for the slanders she told my children and me way back when.

Lucy still every-so-often torments my dreams. I remember many of these nightmares. And most of the time, they usually remain at the forefront of my memories because they startle and wake me.

There appear to be three categories of dreams. In the first, Lucy sits beside me while I do something. She asks about what I am doing, and we talk for a bit. Until, in the dream, I realize I have a Restraining Order against her. Then I try to take my leave or run away from her in embarrassment.

The second style of dreams has Lucy appearing naked or in the process of removing her clothes and offering herself to me. I always wake up quickly, disgusted with myself for even subconsciously thinking this. I cannot describe how abhorrent I find these dreams.

In the final type of these dreams, Lucy and her friends stalk and hunt me down, either with guns or knives in their hands. These nightmares feel as though they last a long time. When I wake from these, I always find myself in a sweat and my heart racing with small, fast beats. I usually cannot get back to sleep for hours after these nightmares. It takes dozens of minutes to calm down. Then, the scenes from the dream repeatedly play in my head for hours while I lay awake in bed.

What is in a title, anyway? Choosing a suitable title for this book has been onerous and has followed a progression. The title has changed three times. When I began the book, it was named *Ascent From Madness*. At that point in my life, I saw myself crawling out of or rappelling upwards from a viper's cave. While this title was fitting, it only represented a point in time and did not encompass the entire story.

Later, while participating in a writer's guild, a colleague and friend suggested the title *Memoirs of a Marriage*. At first, I did not like this title because it irked me to attach such a lovely label to such a wretched story. However, it grew on me and remained for close to two years. Eventually, I began to think it only applied to half of my story. So, in the back of my mind, I pondered other more befitting labels.

Finally, after the courts terminated my marriage while nearing the completion of my book, I thought of the title *Caress of the Bête Noire*. This title advances such a contradictory message. To be lovingly held in the arms of the Bogeyman, or in my case, the embrace of the Baba Yaga. It's not love or a safe place to be. Instead, the title conjures antithetical visions of impending doom and unspeakable horrors, similar to a soft touch of razor wire that cuts and peels your skin. The title perfectly describes my ambivalent perspective of our relationship before, during, and after the divorce.

I will close my story with this final thought process. I have been single since I began our divorce almost four years ago. However, as I contemplated my situation, I realized I had also been physically alone for the past eight years since I bought the farm. In the end, I came to understand the narcissistic relationship I endured. I recognized that Lucy was never honestly a companion of mine.

She was beyond question against me and only there to deplete me emotionally and financially for her selfish cravings. The bleak reality of my situation shows I was alone during the entirety of my relationship with this parasite these past thirty years.

That was a somewhat depressing and pessimistic final thought process. However, it is from the viewpoint of looking backwards in time throughout my relationship with this woman. The silver lining or the bright light comes from looking forward towards the future. I am entirely free of this charmer, and there are no strings to attach us. All my children know what their mother is and are safe from her. My children and I were no longer a part of the legion of minions she controlled.

COROLLARY

Did I mention how much I love our first responders? I can't say it enough.

When in the same line at a shop, I want to tell them thanks, shake their hands, hug them, then buy their coffee or lunch. Shaking hands and giving hugs may be taking it a little too far. I have not done this and do not suggest trying it. However, I have offered to pay for their coffee or meal, which is a great way to show your appreciation. And I wish so much for the rest of the country to do the same. I ask that you please show respect for these individuals who are inevitably there for us during our darkest hours and in our times of greatest need.

I began writing this section before our country descended into riots. It saddens me to no end watching the cancel culture and the woke, silencing the majority and all the rampant hatred. We are the world's melting pot and so much better than what has recently been on display from all sides. Please stop the madness, get along with your neighbors, and show respect for those who protect us every day.

Our first responders have my gratitude in abundance.

www.ingramcontent.com/pod-product-compliance
Lightning Source LLC
Chambersburg PA
CBHW041302240426
43661CB00010B/986